Bosses

BOSSES

by

JIM WALL

Lexington Books

D.C. Heath and Company • Lexington, Massachusetts • Toronto

Library of Congress Cataloging-in-Publication Data

Wall, James A.
Bosses.

1. Leadership. I. Title. [DNLM: 1. Leadership.
BF 637.L4 W187b]
HD57.7.W35   1986   303.3'4   86-45515
ISBN 0-669-13475-9 (alk. paper)

Published simultaneously in Canada
Printed in the United States of America
Casebound International Standard Book Number: 0-669-13475-9
Library of Congress Catalog Card Number: 86-45515

The paper used in this publication meets
the minimum requirements of American National Standard
for Information Sciences—Permanence of Paper
for Printed Library Materials, ANSI Z39.48-1984.

ISBN 0-669-13475-9

86 87 88 89 90 8 7 6 5 4 3 2 1

Contents

Acknowledgments

W ITHOUT the enthusiastic assistance of many people this book would never have surfaced. Thanks are due to my editor, Bruce Katz, and agent, Richard Curtis, for their support of the project. Special thanks go to Joe Reitz, who cheered me along from the start. Mary Post, who adopted many of the stories as her own, deserves my utmost appreciation for her excellent typing and editorial assistance.

I especially appreciate the inputs from my family. Both parents edited the entire work. My wife, Judy, encouraged and tolerated me during the project. And occasionally my daughter, Lindley, left me alone.

Diane England remained cheerful while laboring for weeks on the thankless tasks of editing and printing the final copy. Scott Gaines and Brad Eiffert also deserve my appreciation for their assistance.

My colleagues—Tom Howard, David Baucus, Ron Beauleiu, Chuck Behling, Bill Bigoness, Art Brief, Dave Cherrington, Larry Cummings, Marty Gannon, Jimmy Gentry, Ricky Griffin, Herb Hand, Harv Hegarty, Bob House, Jerry Hunt, Dave Jemison, Tom Kochan, Fred Luthans, Jim McFillen, Dennis Organ, Ken Roering, Jerry Rose, Ken Rowland, Dean Tjosvold—merit my thanks for graciously providing feedback and suggestions on the leaders' commentaries.

Obviously the most important contributors are the hundreds of leaders who shared their worlds with me. Here I would like to thank them.

Introduction

THIS book is about the men and women who keep America—its airports, missile systems, peace movements, Indian reservations, crime rings, sawmills, brothels, bars, mental wards, and everything else—running from day to day. They are the first-line leaders, not the captains of industry or the middle-level bureaucrats who shuffle paper from one pile to the next. They are "hands on" leaders, who tell their stories here.

Many of them are interesting not only because of their personal qualities but also because of the nature of their jobs. For example, the SEAL team leader and his men play and kill with chilling abandon. Along with his deputy, a missile commander sits sixty feet below ground with ten to fifty Minuteman missiles—the seeds of a nuclear holocaust—at his fingertips. Opposing him is the peace camp leader who wants to deny the military its missiles and simultaneously seeks to give women the power to believe in themselves.

Some of the leaders leave us with a feeling of invigoration. The inner-city mission director, filled with a mixture of dedication, optimism, and frustration, is one of these. From a brick foreman we are amazed to learn that some of the men who work under him earn twenty-nine hours' worth of time on an eight-hour shift. And there are many other stories: we are made privy to the routines of a monastery abbot, a Bahai leader, the overseer of a brothel, the owner-manager of a collection agency, an Amish sawmill operator, a hit man, the supervisor of a maximum-security prison, the operator of a body builders' gym, a women's crisis center director, and the psychiatric director of a mental ward, to name but a few.

For the most part the stories these leaders have chosen to share with us are uplifting, but some of them leave behind a cold numbness: the wino leader leads his "merry band" in a quest for drunkenness and for any liquid—Lysol, rubbing alcohol, Listerine, antifreeze, canned heat, shoe polish—that will induce it. In his words:

"Now you might think I'm telling you a lie, but a can of Lysol makes you the best drink you ever drank in your life. . . . Now what you do is take a can of Lysol

*and knock a little hole—just a little bitty hole—to let the pressure off it first. Then
you shake it into a pint bottle, fill it with water, shake it up. Best drink in the
world. . . .*

*"And I tell you something else you can drink too. Canned heat. You know what
that is? All right, you got your red top. You got your green top. You got blue tops.
The red top is the only kind you can drink. Can't the green and the blue; they'll
kill you. But what you do, you take a white rag—I have taken my socks—and squeeze
it out. You can make a half a gallon with one can of that."*

The burglar's directness and brutality generate a similar uncomfortable sobri-
ety in the reader:

*"Sometimes it's just, 'Sit down, I want to talk to you. You're goofing off, and
I won't tolerate it.'. . . Then you got the tough guy. He's just like the mule that
you've got to slap alongside the head to get his attention. So I just tell him I want
to talk to him and bring him into a room. He's completely unaware of why I want
to see him. I'm talking really nice to him. First thing I do is knock him down
and put a gun to his head. And I let him know, 'Now hey, you've been screwing
up for a couple of weeks now. I've let it slide and let it slide, expecting you to shape
up. Right now you better shape up or ship out.'"*

Whether their tales are interesting, invigorating, or numbing, almost all
of these bosses do an excellent job of leading. They survive hectic, often chaotic
days in which they are trapped inside a vortex of pressure coming from 360
directions. As the inner-city mission director declares, his former position as
president of a military academy was similar to a fire hydrant at a dog convention: he was caught between the trustees, faculty, and parents. The abbot
and paramedic director repeat the familiar slogan "the buck stops here" to
indicate that pressure rises from the bottom.

Pressure also comes from the top. As the research director puts it, "The
crap stops here." The women's crisis center director is more specific:

*"They expected me to come in here and know what to do. They threw me in
here and told me what to do but not how to do it. When I first came in, this was
stuff I'd never done before, and for me it was trial and error. They don't believe
in trial and error because it was a new shelter and it had to be run right the first
time or we'd lose the volunteers and the community support. So it had to be done
right, right then."*

In some leadership positions, pressure comes from the sides as well as from the top and bottom. The head nurse is caught between doctors and nurses; the bar manager, between the customers and his bar keepers; the hospice director, between her volunteers, the dying, and the relatives of the dying; the federal mediators' director, between union and management. And, as you will see, the list could go on at length.

The helter-skelter nature of a boss's daily routine is easily recognized by anyone who has ever led. For someone who has not—and who believes that leaders are able to plan, organize, control, and coordinate their time—the reality comes as a stark surprise. Leaders find their days packed with brief, varied activities. Following is a brief sample of these activities. They are a mixture of the mundane, exciting, humorous, and sobering:

Burglar: killed his boss.

Chief test pilot: awarded the "golden boot" to a pilot.

Inner-city mission director: interviewed 25 families (475 during the month).

Wino leader: negotiated with police.

Brothel overseer: installed a handicap ramp in the brothel.

Assembly line supervisor: did not buy a concrete Suki lawnmower.

Women's crisis center director: checked the obituaries for her mistakes.

Air controller supervisor: stepped in to avoid a crash.

Olympics official: explained to his co-officials that they would be allotted only one uniform to wear during the entire Olympics.

Heroin dealer: shot himself to prove he was tough.

SEAL team leader: machine-gunned some motorcyclists.

Antisubmarine mission commander: lost a Soviet sub.

Limestone quarry foreman: used a laser to cut diamond teeth for a limestone chain saw.

Heart transplant surgeon: successfully transplanted a heart.

While muddling through their daily activities, the leaders interviewed for this book demonstrate important lessons about what it takes to inspire and motivate people. The majority of these leaders succeed because they stick to the basics. In addition to knowing the jobs they are supervising, they protect and motivate their troops. Simultaneously, they develop a leadership style that works. Initially they adopt an approach they think *should* work; as time passes, they experiment. They try one approach, observe the outcome, and if the results are not up to par, modify their style, taking the particular circumstances into account as they do so. Most of them realize that just one approach will not be appropriate for every subordinate, opportunity, job, or technology. Therefore, they learn to modify their behavior so that it "fits" the situation at hand. In sum, the leaders' success is based on a common troika: (a) protection of personnel, (b) motivation of personnel, and (c) experimentation with style until finding one that works.

The first of these elements—protection of personnel—is the one most often overlooked. We don't teach it in business schools or management seminars, yet it is essential. Leaders who plan to get things done through others had better buffer their workers. The heroin dealer's commentary, though extreme, makes this point most saliently:

"You got to think and protect yourself and your people. You got to kill, because if you don't, then the other dude's going to kill your people. And nobody wants to work for you if you can't protect him."

Most bosses eschew violence, of course, yet they must shield their subordinates from stress, abuse, or the "bright" ideas of bureaucrats. Sometimes leaders can educate their people about stress or they can structure their subordinates' jobs to fend it off. Such ploys are adopted by the air controller supervisor:

"We have the stress built in procedurally. But we educate toward that. We're not taking John Doe off the street who's never been educated and plugging him into a microphone and saying, 'Here. Talk to this airplane.' We're sending him to sixteen weeks of Academy. We're bringing him in for six weeks here. We're putting him in the least busiest position, letting him get certified on that. Then we send him back to school. It's a little like a confidence course. . . . Here the day-to-day operations and standard procedures are set. The airspace is defined; the operational procedure is defined; the plane flies in this airspace at this speed behind this guy at this distance."

To fend off pressures exerted by customers and superiors, leaders can intervene by handling "hot potatoes" or by warning threatening forces that they had better tread lightly upon the time, resources, patience, and esteem of the leader's team.

Successful leaders keep the second pillar of their success—motivation—simple. They ensure that their people know what to do and that they are rewarded for good performance. While the concept is simple, its implementation at times requires creativity. As expected, the leaders you will read about in these pages use pats on the back, kicks in the rear, pay raises, and warm relations. Even more important, they ensure that the job itself motivates. For example, the heart transplant surgeon encourages patients who have recovered to visit the surgical team that participated in their successful operation. The body-building operator keeps the quality of her establishment high. And to his squad, the antisubmarine mission commander keeps hammering home the same theme: "Our mission is an important one."

What is the best way to motivate? Many leaders choose to lead by example. Not only does this motivate people, it also enables leaders to communicate what is to be done and what is important. The chief test pilot, SEAL team leader, city bus maintenance foreman, limestone foreman, massage parlor operator, and many others—in fact, over 50 percent of the approximately two hundred leaders I interviewed—lead by example. It is a simple stick-to-the-basics motivational/leadership approach. Why does it work so well? Because people follow best the leader who walks beside them, not the one who walks in front or behind.

The last element of the troika is finding a style that works. Sometimes protection and motivation are sufficient. Sometimes not even they are required, because technology, training, peer pressure, and other leader substitutes enable leaders to take a laissez-faire approach. At other times, leading by example suffices. However, most leaders find that they must round out their skills with an active, hands-on style. Effective leaders are not fastidious about which style they choose. They go with one that works, but they are neither hasty nor lazy in choosing it. On the contrary, they painstakingly search for and experiment with a variety of styles. It may come as a surprise to some that leaders think a lot about their style. Some choose to be autocrats; others, dictators; many are very democratic and invite participation; a few delegate both decision making and implementation to others. The wino leader is an "arguecrat," and the marijuana dealer has a down-home, man-to-man style.

Among the leadership styles represented in this book are a number of gems, often mined from humble sources—leaders who gleaned their knowledge in the school of hard knocks. For example, the uneducated head housekeeper, who utilizes a precise, contingency-oriented leadership approach, one that takes into account differences in personalities, expectations, and abilities:

"I find the moods and then react. For example, when I find a girl who wants to please me, I tell her, 'I think you have done a good job!' If a girl is interested in her family and people, then I will take more time off to talk to her. Those who want money, I tell them what to do and make sure they do it. For those that take pride in their work, I act a little like a mother for them and tell them the job is really good."

In the following chapters we will see how even criminals can be excellent leaders. Successful criminal leaders know what they are managing. They protect their followers. They motivate other crooks with rapid reinforcement, interesting jobs, and leading by example. And they develop an appropriate style. For example, the burglar is autocratic. His leadership style fits his personality and his missions, which require precision, discipline, obedience, and timing. The marijuana dealer can afford to have a looser style. As for the hit man, he realizes that his mission requires a strong commitment from his people; therefore, he is democratic as well as charismatic. In his words:

"First you got to cop people's minds by your conversation and get them to believe in you; that's the main thing. You got to believe in what you're doing and get them to believe in what you're doing. You got to explain it to them, and you got to do your best. Then you have to perform, and you see how they do. You put the basic rules down—what we all need to do and then if we all do this then we'll all make money. . . .

"I drive a lot and think up these scams. Then I lay back and think what people would be good to use in them. Then I get the people together, explain things. Get them motivated. I get an idea, and then I start talking it over with someone. Then they start to think they're helping with an idea or if they start thinking it's part their idea, then they get enthusiastic. Then that gives me a turn-on, a natural high. They're fired up about helping me do something. It's a good feeling."

Like their licit counterparts, these crooks have important leadership experiences to share with us.

1

Why Lead?

MOST of us never ask why someone would want to become a leader. Americans love a leader, and we take for granted the virtues of leadership. We are taught from day one to achieve, to excel, to win, and we link all these behaviors to leading. What parent isn't thrilled to learn that his or her child has been elected class president? Being class president is the equivalent of being number one in the class—*the* leader.

We like to think of ourselves as leaders. If you pick any hundred people at random and ask them how good they are at leading, 98, yes, 98 percent will rate themselves as above average, and of these, 70 percent will volunteer the information that their performance places them in the top quartile.

People become leaders because to do so is a part of achieving, excelling, and viewing themselves as winners. The effort to attain leadership is continually reinforced by parents, colleagues, society, and even by our opponents. The position of leader promises self-satisfaction, a sense of accomplishment, and the respect of others.

At least, that is what I assumed—until I interviewed, within the same week, a Bahai leader in California and a robber from somewhere else. The Bahai emphasized that he did not seek leadership and that, when assuming the role, he was unsure of his ability to live up to it. Specifically:

"I became a leader because the highest station you can achieve is the station of servitude. The rewards for servitude are several. The reward in this life is that you've been put into a position to give great service, and you give that service. And there are rewards in the afterlife for those who have given the utmost, and if that means as a leader, that's one effort. But being a leader doesn't mean that one has a leg up on the nonleaders. That is, we don't feel that you're, so to speak, building credits in the afterlife by being a good leader.

"When one becomes the leader, there's a dual emotion. There is an elation that you are recognized by the members of your faith, that you have some capacity, and that you've been asked to give it. There's also an immediate sense of humility, thinking that you're probably not going to live up to the task. . . . But when you're chosen, you serve."

Similarly, a Mosque leader pointed out the obligation to serve and the heavenly rewards for doing so:

"So some people will become leaders to worship God, and then they will be rewarded for this. And in Islam, if people come and they say, 'You are the one who can do the job,' you have no right to decline. That is their consensus, and you have to do it. Likewise [like people who have given money for a Mosque], I will be rewarded [in paradise] for giving of my efforts to be a good leader."

Neither of these individuals saw leadership as a personal achievement; rather, it was an opportunity to serve. I found their comments both surprising and thought provoking. Unknowingly, these gentle men had set me up for the armed robber's harsh testimony:

"You don't lead unless you can't help it. Sure, all those movies and programs like 'Miami Vice' make you think it's cool to be Mr. Big. But leading's a luxury you can't hardly afford.

"Every dude what's working for you when you take down a place has an insurance policy. Now, he can go around and commit any crime he likes. If he gets caught, all he'll do is turn on you—cop to a minor plea and testify against you. He walks on his crime, because the cops want to get me.

"So you don't lead unless you need more hands—to drive the car, hold another gun, scout out the place—or more brains—like to take down a safe. Sometimes after a bit a guy will get scared and start to talk, or he gets to bragging. Then you got to put him in the bushes, and that gets everything too complicated."

This individual was not seeking out leadership either. These three commentaries dispelled the assumptions I had brought to the interviews and generated the question, why do men and women lead? Leading is a tough job. It is difficult to do well even under the best of circumstances. There are stresses, overloads, constant interruptions. And people blame the leader whenever anything goes wrong.

So why do intelligent people take up the burden of leadership? Many different answers emerge from the following pages. As we have already seen, they had better tread lightly upon the time, resources, patience, and esteem of the leader's team.

Successful leaders keep the second pillar of their success—motivation—simple. They ensure that their people know what to do and that they are rewarded for good performance. While the concept is simple, its implementation at times requires creativity. As expected, the leaders you will read about in these pages use pats on the back, kicks in the rear, pay raises, and warm relations. Even more important, they ensure that the job itself motivates. For example, the heart transplant surgeon encourages patients who have recovered to visit the surgical team that participated in their successful operation. The body-building operator keeps the quality of her establishment high. And to his squad, the antisubmarine mission commander keeps hammering home the same theme: "Our mission is an important one."

What is the best way to motivate? Many leaders choose to lead by example. Not only does this motivate people, it also enables leaders to communicate what is to be done and what is important. The chief test pilot, SEAL team leader, city bus maintenance foreman, limestone foreman, massage parlor operator, and many others—in fact, over 50 percent of the approximately two hundred leaders I interviewed—lead by example. It is a simple stick-to-the-basics motivational/leadership approach. Why does it work so well? Because people follow best the leader who walks beside them, not the one who walks in front or behind.

The last element of the troika is finding a style that works. Sometimes protection and motivation are sufficient. Sometimes not even they are required, because technology, training, peer pressure, and other leader substitutes enable leaders to take a laissez-faire approach. At other times, leading by example suffices. However, most leaders find that they must round out their skills with an active, hands-on style. Effective leaders are not fastidious about which style they choose. They go with one that works, but they are neither hasty nor lazy in choosing it. On the contrary, they painstakingly search for and experiment with a variety of styles. It may come as a surprise to some that leaders think a lot about their style. Some choose to be autocrats; others, dictators; many are very democratic and invite participation; a few delegate both decision making and implementation to others. The wino leader is an "arguecrat," and the marijuana dealer has a down-home, man-to-man style.

Among the leadership styles represented in this book are a number of gems, often mined from humble sources—leaders who gleaned their knowledge in the school of hard knocks. For example, the uneducated head housekeeper, who utilizes a precise, contingency-oriented leadership approach, one that takes into account differences in personalities, expectations, and abilities:

"I find the moods and then react. For example, when I find a girl who wants to please me, I tell her, 'I think you have done a good job!' If a girl is interested in her family and people, then I will take more time off to talk to her. Those who want money, I tell them what to do and make sure they do it. For those that take pride in their work, I act a little like a mother for them and tell them the job is really good."

In the following chapters we will see how even criminals can be excellent leaders. Successful criminal leaders know what they are managing. They protect their followers. They motivate other crooks with rapid reinforcement, interesting jobs, and leading by example. And they develop an appropriate style. For example, the burglar is autocratic. His leadership style fits his personality and his missions, which require precision, discipline, obedience, and timing. The marijuana dealer can afford to have a looser style. As for the hit man, he realizes that his mission requires a strong commitment from his people; therefore, he is democratic as well as charismatic. In his words:

"First you got to cop people's minds by your conversation and get them to believe in you; that's the main thing. You got to believe in what you're doing and get them to believe in what you're doing. You got to explain it to them, and you got to do your best. Then you have to perform, and you see how they do. You put the basic rules down—what we all need to do and then if we all do this then we'll all make money. . . .
"I drive a lot and think up these scams. Then I lay back and think what people would be good to use in them. Then I get the people together, explain things. Get them motivated. I get an idea, and then I start talking it over with someone. Then they start to think they're helping with an idea or if they start thinking it's part their idea, then they get enthusiastic. Then that gives me a turn-on, a natural high. They're fired up about helping me do something. It's a good feeling."

Like their licit counterparts, these crooks have important leadership experiences to share with us.

some feel it is their duty to serve. Many feel called; others feel it is in their own best interest. The reasons seem as varied as the leaders themselves. The bar manager considers his operation a mechanism for recycling his money, while the inner-city mission director quips that accepting his post allowed him to continue his prodding of the clergy. For the head housekeeper, leading offers respect, but for the resident hall adviser, it brings only headaches.

In this section, the commentaries cast some insight into the motives of five quite different leaders, and perhaps into our own motives for leading. Sometimes the reasoning is written between the lines; at other times, it glares out at us from the pages. The burglar deserves credit for his honesty as well as for his insights into his own motives:

"There's a special thrill to leading a team. I've got the motivation, the excitement, the compensation, the money; then comes the power. Anyone who's ever tasted it enjoys it. . . . I'm like the baseball player who's getting paid for doing something he's always loved to do. . . .

"You've got to recognize that you're greedy. I'm greedy. I want more than what my neighbor has. I want a better car, better clothes; I want my kids to go to a better school. I want better food in the house. Those are the basics. Beyond that, I want the respect of my community—I want them to know I'm an achiever. I want control. I want to make decisions. Then I want the ultimate. I want the power."

Like the burglar, the abbot was a leader from childhood, but his current reflections on his motives differ. He does not look for power. While he feels he is a capable leader who is fulfilling a responsibility, he is willing to step down at any time the monastery should decide it needs a new leader.

The test pilot fits into the American mold for a leader; he would rather lead than follow. His style, which is a mix of leading by example and coaching, allows him both to command respect and to use his position to help his pilots cope with the stresses of testing expensive supersonic aircraft.

The brothel overseer has his own mission, or quest:

"I want this place to be better than any other brothel. . . . I want to discount and get rid of the idea that brothels have to be seedy and that girls and managers have to be gray-area greasy punks. . . . We have a mission here. We contribute to society. . . . I just fully equipped this place so that it's accessible to the handicapped. . . . The ladies pay Social Security; they pay income taxes; and they maintain high standards of hygiene. . . . Now, your grandmother might not like it, your mother might not like it, but it's a practical solution to something that goes back to the beginning of society."

Burglar

It's absolutely easier to lead people in crime.

There's a special thrill to leading a team. There's power here. Any leader thrives on power and control. I've got the motivation, the excitement, the compensation, the money; then comes the power. Anyone who's ever tasted it enjoys it.

I have three or four men working for me, and we break into drugstores, stores, and warehouses. There's a thrill in it, but it's easy. I like the thrill and having control of the operation. Being a leader sort of fits in with my personality. I've been a leader all my life.

When I's about ten years old, I lived in the projects on the poor side of town—one of these clapboard projects set up to provide apartments for the veterans. It was a very low-life type situation. A thousand kids in the project, and we had our gangs. I had my gang—five or six guys. I was the leader. They naturally just gravitated toward me. Pretty soon we built a clubhouse. "Here's where we build it," I said. Then at eleven years old I'm meeting with other gangs. "This is my territory; we collect the papers over here to sell to the junkman. You guys stay out of here. You tell your guys to stay out of here, and I'll tell mine to stay out of your territory."

Then I moved into a better town, and the city roughness wore off. I adapted to the American-boy image. Now all the guys are still looking up to me and saying, "Hey, what're we going to do now? Where we going?" This was in junior high; they look up to me even though I was younger. I's captain of my high school football team.

Then I had to get out of school. My mother was dying of cancer, and I was needed at home. I had a younger brother and sister; my father had to work. So someone had to look after the children. One was eight years old and the young one only twelve months. I tried to go back and get an education, but she had a relapse. She died; then I ran off and joined the service.

Came out of the service and got a job in the shipping end of a mail order house. There I had some responsibility for hiring people and obtaining some order, discipline, and control. Then I went to work for a distributing company, which is really a euphemism for an encyclopedia sales group. While this is usually looked at as the bottom of the line in terms of credibility, I was *very* successful at it for about five years.

I worked myself into a responsible sales management position, where I had twelve to fifteen salesmen under me. I was responsible for sales meetings every morning. It was a high-hype type of deal. I had to fire up people every day.

High-pressure sales. In fact, my salary was commensurate to what they brought in. If they didn't produce, then I didn't earn a living. For a while I did really well. I had a good paycheck every week. I was very successful and lucky. That required a lot of motivating. It was OJT. I was successful as a salesman, and my superiors saw that I had the ability to motivate others.

My problem, though, and the reason that I turned to crime, was the fact that I would accept a challenge like that. Be successful in meeting the challenge and then have no stepping-stone to reach for. I was stuck right there. They wouldn't promote me. I didn't have the sheepskin—the degree or the formal education—to open doors for me. The organization kept me down. I quit and moved back close to the East Coast end and got involved with some people there who got me involved in this.

I think I carried some of my talents from being a sales manager into this position. I'm very forceful, dynamic. When I turned to crime, I finally broke loose from all the shackles of society that inhibited me—in growing up and on my job—that stagnated me in life. I broke loose from all the shackles and became a nonconformist. The freedom, wow, of breaking loose from laws I didn't agree with was an extreme release of tension and frustration.

It's important to say that I didn't blame society. I wasn't bitter, just frustrated. I was bitter at the time because I was frustrated and didn't know how to handle it. I felt I was now successful in this element of life, where I was a failure in a lot of other aspects. I had a marriage go bad on me. There was an inability to get a job that I was proud of. There was a stigma of being a door knocker or a man who's running a scam. I was a failure; society was holding me back; I was tense. Then when I moved to this job, all that was behind me.

I'm given the personnel to use on the jobs. One of the factors that always intrigues me is that we steal drugs, TVs, and money. And the reports are always different from what we steal. Like one time we broke in this doctor's office and stole about $5,000 in cash, and that wasn't mentioned in the newspaper. Once we stole a bunch of drugs and the newspaper said we took three times the amount we did. And on warehouses, they're always lying about what we steal.

We work about the same routine. I'm told the place I'm to hit, what's there, and where it is. The rest is up to me. Me and my troops might scout it out. We figure out how to shut off the alarm. We see the schedule of any watchmen and cops. I plan it out, and we go in. Everyone knows his part. We don't talk much when we're in there. He knows which drugs to get, where they are. He looks for cash. He maybe is on the safe. Then we haul everything away and put it in the designated place. Someone else picks it up.

My boss provides the people, and I come to a meeting with him. They're very formal. It's not just a bunch of guys sitting around talking in the locker room. He just assumes I know what I'm doing. I'm a professional. He breaks down the job: this is where the drugs are located; this is the route to take. He tells me the dates. It's more of a discussion as how to do it. I take my personnel, rehearse them on what to do. Who watches. Who takes what. What to do if the cop come. What's neat is that it takes more nerve than anything else.

And I don't usually have trouble motivating them. They get money. Money motivates everybody. That's the prime motivator in life—money. They get enough, and I get $2,000 a week. No, not every week; let's call it $2,000 a mission. Sometimes it's more. Sometimes I know what I'm going after and sometimes it's catch as catch can. We take what we find.

But what really motivates me is the thrill. I still don't have that stepping-stone up that I want, but it'll come. I'm unfortunate enough to have ability, an innate ability, to achieve but not the opportunity to succeed. So I'm agnostic. I consider there's only one law, and that's my law. Everybody is out for himself. Now I'm in this, and it's exciting. It's exciting and the money is there, too; so I guess it motivates. I won't do something simply for the thrill of it. The end has to justify the means. I'm like the baseball player who's getting paid for doing something he's always loved to do.

I like the freedom of lifestyle I have, the choice. And I love the way I can dress; the suits, the ties, drive a good car. It's phony, but I feel like I'm somebody. Most people like to feel that way. The average man on the street would like to have all this if there wasn't the element of getting caught. There's a great number of people out there that, if the truth be known, would love to live this lifestyle. But they don't dare do it because they're afraid of getting caught.

I don't like not being able to talk about my job. I want to have children and a family. I can't live the all-American family-man image. There's a part of me that misses that. And there's some frustration that I can't be more powerful than I am. I can't move up. If I want the next man's job, I've got to kill him. If I do take a swat not knowing the next level, then I might be seen as getting too big for my britches, and the other guy will protect his job—kill me.

To lead my people I use money. Just like managing encyclopedia salesmen, it's money; the prime requisite for motivating people is money. Everything else comes with it, and that adds fuel to the fire—the control, the power. Now you throw other things into it to stimulate interest, like dignity, integrity, family care, personal pride.

Crime tends to be more cut and dried—this is a job; you do it and you get paid. It's absolutely easier to lead people in crime. You do the job. If you don't, someone else will take over. And if you know too much, and you don't want to do your job, then you pay the cost—very violent physical harm, death, or just ostracism with a bad rap on your integrity where you can't get anything but street-level jobs, breaking and entering type stuff. So I just remind my people. I don't let them question my authority. I tell them, "This is the way it's going to be." Sometimes you have to intimidate. I'm always capable of handling the job. I prove myself to the guys above.

But I vary my approach to fit the person. First, you got to know the men you're dealing with. You got to be a good judge of the personality and character of the person. What intimidates this guy the easiest? Sometimes it's just, "Sit down, I want to talk to you. You're goofing off, and I won't tolerate it. If you can't change, I'll change it for you." You use this on an individual who's not intimidated by your physical stature but is by what you say, how you're saying it, and by what he thinks you're capable of doing. Sometimes you're running a bluff, and he thinks I'm bigger than I am. I use that to my advantage and intimidate him.

Then you got the tough guy. He's just like the mule that you've got to slap alongside the head to get his attention. So I just tell him I want to talk to him and bring him into a room. He's completely unaware of why I want to see him. I'm talking really nice to him. First thing I do is knock him down and put a gun to his head. And I let him know, "Now hey, you've been screwing up for a couple of weeks now. I've let it slide and let it slide, expecting you to shape up. Right now you better shape up or ship out." You let him know he's not as tough as he thinks he is, and you're not as stupid as he's playing you to be. He thinks because he's been getting by with this silliness for a couple of weeks that either I'm not aware of it or I'm not capable of handling it. So I give him enough rope to hang himself. So now you run it all down to him and he realizes, "Wow, I really messed up. This is a lot more serious than I thought."

If it gets any stronger than that, then I take them out and eliminate them. If you need to do more than scare a person, then that person is a serious weak link in your organization. You've got to kill him. And I do this—intimidate, gun to head, and kill. I never go up to my boss for the muscle. That would show my weakness and my inability to handle the situation. Then people up there will say, "Hey, this isn't the man for the job." I'm tougher than I have to be. I show them I'm so capable that they'll soon be saying, "Hey, we need you up here."

Impressions are important. I want to show my bosses that I'm a strong leader, that I'm getting the respect from the people under me. Mutual respect, earned respect, fear. You got their attention; they listen to what you say, and they produce results.

I don't just want to get the job done. I want to move up. I don't want to be retained at just one plateau. The objective is always to go higher, higher, and higher. I'm a very greedy individual. I'm greedy for money, for control, for power and the means for getting it. That is why I want to be a leader. I've had the natural leadership ability ever since I was ten years old, the gang leader, whatever.

To be a good leader you've got to be a strong individual. You have to be greedy. And I'm calling a spade a spade. Reach deep within people and get to their gut-level instincts. One of them is greed. You've got to recognize that you're greedy. I'm greedy. I want more than what my neighbor has. I want a better car, better clothes; I want my kids to go to a better school. I want better food in the house. Those are the basics. Beyond that, I want the respect of my community—I want them to know I'm an achiever. I want control. I want to make decisions. Then I want the ultimate. I want the power.

Then you understand power. When to use it. How to dress. What clothes to wear. What kind of hair cut to have. What kind of office furniture. Where people sit in your office. You got to recognize these points and use them. Be ruthless. That's an element of your character if you're going to be a leader. That doesn't mean that you hurt people, even though you might at times.

Then you motivate people. You use money. Plus you always give them job opportunities; let them know they can advance. You got to give them something to reach for. Money isn't enough. Create jobs if you have to.

And you judge people. He's a loser, and nothing—money, title, prestige—is going to motivate him. Keep him at the bottom, or eliminate him. Intimidate the milquetoast. Put the gun to the head of the tough guy. Eliminate the weak link. Never lower your standards so that whatever people do is okay.

You recognize opportunities, and if it's what you want, you go after it. Don't be afraid to go after it. Again, it's the greed. Be brave enough within yourself. Another thing that's important is that you've got to realize that sometimes opportunity doesn't knock. You have to create opportunity. There's no room at the top, so you make room. That's how I got this job; I killed my boss.

Monastery Abbot

*If you've got stamina enough to play at night, then you've got enough
energy to pray in the morning.*

I could almost say that I stepped into authority by accident or osmosis.
I'm the second oldest of a very large family, so as a very young child I helped
around home and became responsible. And all my life I've been a responsible person. I found myself in leadership roles as a young person and as a
teenager. Even without thinking of someday being abbot, I found myself being put in leadership roles. And there came this partiuclar time, and I was
elected. I didn't strive for it.

I like being the abbot because of the service I have to offer to other people.
I don't look for the prestige or power that comes from the position. That's
not a big thing for me. In the *Rule of St. Benedict* he warns against ambitiousness
and he stresses the value of humility. It is not a democracy here. It's an
autocracy, but it's one that is built upon a system of counsel that is spelled
out for us in detail. Benedict set up a very systematic type of community,
and he basically established the abbot as the person of authority in the
monastery. He stresses that the abbot is to take counsel in all that he does,
but once he has taken counsel, the abbot is to make the decision, weighing
everything, praying over the matter. He is the one who ultimately makes the
decision. And St. Benedict exhorts the monks not to adhere to their own
will when they conflict with the abbot.

I suppose what comes to mind is a little plaque that was on Truman's desk.
It said, "The Buck Stops Here." And that's exactly what Benedict meant.
There comes a point when someone has to say, "I have to make the decision
and take the responsibility."

As the abbot I am elected by the community—the monks who are in final
vows. I in turn appoint my assistants, the prior and the subprior. That's the
chain of command. In addition, there's the abbot's council. The size of the
council depends upon the size of the monastery. The council is made up of
people elected by the community and those appointed by the abbot. My council is four men—the prior, the subprior, and two elected by the community.
Now, there is little I decide on without first taking counsel with the council.
As the superior, I have the ultimate authority, but I must give account of
these groups of people. I'm very accountable to the community. When you
read through Benedict's *Rule* you recognize that on the one hand the abbot
has a lot of authority, but if the abbot interprets it [the nature of his author-
ity] correctly, he is very accountable.

The prior handles the day-to-day matters, and that frees me up for the spiritual matters. My schedule in doing so is about the same each day:

5:45 A.M.   I usually get up at quarter to six, and after cleaning up I will spend a period of private prayer. That will vary, and it varies depending upon the season. I personally am very much into exercise, so in the summer months I get up and jump rope and then spend time in prayer.

7:00 A.M.   We have community morning prayer at 7 in the morning, followed by a period of what we call *lexis*, a period of private reading of the Scripture or whatever. As a community we're all involved in this, so from 7:00 to 8:00, we have an hour of prayer.

8:00 A.M.   Breakfast. After breakfast we go into our work period, and I spend that period of time meeting with monks if they want to. I may have classes with the novices. I have correspondence. It's a lot of desk work.

11:00 A.M.   We have the Eucharist ceremony from 11:30 to 12:30.

12:30 P.M.   Lunch. Then, in the afternoon, there's a period of work. Myself, I might be at my desk or about the various areas of the monastery, visiting where others are working. I might have appointments in the city. Or, if I haven't exercised in the morning, I usually take a period in the afternoon to exercise.

5:00 P.M.   We have our evening prayer at this time, followed by supper at 6:00.

6:00 P.M.   Supper.

6:45 P.M.   A period of community recreation, which is really the only time for all of us to come together for fifteen to twenty minutes to sit down and relax with one another in a very casual conversation.

7:15 P.M.   Night prayer. The rest of the evening is spent in any way that one might choose.

10:30 P.M.   I usually get to bed between 10:30 and 11:00.

I can truthfully say that this is a very difficult job—to be a leader in the Church, to respond to the various kinds of individuals, to really know and understand each person, to really get under the skin, so to speak, of each individual, and to be sensitive and understanding. That takes a lot of time and emotional energy. There's also the administrative responsibility. Even though I delegate to others on daily business matters, they are still account-able to me. I have to be responsible for the finances and to know that they're going okay.

It's one thing to be a spiritual leader, but if you're going bankrupt it won't do any good. So I have to make sure we're not going bankrupt also.

Admittedly my main job is being a spiritual leader. I work with the monks on the personal side. The nature of our life is a very introspective one. To go through the training, we not only study Scripture, the Church fathers, and Church history, but it's also psychological in that we look at ourselves.

In our community of monks we've got men of all ages, so, like people else-where, monks of different ages have their own problems, their own strug-gles. In the twenties it would probably be a problem of adjustment in that the monk has not been in the community long. He's come from college or from a work situation. He's let go of relationships—girlfriends, family—that he's had. He's let go of possessions, and the adjustment is to a new group of people living in close contact. Our daily routine is somewhat structured, more so than his regular life, and at that point in time it is a routine that seems somewhat restricted. And so he would be adjusting to a new environ-ment and probably at this point in time asking seriously whether this is what he wants or whether he would want to go back to another lifestyle.

Consider a monk in his late thirties or early forties. That person in a monastery will experience the same midlife crisis and adjustments that any other person does—the sudden realization that life is moving on, "What have I done? What have I accomplished?" He may feel that there are things he has missed out on by being in the monastery and also that he's accomplishing anything there. Such a person needs to rely upon his faith and his belief in God to deal with these problems. But such a person also needs to rely upon wise counsel. He will talk to me not only as an abbot but also as a person he can trust.

The older men need to make adjustments to changes in their health, to not being as productive. Interestingly enough, most Benedictine monks have been very productive in their lives. Many, for example, have been college pro-fessors, high school teachers, etc.; so after teaching for twenty to forty years, they find it difficult to let go. Also, they've been a part of the governing group, and they're being replaced by a younger generation. You see these same problems in the aging businessman, engineer, salesman, or professor.

And there are some rather unique problems for monks. I've not come upon any who question the existence of God, but I've come upon some who struggle with how they communciate with Him. When you talk about communication with God, you're talking about an intangible, and we are a people who like to see our results. My responsibility, then, is getting the person to live with the intangible. I believe you must live the intangibles. I also think those times when people experience difficulty in communicating with God corelate with other personal problems. Sometimes we find God in our difficulties. That's when our faith grows strongest. But in difficult times, we also really question.

For example, I think of a man in my community who has been diagnosed just recently as having cancer. And I see the change taking place in this man. He's going through the five steps that Elizabeth Kubler-Ross describes. While he's doing that psychologically, he's doing that from a faith perspective, the anger, the detachment, the letting go.

As the spiritual leader, I give counsel in these matters. On the administrative side, I have a lot of authority but I seldom use it. I seldom say, "You have to do this or that." On rule violations, this is where the prior comes into use. I step in only when it becomes a repeated type of thing or a matter of principle. I look at it as my responsibility to set down the guidelines and principles, and it's the prior's responsibility to see that they're carried through on a daily basis. If they're not, then it is understood that he is the one who deals with these problems and confronts the individual. If he can get nowhere with the individual, then he brings it to me and then the three of us sit down.

A good example—I have few absolutes—would be community prayer. An integral part of our lives as monks is that we come together several times each day for community prayer. Unless excused, I consider it very important that we observe these times of prayer together. Within my community no one is excused from prayer on a general basis. Sickness is an excuse. If, for example, a person misses an hour of prayer, then it is up to that person to excuse himself to the prior. And it's known that we don't do this on a regular basis. We have a responsibility as a part of our life to meet in prayer. If a person were to repeat this behavior, then it would come to my attention and I probably would sit down with him.

If the person were in a period of formation—if he were a novice or in his three years of temporary vows—I would have to seriously question whether or not he should stay within our community. If he had taken his final vows,

I would have recourse to other action. Probably I would ground him. We do accept invitations to go out in the evening to the theater, to a ball game or whatever. So I would say, "If you've got enough stamina to play at night, then you've got enough energy to pray in the morning." Of course the most stringent punishment is excommunication from the monastery. I've done that only once.

In managing conflict among the monks, my approach speaks of my own training. I have a graduate degree in communications from a secular university, and so, having been trained in the process, I'm very much in tune with talking things through honestly together with them. If I know two men are involved in a conflict, I will first encourage them to work it through without me. I will step in and try to work it through only if I see that they're not going to work it through just with each other. I think that the interdynamics of two people are very important, so I seldom use the authority I have here.

I would hope there's a difference between conflict resolution here and elsewhere, because this is a religious setting. I don't think the religious setting contradicts the human dimension; rather, it just builds upon it. As St. Thomas Aquinas said, "Grace builds on Nature." And that's how I approach a conflict situation. We resolve it on a human level. Built into that is the Christian principle which I frequently call up and refer to. If I feel it would be helpful, I would not hesitate to refer a person to a particular scripture or passage. I would not hesitate to confront what I would call un-Christianlike behavior with a Scripture passage. And I would ask the person to look at himself, or I would ask him to read the passage and reflect upon it.

There are some frustrations in being an abbot, but I'm not sure I would change these. You have to sacrifice much of your personal life because of the role relationship of the leader. Again it's the old adage. The top position is always a lonely position. You know the president of any group does not have any peers. It's not something I would want to change because it's part of the breakdown of responsibilities; yet it is a difficult thing to live with on a day-to-day basis. I listen a lot to the needs of other people, but I don't have anyone within the community that I can go to.

Having a spiritual relationship helps in that I can go to prayer. I also have some close friends outside the community. I have a spiritual director outside the monastery who I talk to very freely and relate to very well.

But in the spiritual sense I am in the middle. I give counsel to the monks and assist them in their struggles. Then I go to my spiritual director, who does the same for me. Because he helps me, I can better help the members of my community.

I feel that I am doing a good job, that I am capable of the leadership and that this is my responsibility. But at the same time I can truthfully say it is a difficult job. I do feel that I am serving God, Christ, and man by being a good abbot. Yet I am honest enough to say I will hold the position only as long as I believe I am doing a good job. When the time comes that I think this community needs a new leader, I will freely step aside and allow for a new person to take over.

Bahai Leader

> I became a leader because the highest station you can achieve is the station of servitude.

As a Bahai leader, I am totally without any authority. It is only the assembly, my group of worshipers, that has authority. It makes its decision and in so doing exercises its authority. So as the leader, when I speak in the group, I am just like anyone else. Being a leader doesn't make any difference. The Bahai Scripture says this is the time for working in groups, and we understand that a local assembly, working in the right way, will receive God's guidance in making its decisions. But no individual is vested with that authority or ability.

Being a leader brings with it no monetary reward or privileges. I am respected, but in a way that is different from the outside world. The respect that people had for me enabled me to become the leader, but they have no more respect for me just because I am the leader. Respect doesn't come with the job; the job comes because of the respect.

Not only is the leader without authority, it is also absolutely forbidden for him to seek leadership. In choosing a leader, the members of the local community vote for people who have exemplified both a capacity for and a degree of spirituality that they feel should be in those who guide the affairs of the community. So the criteria that they're looking for aren't the same that you would normally have in any other organizational setting. In most organizational settings, you are looking for people that are assertive, who are going to lead, who will take the lead. That kind of person isn't excluded in the search for a Bahai leader, but it's specified in the teaching that the emphasis is to be on other criteria. How has the person conducted his life? What has he done, and is he really making an effort to lead a spiritual life?

I became a leader because the highest station you can achieve is the station of servitude. The rewards for servitude are several. The reward in this life is that you've been put into a position to give great service, and you give that service. And there are rewards in the afterlife for those who have given the utmost, and if that means as a leader, that's one effort. But being a leader doesn't mean that one has a leg up on the nonleaders. That is, we don't feel that you're, so to speak, building credits in the afterlife by being a good leader.

When one becomes the leader, there's a dual emotion. There is an elation that you are recognized by the members of your faith, that you have some capacity, and that you've been asked to give it. There's also an immediate sense of humility thinking that you're probably not going to live up to the task. I've felt this, and I've seen this in the members of the House of Justice in Israel [the international leadership body].

But when you're chosen, you serve. I'll give you an example. One of the members was elected to the House of Justice, and, at the same time, he got the job that he had spent his whole career working for. It was in a particular field of medical education he told me that he had wanted this job for twenty-five years. But he turned it down because of his obligation to serve. So every Bahai leader has these own little personal reflections as to what it means for them to serve.

Since we don't have authority, we accomplish tasks very slowly. First we use a lot of open and frank discussion. *Consultation* is the term the Bahais use for this process of arriving at the truth. Let me digress for a minute. What this means is that in a Bahai meeting, when you speak, your words leave your mouth and belong to you no more. They belong to the collective that's heard them.

Even though I am the leader, I share my work with committees. The community forms committees and gives them responsibilities for certain areas. For example, there is a finance committee and committees for teaching the faith, planning activities—topically, I could name ten. Those committees also have no authority. Rather, they report to the assembly and make their recommendations. Sometimes, especially in a small community, if there is something to be done, a member takes it on herself or himself to go do some work first, with another colleague perhaps, and then reports back again so as to execute what they have found.

The assembly can delegate to the individual the authority to do something, but again the emphasis remains on the corporal unit. The assembly never divests itself of its authority. In doing things this way we get things accomplished, plus we keep harmony in the group.

The group seeks this harmony at all costs. Again, one of the primary premises of the Bahai faith—and we perceive it as our function in life—is to help bring about the unity of mankind. And when you believe in this as a principle, that means you have to believe it as it relates to you, your institution, and the conduct of your personal affairs. You try to accomplish a harmony. The fact that the Bahai faith has not splintered, as all other religions have, is a tribute to our obedience and to this operational principle. The strength of the faith, one of the strengths, is our continuing effort to maintain a harmonious relationship.

That we seek harmony is not to say that we don't have problems. As a leader I face about three types—committee, personal, and conflict. In dealing with these, one of the major difficulties is the natural tendency for me to be impatient. When you're working out problems, especially with a group, it never goes as fast as it would with an individual who has the authority to make decisions and execute them. Again we Bahais sacrifice this expediency. When one person is running the show, his view is heard but we feel it is more important to see the collective view and obtain the collective agreement.

So I am patient in using committees. The committee brings the problem before the assembly, and I consult with the committee. Maybe the committee's charter wasn't very clear. Maybe the membership is having personal problems—they've got too many demands on their time. All those things should come forth, and then a decision can be arrived at as how to correct the problem. I remember a committee that wasn't discharging its responsibility as envisioned, and there was some personal difficulty. So we had assembly meetings to open the sore wounds. The problems turned out to be the normal human ones—someone was upset with someone else, and they were stewing in their own mess. When such problems are handled openly, in a loving and kind way—when the motive isn't to put someone down but to identify the problem—then finding the solution becomes a less threatening endeavor.

Now I wouldn't mislead you by letting you think that in every instance everyone walks out of the room happy. I wouldn't say that for a minute. It takes a very mature person to deal with the fact that someone is displeased with what he has done and to remove himself from the situation so that he can recognize the problem.

When someone in the assembly is generating a problem or fostering disharmony, it is handled somewhat differently. Again the leader doesn't handle it. And there are gradations in this situation. Maybe someone is generating disharmony because he is having problems in his own life. Here the assembly will consult with the individual collectively and ask what is happening to cause the difficulty. They don't have the authority to order him to cease or desist unless the behavior is so egregious that he is openly violating the laws of the Bahai faith. In that case, an investigation is conducted by an assembly member to verify whether or not this behavior is violating the tenets of the faith. If they do find that, then a report is made to the national assembly, and they may find that this person is a covenant breaker. [This term refers to a person who willfully chooses either to disavow his or her beliefs or to openly and flagrantly violate the principles of the faith.] For example, let's say someone has a drinking problem. He simply refuses to abstain, and he won't go to treatment. He acknowledges that he still is a Bahai but he doesn't have sufficient willpower to seek medical relief. That person may have his voting rights taken away. More serious would be the person attacking the faith itself or setting himself up against the faith. In this case, the person risks being thrown out of the Bahai faith.

Again, when we have conflict between individuals within the group, I as the leader won't necessarily try to resolve it. I would serve as a facilitator but not as a mediator. If I tried to mediate, that would imply that I have a position. But there is no position until the body adopts one. I would not meet together with the conflicting parties. I would not offer agreement points. I would not point out the areas of disagreement and areas where compromise is possible. Rather I would bring the parties together at the assembly, and the assembly would assist them in resolving the conflict. I would not sit down with them to resolve the conflict because that would be assuming leadership authority.

I would use members of the ancillary body, called the auxiliary board, to serve as mediators *if* this conflict is serious enough to be causing a rift within the community. Their role is not to solve the problem but to let the expression of concern be brought forward and to help to mediate by letting the conflicting parties openly express their views.

I think in our American culture we find leading in this way is very strange. However, other societies do not find it difficult to understand, if they have a strong group tradition. In fact, this type of leadership fits in very well [in such societies]. For example, the Bahair faith has grown very quickly in the Pacific Islands. The islanders always have had a council. And among the Navajo Indians in America, we have a large community. I think in those groups, they are very comfortable with the notion that there's a ruling council. They've always had a chief, but the chief draws his authority from the council.

I have observed in the American business culture that working in groups this way is alien. But I would suggest that some of the things creeping into the American business culture, like Japanese quality circles, are examples of the same principles at work. People end up structuring things to foster and nurture the development of everybody instead of just one individual. That is something that has quite a positive quality to it.

Chief Test Pilot

The "right stuff" doesn't entail Monday-morning quarterbacking.

The fact that I'm the leader is nice. I prefer to be the leader rather than the follower. I think most people who are in the professional world aspire to some level of leadership. Here I've got the best of both worlds—I'm the leader, plus I get to be out there flying. On the flying side, there's a lot of stress. Stress is a major part of every test pilot's life. For one thing, we're under stress because we're involved in testing a very expensive piece of machinery. The early airplanes, especially the ones that came off the line, are many times more valuable than the later production airplanes. If you're talking about an airplane that costs $30 million a copy, then the first ones to fly cost $130 million a copy.

The company doesn't put any pressure on you. You clearly know the plane is expensive, but you can't do a decent job flying an airplane if you're scared you're going to put a dent in it. It's just an obvious piece of knowledge, so you're under constant stress from being charged with a pretty expensive piece of equipment, pretty expensive program, and anything that you do to screw it up is going to be problem for you. It will be a problem for you personally because you know you shouldn't have made the mistake. It's like when you make an error in the field while playing baseball. You don't feel very good about that, and at the same time, it hurts the team.

So that's a stress. I don't know how to categorize that. It's not a load that the company places on you. It's something that's there, and everybody is aware of it. It's a very expensive process, a very expensive piece of machinery, and you want to do the very best you can to do the job right.

The fear for your life—I think anyone is naive if they say it's not there. It's something that is tucked away in the back of your mind, but nobody dwells on it. Nobody thinks a whole lot about it. It's a low percentage, but the risk is higher in this type of job. Since I've been here we've lost about half a dozen people, and just before I came here we lost three or four in a row in a big hurry because we had some real problems with the airplane. You don't dwell on that; nobody thinks about that a great deal. But it's there, and if you weren't aware of it, you'd be very naive or very dumb. Something can go wrong and cost you not only your $100+ million plane but also your life.

The stress of the job on a day-to-day basis is there, too, because it is a fairly intense type of work. Even though you're not flying three or four times a day—you're flying about once a day—it's a mentally taxing, as well as physically taxing, task. During your whole day you're thinking about it. You're thinking about the flight when you wake up in the morning, about that flight that's coming up at 10:00 or at 1:00. You're going through mental preparation, you're thinking about it. When it's all over, there's a relaxing period, and then you start thinking about the next flight.

Now I shouldn't say that every flight is that taxing, because some are very routine: you can walk in five minutes before you start to dress for the flight, take a look at the flight cards, and do it. But that's the exception.

As for us as test pilots—me and my pilots—our daily routine at Edwards, in general, is one of going to work just like anyone else. Sometimes we carpool. You generally have a pretty good idea before you go to work what your flight schedule is for that day; for instance, you know if you're scheduled to fly a structural integrity flight. You go to work, sit down, and review the schedule for the day. If you have a flight coming up, you start thinking about it—start planning for it. This involves reviewing the flight cards with the engineers, maybe on an informal basis early on; later on, on a formal basis. You keep tabs on the status of the airplane or airplanes that you're going to fly for the day, when they're scheduled to be ready. You check weather. You look at other constraints to the schedule, and so forth, and just pretty much plan your schedule around that.

Now in addition to flying the airplane and planning for the flight of that plane, you've got all types of routine paperwork that has to be done. Reports have to be written for flights you've done in the past. Administrative activities go on in a pilot's office just like in any other office, and as leader of that office I am in charge of that—budgeting, scheduling flights and people's vacations, things like that.

And then there's flying an hour, maybe two. Some flights might require only fifteen minutes. For some flights—for example, when we are doing the low-altitude speed work—we jump in the airplane, fly up to twenty thousand feet, push everything to the firewall, point the nose down, and get down to eight hundred knots on the deck. Then we're out of gas, so we come in and land.

But you have to remember, all of this is flexible; everything is subject to change. You have a general idea as to what will happen, but it very seldom fits into an ordered routine. So you have to be flexible and be able to move your hours around during the day.

The time you're not flying or involved in getting ready to fly, you're doing administrative work or coordinating with the engineering staff. It's a full day, actually, but a very small portion of it is actually spent flying. In a normal month you might fly twelve to fifteen flights; there are times of intense activity in which you're flying two or three flights a day.

When you're in that plane it's a different world, an intense, concentrated period. You have to be *very* concentrated on what you're doing. There's no visible fear because you're so busy doing everything else that you just don't have time for that sort of thing. Obviously, in the back of your mind, you know something could go wrong, and you're kind of on the alert for it. So you're pumped up, especially in some sorts of maneuvers.

And everyone enjoys flying, so test pilots like to get into new planes and fly them. But it's still work. There's a lot of physical work involved when you're doing a lot of maneuvering. Sometimes you come down soaking wet from the physical exertion. Also there's a lot of mental work involved because it is an intense period. Oftentimes you are busy from the time you take off until you land—recording data, turning switches on, maneuvering, turning switches off, talking with people on the ground.

There's just an increase in interest when you step into an airplane. It's a new environment, and there's the special thrill of being the first person to fly a plane, the first plane in the newest model. Someone has got to be the first one to fly it, and it's a thrill when it's you.

When a new plane or model comes out, every flight is a new event; you're testing the handling qualities, the propulsion, the structure, the weapon system, and so on. Until you get ten or twelve airplanes built, the flight of each one is a new exciting event. After you've got seven to eight hundred built, it's more routine.

The test pilots, myself and the fellows who work for me, are people who want to fly, who always have wanted to fly. They really like it, like expanding the envelope in a new airplane and seeing things that have never been seen before. Generally they are people who really enjoy flying and become very good in the test-pilot business by virtue of going through a military test-pilot school or by soaking up enough information and experience from on-the-job training.

Most of my test pilots were fighter pilots. Then they went beyond that by becoming well versed in recognizing the symptoms of the airplane, its system, and what makes the airplane do things. In some cases they know what must be done to fix things that go wrong. Test pilots have a strong technical background by virtue of their education or by having learned on the job. So, for example, if an airplane handles in a certain way, they can very generally say why. A plane might have poor roll characteristics—you have a high-performance aircraft, you fly it out to six or seven hundred knots and find it's not rolling very quickly—you move the stick and it doesn't move very quickly. That's not good, obviously, so you've got to figure out ways to fix that, and the test pilot can be a vital link between what's happening in the airplane and the engineering group that works on fixing that sort of thing.

The test pilot has to be able to fly his plane and relate very well to the engineers, at least talk their language. He doesn't have to be an engineer to the extent that he fixes it himself, but he does have to relate to them and talk to them. In short, he's more technically proficient and articulate than the fighter pilot. In *The Right Stuff* the test pilot comes across as crazier, but that's baloney. Some people might say he's crazier in that he's willing to go out and fly a plane that's never been flown before. He does things with planes that have never been done before. If that's their version of crazy, then he's crazy.

The pilots are free spirits, but they're out there to do a job in a very structured system. There's a lot of people depending on them, backing them up, and there's a lot of structure because of the coordination that is necessary. You might have 200 or 300 engineers at Edwards, 6 or 8 test pilots, 12 airplanes, a shop force that includes 2 shifts' worth of people down in the shops, maybe 150 people down in the shops. It's a big, big, expensive effort that depends on my test pilots. And it's very structured, very systematically approached with a lot of safety constraints. By the way, we have our own radio man out there, we have our own radio. We'll have a support aircraft to run back and forth to get spare parts if we need that sort of thing.

In *The Right Stuff*, the test pilots were described as nonconformists. If you told them to be sure to have a good breakfast, they would drink only a cup of coffee and then go fly. That's inaccurate; test pilots won't do the opposite of what you tell them to do just because you told them to do it. But they are individualistic. They don't like being told to do things they feel are unimportant, or silly, or that waste their time.

When it comes to leading test pilots, you've got to keep in mind, first and foremost, that *I* am a test pilot. I do what I lead. As chief test pilot at Edwards, I have about six pilots reporting to me. I kind of keep an eye on the constraints and the rules and regulations, and I suppose I do some norm setting by example.

Everything is pretty well structured from years of background and so forth. Everyone knows pretty much how to do their thing. So what I want to do is set a good tone of coordination between the pilots and the engineers. I like to set a standard of quality and excellence, dedication, commitment, and that sort of thing. I like for my guys to work together well, and I like to keep them acting professionally, but that's not difficult to do with people like this. They're high-level people to begin with. They're well educated; they're dedicated to their work. So it's mostly just administering to the details and setting the scheduling and spreading the work out equitably.

My leadership style has always been a laid-back style, democratic or whatever you want to call it. I believe that most of the guys that are working for me are probably a heck of a lot smarter than I am, so I don't try to tell them what to do. I give them as much free rein as possible to do the thing that they are responsible for doing. I provide help as much as I can—keep the administrative problems off their backs and act as a buffer. I don't get into the heavy discipline or the autocratic style of leadership; that's just not my thing. And I think I can maintain a friendly relationship with most people. When I do give negative feedback, when I have to discuss something with a guy, I'll just sit down as comfortably as I can and approach the problem bluntly. But in all honesty, that hasn't happened very often.

When I find something going wrong, I'll say that we've got to sit down and chat about something. We'll discuss the reason for it, in as pleasant a way as possible. It's almost a coaching style. I wouldn't say, "You screwed up here, here, and here." I'd say, "That's the type of thing we try not to do around here," or "That's just not the best way to do it."

For example, I can recall an early thing that I myself did wrong and then, not too long after that when I was in a supervisory role, one of my guys did it. You go out and you start a test flight with a plane that has redundant hydraulic systems. That means if one system fails there's another one to back it up. We're so safety conscious that if you were to lose a hydraulic, the normal thing is to bring the airplane back, because you're now flying on the system and if you lose that system, you've lost the airplane.

Well, in my younger days and in other guys' younger days, the inclination would be to say the heck with that, we'll just go on and do our mission with just one system. I got chewed out early on when I did this, and I had to tell a guy who did the same thing when I was running the show that we just don't do that sort of thing. Our safety record is something that we've got to work at all the time, and we just don't take chances like that. It's not worth it; it's not a good trade. Bring the airplane back when you've lost a system and don't play games like you would if you were out as a fighter pilot.

That's one of many things a guy can do wrong, but you don't want to get in the habit of playing Monday-morning quarterback with him. You can say, "Hey, you did that wrong." But you can say the same thing about the quarterback on the field. He's doing the best he can, and at any given moment, it's not necessarily the wrong thing to do. So you don't Monday-morning quarterback him. There's a difference between doing something that you can see is wrong in retrospect and doing things that are flagrant violations of rules, regulations, practices, or common sense. You don't have a whole lot of the latter in the test-pilot business. Pilots are a pretty disciplined group of people. They have a pretty good idea what the constraints are and the reasons for them.

My people like to have fun, joyride with the plane. There's always that, and I guess the biggest complaint in the test-pilot business world would be that you never have the opportunity to just relax and enjoy it. I tell my pilots, "If you've got five minutes of fuel left and you've run all your test points, then go fly some acrobatics." There's nothing wrong with that—it's just a matter of getting some of the ol' juices flowing again. As their leader, I don't have any problems with it, as long as they're not down buzzing at two hundred feet or something like that—as long as they're doing things that are legal, within the envelope of the airplane. If they've got five minutes to enjoy flying the airplane, to get a better feel for it, there's nothing wrong with that. But again, it's all a matter of constraint and discipline. They don't go flying under a bridge. They don't go breaking FAA regulations. And they don't go supersonic where they can break windows. So they keep it within limits.

A lot of my job has to do with scheduling and helping the pilots cope with stress. I've got a lot of risky flights and some mundane ones. So I try to break up the stress by scheduling some routine flights in among the stressful ones. But there are other things to consider, too. There's a number of programs going on. I have ten airplanes out there and nine or ten or fourteen separate programs going on. There may be a structural-integrity program; maybe a cruise-control program; maybe an autopilot program; a spin program; a high-angle-of-attack and out-of-control program—things like that. And generally I have the pilots assigned to the programs. So I've got one guy who's going to do this engine work. He does most of the engine work on a specific airplane. So to the extent he can do it, and to the extent that it's not too much of a burden on him, he'll do all the engine work on a given plane, because he's very familiar with the engine; he's been working with engineering to get ready for the program. So he's the guy on that program. So for the most part, I'm not going to back him off to give him stress relief. Occasionally I might.

Every five or six flights I might say, "Let's let someone else fly this flight and you take that one," if it's a very high-stress program. You don't say, "You need a break." It's more tacit; he understands what I'm doing.

But stress doesn't really get to be a big consideration very often. What I'm more likely to do is to spread out the flying so that everybody gets a chance to do something interesting and challenging, rather than the other way around. It's not so much a stress reduction as it is an opportunity for other guys to participate in those challenging programs. The stress reduction is sort of a fallout, and you kill two birds with one stone. You also get new inputs, a fresh look into each testing.

I encourage my pilots to discuss the problems they encounter; this relieves stress and helps solve some of the problems. You're up there and things go wrong, so you communicate that back immediately. We talk about our problems all the time—how we're going to get this particular piece of data, how you go about achieving a particular point in the flight envelope. Now fears—that's a different thing. We don't talk about them; we don't sit down and talk about how scared we might be and what particular element scared us in the last flight. We don't talk about our fears. But problems are another thing; we always compare notes on problems and how we can solve them.

Other than doing these things, I back off as a manager. I have to watch in handling test pilots that I don't get too involved in the individual pilot's program—in other words, being a micro manager rather than a macro manager. I always feel the guys who are doing the programs are perfectly capable of running their programs. I always ask them how the programs are going, but I never get in there, in the nuts-and-bolts sense, trying to do something they probably could do better than I can. I've got to allow a test pilot who has a lot of individual skills anyhow to do his thing, and not try to do the job for him. That's true of any leadership role, I think. But it's even more true of this one, because here's a guy who's charged with a pretty important role, a pretty important piece of machinery, and if I don't have confidence in his ability to do it by himself, I better get somebody else in there.

I think I need to give positive feedback when a pilot does a good job. Too often I think it's self-evident when they've done a good job, and I need to do more of that. I assume too much, that people know when they've done a good job. They're experts; they're professionals; and if nothing goes wrong then that's a good job, and they know it and they get turned on by it.

That's *not* necessarily the case, and there should be some more positive feedback. On the other hand, I don't think they're out seeking feedback as to whether or not they've made a mistake. In this business that's self-evident.

At the extreme, you simply don't come back. Most often it's not so severe, but it's obvious. Everyone knows it, and we don't make a big deal out of a mistake unless it's important and we want to highlight it. Then I do it privately, obviously. But if a guy lands the airplane with the gear up, it couldn't be more evident to anyone than it is to him. That's an exaggerated example, but everyone makes a mistake; no one is perfect. There's always the human element in this business.

Actually, when pilots make mistakes, I joke about it to relieve their stress or distress. We have a standing joke. One of the things you can do in a high-performance airplane is to get on the brakes too hard when you land. The analogy is you press your brakes too hard in a car and screech to a halt. In an airplane you blow the tires out when you do this, and that can have more drastic implications, but generally, if nothing else goes wrong, you just end up stuck on the runway with a blown tire or tires. And if that's done just because of a heavy foot, we have a golden boot that we pass around to the last guy to blow a tire. The boot just sits on his desk, and he is the lead foot for the day.

I think one reason I have a laid-back style and joke about pilots' mistakes is that there are a lot of factors in their world I can't control. I have very little control over the dangers that pilots face. And there's the actual physical stress or punishment that they go through. There are times when you're knocked around in the plane. That happens sometimes, especially in the high-angle-attack programs. You come down wringing wet from trying to muscle the plane around at six to nine g's. It's very physically stressing, demanding. When they're coping with all that, pilots don't need also to cope with an overbearing leader.

Brothel Overseer

People need to understand why they're doing things, not just that they're being told to do them.

Lying on flat terrain, the brothel is easily accessible by taxi or private car. After clearance from the security guard at the gate, a customer enters a homey, open reception room in which about ten girls introduce themselves. The customer selects one or two girls. Having made his selection, he is escorted to another room, where he chooses from the items on the menu. The options include massages, a "French," the "reverse," the "99," and other sexual favors. After choosing an item, or a combination of items, the customer is quoted a price, and the rest is up to the work-ing lady or ladies. As for management of the establishment, it falls to the overseer.

I want this place to be better than any other brothel. Most peoples' im-pression of a brothel is that when you walk in you keep your hand on your wallet. You don't hang your coat up without watching it, because someone is going to steal it. It's a part of the world that is just sort of seedy.

I'm trying to make our place the direct opposite of that, and I think we've been successful. For the working girls, this is like a sorority. In their spare time they watch TV or swim in the pool I put in. They watch Jane Fonda workouts, run on the treadmill, ride bikes, or go jogging.

What I've established here is a real homey atmosphere. It's not dark. The sun is shining through the windows, and it's clean. It's like someone's kitchen or dining room. And it's a secure environment. When a fellow takes off his clothes in a room, sometimes his wallet falls out, or he takes off his watch and leaves it. Watches get left here all the time; we mail them to New York, Florida, and L.A. And we mail wallets, lots of money. Those kinds of things.

I want to discount and get rid of the idea that brothels have to be seedy and that the girls and managers have to be gray-area greasy punks. Here it's all above board. We don't break any law—selling sex is legal here. Coming here is a refreshing experience. Families drive up here, and the husband sneaks in to purchase a menu. We say, "Bring the whole family in." We've had grand-mothers, great-grandmothers, four generations sitting on the couches in the parlor, taking pictures with the working girls so that they can go back and show their friends in Iowa.

We have a mission here. We contribute to society. I show society that this business can have positive aspects. One example: I just fully equipped this place so that it's accessible to the handicapped. Handicapped people don't get a fair shake in society when it comes to the freedom to have sexual rela-tionships. They're ostracized. Here it's really refreshing to see a paraplegic come in. The women are sensitive to his needs, and they send him out feel-ing like a whole man.

Comparing legal to illegal prostitution, I know I'm making a contribution—to the individual ladies and to society. Example: society derives licensing fees from the working ladies. The ladies pay Social Security, they pay income taxes, and they maintain high standards of hygiene. I have a doctor here who checks each lady once a week. And I have doctors and nurses to present seminars, answer questions, and show photographs for symptom recognition.

In illegal prostitution, the working girl is deciding to be an outlaw. That makes her associate with other outlaws—drug dealers, people who will rip off her customers, harm them. So she becomes an outlaw not just in prostitution but in drugs, robbery, etc. And all that money is accumulated tax-free and is pyramided toward other illegal endeavors. And the police force spends tremendous amounts of money, tremendous numbers of man-hours trying to accomplish the impossible. They can never stop prostitution. So I want to demonstrate that this is the answer to it. Now, your grandmother might not like it, your mother might not like it, but it's a practical solution to something that goes back to the beginning of society.

This brothel has a fine history. I think it's the Rolls-Royce of brothels. The women who work here are the girl-next-door type; they're not the type you see portrayed in the movies. They're bright women, mostly college-educated, who are looking for a shortcut to achieve goals in five to seven years that normally would take ten to twelve years to acheive in a straight job.

I have certain guidelines as to what girls will and will not do; however, within those guidelines the girls are essentially private contractors. They negotiate with each customer. We have girls here right now from New Zealand, Indiana, Washington, Alaska, Florida, Kentucky, and elsewhere. About half of the staff is permanent—they've been here for two to three years—and that's unique in any brothel. The other half turns over every six to eight months.

My job, to say the least, isn't boring. I manage twenty beautiful women. In addition, I have a cook, a handyman, a gardener, shift managers (housewives from this community), a private limo man, plus taxis that don't work directly for me, and two security guards. Supervising all this keeps life from being boring; there are a lot of facets.

The style I use is to tell my employees what I want, but I don't limit them as to how they accomplish it. As long as we get to the right point, I give them considerable latitude to use their own approach. Now, if I see some approach I don't like, some subtle nuance that I want changed or corrected, then I mention it. Yet, I generally like to give as much freedom as possible.

I put myself into the shoes of the people who are working for me. I know that for me, the more freedom I'm given, the more opportunity I'm given to be creative, then the more I'm going to enjoy my job, want to come to work. Then I'll do a better job when I get there. It's the same with my ladies. The more freedom I give them, the more they'll enjoy the work and the better job they'll do.

I didn't use to manage that way. I'd chase people down and egg them on to get their work done. Then I realized all the attention and effort I was giving them was just contributing to their irresponsibility. I was just making it easier for them to depend on someone else. That was a valuable piece of information for me to pick up. Now I make it very clear what I need, and very clear that they can do it. Then I don't contribute to their irresponsibility.

When it comes to hiring working girls, I consider myself a good judge of character. In fact, it's easier to hire a good working lady than it is another staff person. Of course, it's important that she be attractive. But in this brothel, that's only 50 percent of it. I tell ladies that the other 50 percent is that they need to be great-quality company; they need to have a good personality. I subscribe to the *Wall Street Journal* and other magazines for them so that they can improve their ability to carry on a conversation. I tell the ladies, "You are more than just prostitutes. You are courtesans. You supply sexual favors, but your greatest asset is the quality company you provide to the customers."

And I'm right. Customers come here and spend six, eight, ten hours with a lady, and only one-half hour of that might be sexual. The rest is quality companionship. So I tell a lady when I'm interviewing her, "It's obvious that you are sexually attractive. Now show me what kind of conversationalist you can be by asking me questions and talking with me. Role-play like we're in a room and I'm a customer."

I'm silly on little things, too. If people give me a resume with a misspelled word on it, then that tells me something about the person. I look at grooming. Do they look me in the eye when I talk to them? And I always expect people to ask me questions; if they do, I'm real pleased. That indicates that they're interested in the organization here, and that they care.

Once I've hired a working lady, my major concern is keeping her serious, tuned in to being good at her job. I want the ladies to do their best, to be alert all the time for ways of doing the job better. I'm constantly stressing that. A gentleman comes here, picks a lady, goes to a room with her, spends some time with her, and leaves. His total impression of this brothel is, in essence, his impression of her. If she's in a bad mood, not looking good in the lineup, or not doing something the best way she can, then it hurts all of us. If she thinks she's just hurting herself by not performing well, then she's mistaken. She's hurting everyone in the house, from the cooks to the gardener to everyone else, because we live and die on our reputation. Each lady and every staff person has the obligation to enhance that reputation to the utmost. So I'm constantly having little meetings and individual conferences—pep talks—about that, and I give them plenty of avenues and opportunities to step out of the picture and reflect on it. If they're ever so tired that they feel they can't represent us well, then they can voluntarily step down for a while and take some mental-health days, then come back when they can put their best foot forward.

I think my leadership style reflects my managerial philosophy: leaders should be able to do everybody's job. You have to know how to do it before you ask someone else to do it. And you need to have compassion and give people an opportunity to have a bad day. Don't be unrealistic about this. People's lives are stressful, and if they need a day off, give it to them. Here, if someone wants a day off, they don't have to call in and say that they're sick. They just say that they want a mental-health day. I'd rather have someone look me in the eye and say they need a mental-health day than have them lie.

Taking time to explain the "why" to people is also extremely important. When I ask my people to follow certain procedures or practices, I explain why. If I don't want certain furniture in a room, I'll explain why. I don't just say, "Do this because I say so." It's just like explaining the solution to a math problem. Do you put these numbers here and move these over there because the teacher said to do so, or do you do it that way because you think there's a reason for it? People need to understand why they're doing things, not just that they're being told to do them.

Managing this brothel is one of the most invigorating experiences you could have. There are warm moments, excitement, and amusement. A while back an elderly couple in their seventies came in and sat down in the parlor. The wife picked a lady from the lineup for her husband. It was his seventy-fifth birthday present. Then she sat and watched TV with the working ladies while the husband went to the room with her pick.

And a woman came in here who had lost a couple of babies prior to term. She was pregnant again; so she brought her husband here and bought him a party as a present, to show her love for him. Her doctor had told her that she ought not have any intercourse during the entire term of her pregnancy.

We occasionally have women call up here whose husbands are having a fortieth birthday, and he's always had the fantasy of being with two women. So they arrange that for him because they love him.

As for amusement, one time I got a little shook when we had a parlor full of Japanese tourists. These Japanese guys were sitting in the parlor during the afternoon with the window open. They saw the sheriff coming in. He always comes in and has a cup of coffee when he's out here. Their eyes got big and they started jabbering a mile a minute, because they were sure it was a bust and they were all going to be thrown in jail.

My relationship with the working ladies is a special one. I honestly want these ladies to be able to look back five to seven years from now and say that the sacrifices they made here were worth it. I give them investment seminars. They are used to a cash-and-carry world. When you go to buy a car and you're a prostitute, you don't put that down on the credit application. They're not used to credit or investments, but now they have money. So I help them with it. Tomorrow, in fact, we're having a seminar on gold and silver investment. At other times I bring in $100-an-hour tax consultants and financial planners to help them.

Their job is the most stressful in the world. Air controllers are supposed to be in a high-pressure job, but that doesn't hold a candle to being a working girl in a brothel. It's not only physically demanding; it's also emotionally demanding. There are tremendous sacrifices. But I want them to be able to earn money, invest it wisely, have something to show for it and not just blow it all.

2

Helter-Skelter

H ELTER-SKELTER is an apt description of most leaders' jobs. They are
packed with brief, varied, and fragmented activities that make the job
one they "hate to love." Researchers have found that a typical leader's day
contains between 200 and 1,000 events. What kinds of events are they? That
is, what do leaders do?

As the reports in this book show, the answer depends on the line of work.
In general, leaders give orders to subordinates, take orders from superiors,
answer questions, deal with crises, evaluate progress, answer phones, listen
to complaints, and so on, from day to day. The assembly line supervisor does
all this and, in addition, tracks down drunks; runs a bond drive; and observes,
controls, and perhaps participates in gags. The wino leader's life is more placid;
still, he has a variety of responsibilities. Caring for his drunks translates into
initiating a cave excavation, negotiating with police, procuring money and
firewood, and, most important, converting mundane liquids into intoxicants.

The inner-city mission director offers insights into the complexity of two
jobs. His former post as president of a military academy was high-pressured:

*"Your trustees want you to operate the school and make it financially sound, which
means you have to get money. You have to spend very little money. You have to
get students. At the same time, the faculty are saying to you, 'We've got to be sure
we hold the academic standards of the institution high; therefore, we can't take in
just everybody!' . . . and they wanted tremendous raises every year, all the equipment in the world.*

*"Then, also, I had the parents. I'd hear, 'I paid five thousand dollars for my
child to come here and, by golly, he's going to get an A.' In addition to that, there
were the students. I think one of the greatest things about this current job is that
I can come in on Monday morning and not have to worry about a situation that some*

dumb fourteen-year-old kid created on Saturday night. He got a beer, got half-soused, got caught, and it's my fault, when I'm twenty miles away."

His current job "isn't a big job, not a pressure job." He works with people who give him money, food, clothing, and so forth, supervises four or five volunteers, coordinates with the public health nurses, and deals with about four thousand families a year. Dealing with the families means personally seeing each one, deciding whom to help and whom to turn down. He chooses not to delegate the interviews or the decisions.

The missile commander's tour is one of variety and stress, with both occurring in a feast-or-famine cycle. Continually he and his deputy must monitor ten Minuteman missiles. Their communications gear—three voice radios, two data radios, a teletype system, and a speaker phone—along with a couple of computers, must be checked out and kept in running order. Problems—environmental, security, power, communication, missile, or warhead—must be solved immediately. "And if something breaks, perhaps it's Murphy's Law, everything does and at the worst possible time."

The resident-hall adviser was also graced with feasts and famines. In times of feast, he had to control rampant false-fire alarms and pyrotechnics. In more placid times, he simply talked with students, attended meetings, directed other resident advisers, delegated "female to other females, problems" rushed suicide cases to the hospital, charged football players with assault, attended hearings, disciplined drunks, and, we assume, attended classes in his spare time.

The resident hall adviser's report portrays a leader caught in the middle, operating in a stressful helter-skelter world. And it reveals some leadership gems. The adviser's natural or preferred style was one of "moral persuasion"; he got people to cooperate out of respect or friendship. Operationally, he built idiosyncratic credits with people and then traded the credits for others' cooperation.

For this setting, it was a perfect style, because, as the adviser notes, he had few rewards or punishments at his disposal. Perhaps the adviser was just lucky that his style fit the situation. Or maybe the situation forced him to adopt that style. Whichever was the case, his style fit the situation and he was a very successful leader, until he quit working hard at it.

The most important precept is found in the last paragraph of the adviser's commentary. A leader's style must fit not only the situation, it also has to be suited to the leader: "You're not going to be very effective with a style if it drives you bonkers to use it."

Assembly Line Supervisor

One year of experience, six times over.

Day to day, my job is helter-skelter. This fellow asked me last year how much experience I had as a supervisor. When I said six years, he asked me if I actually had six years of experience or if I had one year's experience six times over. That got me thinking about myself and my job.

What do I do? You name it. For one thing, I keep people from coming to work drunk. Like with this fellow Tom Ropes, that upper management traded for gloves. He'd go out and get pickled during lunch. So I caught him coming in and wrote up a reprimand. He kept doing it, so I found the bar where he was going and caught him there. I'd taken my superior so that we had him dead to rights. Of course he went through an appeal procedure, with the union backing him all the way. And the management let him off. They traded him for some gloves.

The workers were issued these gloves to use in some heavy, rough work in the plant, and if they lost them, they had to pay for them. Well, every so often they'd have to turn in the old ones and get new replacements. Since the old gloves many times were in good shape, the workers would want to keep them or would claim to lose them and refuse to pay for the lost gloves, because they were going to be thrown away. So the union backs them on the lost gloves issue, and management struck a bargain: through some horse-trading, Tom Ropes was reinstated, and the workers—the union—agreed not to "lose" but a certain number of gloves per year.

Dealing with the workers can a lot of times prove to be a real challenge. I remember how important it was for us to get 100 percent participation in the payroll savings plan to buy U.S. Savings Bonds. One hundred percent was quite important for a supervisor's future advancement in the company. I worked night and day to get my people to participate and got all of them but two to do so. One of these fellows, I found out, was henpecked, so I went to his wife and sweet-talked her. He came in while I was there, and she told him that I'd explained to her what a good idea it was, and that he *was* now participating in the program.

The other guy was a tougher holdout, but I found that he had this farm that he worked on the side. One day I told him he was the last holdout we had. When he laughed, I asked if he would participate in the program if I agreed to work for him on his farm every Saturday for a year. He laughed again and said, "Sure." I had him.

We make washing machines in this assembly line, so the work is noisy, repetitive, and, worst of all, boring. It comes as no wonder then that workers start pulling stunts. They act like kids. You understand why, but you've got to keep it under control because it can get out of hand. For instance, we have this porcelain dip that the exterior of the machines goes through. Each exterior is dipped; then it is baked; then it has the motor, etc., installed. Well one guy goes up to this unit that has just been dipped and is moving toward the ovens and with his finger writes a four-letter salutation on the side that rhymes with duck. I guess he thought people down the line would see it and get a big laugh out of it. Well, this unit makes it all the way through the line and is delivered to some little old lady in Omaha or somewhere. It comes in a crate; they open it up for her, and there is this nice greeting. Management didn't think that was very funny, so they traced back the serial number, found the production line, and fired the guy.

That's just one example of what we face on a daily basis. Usually the fun and games don't have such negative consequences, so I let them go. For example, "Paul Peters" was an inspector who worked with about thirty other inspectors. He had eyes like that movie star Jack Elam that go off in different directions, and he wore thick glasses, and he didn't have many teeth, so his gums were kind of loose and flopping. And he was real gullible and weird looking—walking around with his hat on sideways, looking at you with these eyes. Oh, he was gullible. He'd believe anything that you told him.

Then there was this other fellow, "Whit Shoe," a real operator, who was a pig farmer. He's a tough, crude-looking guy, but he was real smooth, and he'd come up and could sell you anything. He'd make up stories, and he knew Paul was gullible, so he'd come up to someone who was working near Paul and he'd start telling them a story just loud enough that he knew Paul could hear it. Of course, Paul was a basically nosy sort of person who liked to gossip, so he wanted to pick up these tidbits and go around and tell people about them.

One of these episodes involved me. Whit came up to me while I was standing near Paul and said, "I hear you might be interested in buying a car. If you decide you are interested, I'll get you a deal on one." So he turned around and left. Immediately Paul looked at me. He kind of was looking at me—his eyes were looking in different directions, but one of them was looking at me. And he said, "Don't you ever buy anything from Whit Shoe. He'll skin ye. You know the last time he sold someone a car in here, you know what he did? He found a bunch of Pontiacs they were floating on a barge down the Ohio River. And the barge turned over, and all those Pontiacs were at the bottom of the Ohio River, and a salvage company went down there and pulled them all up and sold them to Whit Shoe at a real low price. So you know what he did? He took them back to Lebanon, cleaned them out as best he could, and then dumped perfume all over them so they would smell okay. And all of these people I know who bought these cars found that after a few months, they all began to smell like fish, and they never could get the fishy smell out."

Then there were the Suki lawnmowers. Paul told me a while back that Whit was going around selling people Suki lawnmowers. And people were buying them, but after a while they found they were falling apart. What he did was to go over to Europe to buy parts, and then he made these Suki mowers in his basement. Paul said that Whit made the engine blocks out of concrete, cheap concrete, and the pistons were made out of old gunshell cases. When he went to Europe, he bought some cannon shell casings and cut them and used them as pistons. So Paul said to me, "If he ever tries to sell you a lawnmower, don't buy it."

He also said to me, "You didn't know old 'Joe Howard,' but Joe died and Whit went over to his widow, masquerading as a preacher, and convinced her to let him give the eulogy. They tell me that Whit Shoe saw the funeral announcement in the paper and got on to that poor widow and got her to agree to let him be the guy who gave the eulogy. So Whit Shoe came in there slick as he could be, all dressed up in a tuxedo and fit to kill and stood up there all holier-than-now and gave the eulogy. Then he bent over the casket to say a few final words, with his back to the audience, and took that diamond ring off of Joe's finger!"

You see, Whit would start these stories or go around to someone who worked close to Paul to start them. For example, "Red Coat," a friend of his, would walk up, preplanned, as Paul was looking up into space and say, "Hey, Whit, that lawnmower you sold me is broke again. It's all cracked and it's falling apart. I've only had it a month and I want my money back." Of course, Whit Shoe would yell back, "That's tough luck, buddy, you should have known better when you bought it! You can't abuse a lawnmower that way and expect it to hold together." Then Red Coat would lean down to Paul Peters and say, "The block is made out of concrete, and it cracked right down the middle!" Then he'd bring in a piece of concrete from the road outside to show Paul a piece that had fallen off the engine block.

As a supervisor, I also have to keep workers from stealing stuff. That's tough, because they're ingenious. But someitmes the workers do themselves in. We had a big tunnel that went from the factory for about three to four hundred yards underground, under a street to a guardhouselike deal. There we had a lot of gates side by side, like you find going into a football stadium. When the bell rang at 3:30—when we let out of work—all the workers would punch their cards, and thousands of them would push through this tunnel, running up to the guardhouse and the gates. As they went through these gates, the guards would look into anything they were carrying. If they had a lunch box they had to open it, a sack, a briefcase, whatever they had they had to open it. The guards were very careful, and they had to do that because stuff was getting stolen.

So one day these guys were going down there, running like a bat out of Hades, and one of them collapsed as he got out of the tunnel to the gatehouse. And the gaurds started to do all this heart restarting stuff to save his life, but when they opened up his shirt, he had this copper wire wrapped around his whole body from his waist to his armpits. What had happened was that back up in the factory, he had decided to steal this wire—it was worth a lot of money—so he had taken off his shirt and held his hands over his head while his friend had coiled it around him. Then he lowered his arms, put on his shirt, tucked it in his pants, and put on his coat. Then when the bell rang, he took off running. What had happened was that the guy must have wrapped it too tight for his normal body position, and as he ran through the tunnel he must have hyperventilated [*laughs*]. So he fell down at the guardhouse, and they toted him in.

Wino Leader

Now you might think I'm telling you a lie, but a can of Lysol makes you the best drink you ever drank in your life.

The interstate passes over the abandoned railroad siding near an ageless textile mill. Underneath the expressway lie two bald dirt banks underpinning the concrete structure and sloping gently down toward two lonely rusty rails, numerous mattresses, one empty wine bottle, two broken ones, a 55-gallon oil barrel that has survived innumerable fires, and a band of "bridge people." Their number varies from a high of twenty to a low of five, depending on circumstances, the elements, their own motivations, the law, and other factors.

Currently their forces are low. Two died of heart attacks during the past winter. Another, lying too close to a bonfire, rolled north when he should have rolled south but never perceived his mistake. They found some of his remains the next morning. As one of his colleagues noted, without humor or sadness, "From ashes to ashes."

One of the bridge people froze to death in the trunk of an abandoned car; he thought he would be warm there. Another went in the hospital for something, having passed out and not awakened. Maybe he is still unconscious, or dead. In any case, he has not appeared recently.

Still another, Roger, might be in the hospital but probably is out because he wasn't burned too badly. Like the others, one night he was drinking and smoking while Bart, who has been to Nashville, played his guitar. When Roger fell asleep, his or someone else's cigarette ignited his polypropylene mattress. He awoke in time, someone ran to call an ambulance—it always comes—and he made it to the hospital. But no one knows where he is now.

Two of the bridge people were caught trespassing at the car wash, so they left town, while another went for a walk a few nights back to find some beer cans to sell to the recycling unit. She didn't return.

This cut under the overpass, along with a larger one a quarter of a mile north and a cave dug across from the local liquor store, make up the bridge people's territory. Early each morning they pick up their bottles or beer cans and scavenge through the dumpsters for food and recycleables. Prior to their search for bottles, cans, and food, they go on a quest for water. Most businesses and public facilities have removed their outside faucets; therefore, finding relief for a sandy mouth is difficult.

If the dumpsters yield sufficient funds to buy a bottle, the people return to their abode; they sit, drink, talk, urinate, argue, and pass around generic cigarettes. If someone is starving, he is fed first; food has a higher priority than alcohol. With regard to alcohol, all share and share alike if they have contributed to the "circle." An exception is made for the fellow with DTs; he gets as much as he needs.

If scavenging generates adequate funds, then everyone gets drunk. If the funds are too low, all parties consider methods for making them sufficient. At night, about five kvet to the all-night convenience store that gives out free coffee. Not "too many" go. They drink the coffee, stay as long as they like, and they "behave themselves." The proprietor allows them to hang around and drink, since he has never been robbed when they were there. This routine changes abruptly when Tommy's check comes in. As with all money, his $440 a month from Social Security disability is shared among all. After his check is cashed, all stay drunk until the funds are exhausted. Then it's back to the standard operating procedure.

Larry, the leader of the pack, serves as the group's spokesman, catalyst, innovator, and historian. He is articulate, strong, and handsome. His blond hair is tucked under a baseball cap. He also sports a clean-shaven face, along with white teeth. His memory, long- and short-term, is sharp, which relegates him to a small minority among winos. His past experiences seem varied. He is a traveler, and he is sustained by his youth—age, 29.

Most people'd think a bunch of drunks wouldn't have no leader. But there's a lot what's got to get done. Now I'm not telling people, "You do this and you do that." It's a democracy; no, it's a arguecracy. Here, whatever our conscience guides us to do, that's what we do. Whatever happens, happens. We live from hour to hour. Well, we get a lot of suggestions from everybody in the group. We sit around, argue, and then all of a sudden we just get up and go do it. We're taken care of for the winter now. Railroad came by about two months ago and tore up them ties, so we got plenty of wood. All we got do to is go out there and take it.

But sometimes, somebody has to make decisions. Like a while back, we were so cold that I decided we ought to dig a cave. You could get two people in there easy and you could get this mattress in there. One night me and Phil Darter slept in the cave. (You'd like Phil. He's dead now. Died up there lying in the back of an old junk car. Phil died in January of '81.) We got up on a Saturday morning, and it had been pouring down rain that night and Sedth Whitman—he's dead too—had crawled up in there drunk. Me and Phil was sick that morning. I came climbing out first. Then he come climbing out of the hole. I thought I's going into DTs 'cause he's red all over. I thought the devil's coming out of the ground after me, and I started screaming. But it was just Phil with mud all over him. He climbed out of the bank, and we went across the street and bought two liters of wine. Got boiled that day.

Well, we came back 'bout half drunk and found the cave done caved in on Sedth. So we start digging with our hands and then we called the rescue, and they camed to digging. And they got fire trucks and everything and they're digging like crazy. So Phil and I are there watching when Sedth comes up drunk behind us and asks who's trapped in the cave. He'd done crawled out and got drunk like we did.

I leave, get some work, and come back here to take care of these [*he points*]. Do it all the time. While I was married I'd come down here and bring them food down here. Buy 'em wine. Buy 'em liquor. I done it because I knowed they needed it. My wife didn't like it that much. And when they get sick I take care of them. Call an ambulance. Just as fast as I can, and somebody comes down here to get them, wherever we're at.

But now, about two and a half months ago Tommy there and Holt Boltman left me laying over there. Well, when I'd start to walk I do like this. [*Gets up and stumbles, leaning backward and dragging his right leg.*] I'd do this. I couldn't move. I's having some kind of seizures, and they left me lying over there. And I ain't forgotten that either, Tommy. And church was going on, and I fainted over there, and a deacon come out over there, called an ambulance for me and they come and took me to the hospital. Gave me four shots of something or another.

I negotiate with the police. They leave us alone if we stay down here. Once in a while you have trouble with blacks coming down through here wanting to start a fight or something. I fight them or just tell them to go on. Then we all get up and there's more of us than them so they don't fight. We're all going to help each other.

Our problem's over at that parking lot. People's ripping off tapes and stuff and tearing up cars and we get blamed for it. We don't do it. We don't steal. So I went up and told the police that. And I think they believe me; least they leave us alone. But the people around here think we do it.

I have to break up fights a lot. We all fight with each other, but we don't mean nothing. We all get down here after we get drunk and we might get in a fight and an hour later we're buddies again. But you got to make sure nobody's hurt. If he's hurt I call an ambulance.

Main thing I got to do is get these drunks something to drink. Weren't for me, they'd stay sober half the time. I like vodka myself. Have drunk Listerine. Drunk Lysol, rubbing alcohol. Now you might think I'm telling you a lie, but a can of Lysol makes you the best drink you ever drank in your life, if you can get to water. Now all the people around here done took their outside spigots off.

Now what you do is take a can of Lysol and knock a little hole—just a little bitty hole—to let the pressure off it first. Then you shake it into a pint bottle, fill it with water, shake it up. Best drink in the world. Got to use water or it will burn your throat out. I drink lemon extract: that's 80 percent alcohol.

One time I went blind. I's in Chattanooga, Tennessee, one time and I's in the county courtyard. City police couldn't bother you on county property. I's up there, and we were drinking rubbing alcohol then, and I did start to seeing double, and they took me to the county hospital, and I stayed in there seventeen days. Because I'd drunk so much of it, I was seeing double. I could see a cigarette and I'd put it in my mouth and I'd be lighting the wrong cigarette. Drank that because it was all I could afford. Up there you could get a bottle for twenty-nine cents and you could make a half-gallon.

And I tell you something else you can drink too. Canned heat. You know what that is? All right, you got your red top. You got you green top. You got your blue tops. The red top is the only kind you can drink. Can't the green and the blue; they'll kill you. But what you do, you take a white rag—I have taken my socks—and squeeze it out. You can make a half a gallon with one can of that.

You can drink shoe polish. Can't strain it through no rag. Take you a piece of loaf bread. All right, take you a piece of loaf bread and put it over a cup and pour your shoe polish through the bread. That strains the black out of it. There is your alcohol going down in there. Now you can dilute it, but it's better to just drink it straight.

Paint thinner? I've drunk a many of a gallon of it. Now you go up here to hardware store and get you a gallon of that and make you five gallons to drink.

I just got back in town four days ago. Been in jail in Spartenburg. I was passing through there from Atlanta. I come out of a bar and these two black dudes jumped on me and I hit one up the side of the head with a pop bottle and I got 120 days in jail. The black guy said I tried to rob him. The other guy ran away, but I knocked this one out.

We have a good time. Police don't give us trouble. I stayed down here nine years before I got married. My wife left me on January twenty-ninth of this year, so I'm here. I'm supposed to go to work tomorrow on heavy equipment.

I go out a lot and then come back down here. I could go to my daddy's house but then I'd have to put up with my stepmamma. She don't like me, because she found out I was carrying on with both her daughters before my daddy and her ever got married. She's got a grudge against me about that. I don't hold grudges.

Now I got me a good daddy. I could go up there and call him right now. Well I couldn't right now; have to wait 'til he got off work, and he'd come get me or give me money. But I ain't done that in about two years.

I like the companionship; we have a good time. We live from hour to hour. Have a good time. We all get around drinking and carrying on and you let Bart get his guitar and . . . have a time. Drink anything we can get our hands on. No stress, no problems.

Inner-city Mission Director

If you're going to cheat me, cheat me in January.

This isn't a big job, not a pressure job. I have had all of those that I want. Not a lot of big decisions to make here. Sure, there are a lot of decisions, and they are important, but not big. Someone comes in and says that they are in trouble and need money to pay the rent or that they are starving and need us to find food for them. With these problems you just solve them on the spot; actually, there is no pondering involved. You simply solve the problem.

As the director, I am in the middle of two processes. The first is personal. People give me money, clothing, and other stuff, and I give it to those who need it. Second is the organizational. I am the only paid employee in this mission. The rest are volunteers—about four or five church people who come and help and about the same number of clients, people who we've helped and they give their time. The ladies you see out front, hanging clothes, helping people try them on, and filling food boxes, are clients; they come in every morning. In addition I have a lot of people who work for me on an if-you-need-me basis. For example, I have a man who'll bring his pickup truck, and we go haul things. We also have public-health nurses who don't work for us but refer families to us. They're out in the homes, and they'll call saying Betsy or Clyde needs some oil because they're freezing to death; so we send it. As you can see, we have a rather odd, great organization—volunteers, church people, suppliers, nurses. We are seeing around four thousand families a year.

Just prior to taking this job, I was president of a military academy, and for thirteen years before that I was the assistant to the president of the college. Coming here has been a really big change. I think the best way to describe being the president of a military academy is to say that now I know what a fire hydrant would feel like at a dog convention. To handle an organization of that sort is one of the most high-pressure situations you can be in. Your trustees want you to operate the school and make it financially sound, which means that you have to get money. You have to spend very little money. You have to get students.

At the same time, the faculty are saying to you, "We've got to be sure we hold the academic standards of the institution high; therefore, we can't take in just everybody." Well every time I didn't take in somebody I saw five thousand dollars a year going out the door; therefore, I had a tendency to say to the faculty, "Look I'll get the youngins and you take care of them. I'm going to get them, and after all I'm hiring you to teach. I'm not supposed to get you good students, and then let you get the glory for turning out A students when they were A students when they came in. Do something with them." But the faculty didn't see it that way, so I was being bugged by the faculty about this, and they wanted tremendous raises every year, all the equipment in the world.

Then, also, I had the parents. I'd hear, "I paid five thousand dollars for my child to come here and, by golly, he's going to make an A." In addition to that, there were the students. I think one of the greatest things about this current job is that I can come in on Monday morning and not have to worry about a situation that some dumb fourteen-year-old kid created on Saturday night. He got a beer, got half-soused, got caught, and it's my fault, when I'm twenty miles away.

As a director here, I do the work myself or ask people to help me and thank them when they do. But I usually do it. We simply don't have the money to hire staff. When someone needs money I tell them to come in and discuss it. They do, and I get the money for them. And a lot of people want just to come in and talk about a problem. So I sit down and talk with them about it. I like that. When I can give more than the material things it takes to solve a problem, that is a tremendous satisfaction.

When a client comes in for help, I need to discern whether or not I will help them. Does this person need help or are they trying to live off the system? I do that by asking several leading questions about their expenses—why they're where they are. Intuition is usually the best guide, or the figures don't add up. Some I help, and others I decide not to. When I turn people away, about 50 percent say thank you anyway. The other half of the time it varies between having someone refer to my canine ancestry or saying, "Well I don't know why you can't give to me when you give to everybody else."

Operating this way has its costs. There's overload, but don't misunderstand what I'm saying. If someone comes in here and says, "I'm cold and need a coat," I give it to them. I don't do a great big interview. I got all the clothes I want.

But 50 percent of the cases are people who want food or oil or money. Those, you have to talk with. Some times are hectic times of the year like in January I personally saw 475 families. Admittedly if a person wants to cheat me, then cheat me in January, because then I don't have time to do a thing.

Being close to the people—doing the job myself—exposes me to a lot of frustrations. It's also pathetically comical at times. I had this gal come in and ask for some food or clothes; I've forgotten what. One of the first questions I always ask is, "How many children do you have?" And she said, "Three."

"Well, you know, are you married?"

"No."

"Well, have you been married?"

"No."

I said, "Well, you know"—and this happens on many occasions—"you shouldn't have children if you're not married." This was said parenthetically; I wasn't trying to make a big criticism out of her not being married.

She said, "God told me to have four."

I said, "What?"

She said, "Yeah, God told me to have four. Got to have another one. God told me to have four, but He didn't say anything about getting married."

That happens quite frequently, by the way.

There are frustrations, but in general I love the job. In fact this is probably the second time I've really looked forward to going to work. (When I was at the college I had a ball.) I think it's the helping here. The people I'm seeing are either one of two kinds of people. One is the person who needs help. Now it's a great satisfaction obviously that I can help. Maybe all of us have always wanted to help people who were hungry but couldn't walk down the street and knock on the door and say, "I want to help you." So just to have finally gotten into the position to be able to solve the problem is satisfying. When someone comes in and says they're hungry—for instance, a wino says he's starving—I don't have to say, "Let me see who I can send you to." I go ahead and get a box of food and hand it to them. That makes for a great deal of satisfaction.

The other people are those bringing me the stuff—the money, the clothing, and the food—to give to the poor. Now those people are fine people. Obviously they are good people or they wouldn't be bringing the stuff around for me to give to people. That's just tremendous. The friends that I have who are supporting me have been a great source of satisfaction.

The hours also are fine; there's no stress. I go home at 4:00 P.M. There are very few real emergencies that must be taken care of today. I can leave when I like. For instance, today I have a meeting—so I couldn't wear my bluejeans—at 12:00, and it will go to 1:30. Well, normally I open at 1:00. Today I'll just put a sign in the door that says, "Be back at 1:45. Wait!" That's not going to hurt anything.

As for problems, I have few leadership problems. The people I work for are fine, and the people I work with are fine. There's no stress, and the job is manageable. But there are some frustrations in the job. I'd love to have more money to be able to help people. The thing that bothers me the most is feeling that someone might have been in more often than they should have, and I think because they were in here two months ago, I can't help them this month. Then when they leave I get to thinking to myself, well now, if they were in a serious enough situation two months ago so that they needed help on their power bill, then why would I think they suddenly would have become rich and could pay it? Then I realize that I cannot get into the business of maintaining people for the rest of their lives. It's that conflict; it's my decision, and I can't delegate it.

This ministry is supported by the efforts of laymen. Now that shouldn't be. It's fine that laymen support it, but there is a lack of the clergy involvement.

Sure there are some clergy that support us. But by and large that isn't true. It bothers me that the church has not played a part in the lives of so many of my clients, in terms of anything—helping them with their poor self-image, helping them with their crisis situation, giving them money, clothes, and stuff they need.

Today, the clergy is not being taught to deal with this poverty, this type of need. Rather it's being taught to be a counselor. And this bothers me. I think the Christian Church has the answer to most all of our problems; yet we're sure not teaching it. Also since the clergy are the ones who have supposedly said to the world, and to God, "'We're going to give our whole lives to teaching and doing," they should be doing. But they're not. Might be the clergy is just failing. In our mission here, if it weren't for lay people we wouldn't do anything at all. If we had to depend on the clergy, we wouldn't do anything at all. The institutional church pays the overhead, but that's it. The clergy is not involved, and that's been a great disappointment. When I've communicated it to the relevent clergy, they won't listen to me, to anything I say.

I think one of the big reasons for this insensitivity and lack of involvement is that so many ministers have never had to work. That sounds terrible to say, and I don't mean to say that to be a clergy isn't to work. I'm talking about the fact that most ministers have never had to be in a situation where they had to worry about a job, where they had to worry about what was going on, or where they were unemployed. I think all preachers should have to work five years before they go into the pulpit. Then I think there would be a feeling and a concern for people that we're talking about. Christ says to take care of the "least of these." But the clergy doesn't know what it's like to be the least of these. They might be the most sympathetic guys in the world, love everybody in the world, but they cannot really feel for that guy who's got to go home tonight and face a wife, children, and an empty refrigerator.

I've tried to build a fire under the clergy about this. I talk a lot. In fact, that's probably the reason I'm in this job. For about fifteen years I've taught a Bible class over the radio. I started this when I was at the college. There and elsewhere I had always said the church was not necessarily doing its job. It should go outside the four walls. It ought to be helping people. So when someone said, "Will you take this job?" what could I say? It was almost like saying, "Put up or shut up." And so I decided, heck, I'll just put up so that I can go on talking.

Minuteman Missile Commander

Basically, my job is to set priorities.

A Minuteman missile complex consists of fifty missile sorties or silos, which are divided into five groups of ten silos each, commanded by a capsule located sixty feet below ground. While each capsule is responsible for ten silos, each holding one Minuteman, the capsule, if required to do so, can control and fire all fifty missiles.

Like the capsule, each silo housing its cold, green occupant is buried. Viewed from the surface, the silo site resembles a large, fenced-in baseball field minus the backstop, covered in 3/8 inch gravel. Antennas and wires that appear to be sensors are located in and around the fence, along with sufficient signs indicating that everyone is to keep their distance. Where the pitcher's mound should be, there are three rusty railroad tracks for removing the thick mobile cover of the missile that can quickly blast to fifteen thousand miles per hour and deliver death to thousands in less than half an hour.

The interior of the capsule is almost exactly like the one depicted in the movie War Games—*about twenty by six feet, with electronic equipment covering the right and forward walls. By the left wall is a vinyl bench, and a chair faces each wall of equipment. The crew commander's chair fronts on the forward gear, which displays the missile status buttons for the Minutemen, while his deputy's chair slides along a long, floor-bound rail in front of the communication gear, the computer, and several banks of lights.*

Four perceptions impinge upon your mind almost concomitantly when you enter the capsule. First, for those of us who are accustomed to working with modern computers that are compact and have small, delicate external wiring, the bulkiness of the electronic gear and wiring is surprising. Large black cables connect most electronic parts, giving the station the appearance of the control station of a World War II battleship.

Second is the potpourri assemblage of items. The moveable chairs are steel and gray, with a red fabric covering the cushions, while the bench is covered in brown vinyl. The computer keyboard looks new, but the locked red box holding the launch keys appears to have been welded in the Depression. The status lights appear to have been molded out of translucent space-age plastic, but the file holding the classified coding books has been pieced together out of one-quarter inch plywood and has suffered through multiple coats of high-gloss paint, the last coat being bright blue.

Third, the plastic keys transmit an eerie, uneasy feeling that at first you cannot understand or explain. Then you become more cognizant; the buttons, like those on your typewriter, washing machine, computer, or microwave, are etched with letters, symbols, numbers, or words that are worn. *The keys are worn. You look at the keys of a missile station commanding ten or fifty missiles, untold kilotons of punch, and they are worn.*

But most striking are the ten sets of small, rectangular, opaque pieces of plastic. Each missile has a set of plastic squares; each square has a different-colored light below it. You stand there staring down at this matrix of plastic chips, glancing to your right at the recepticle for one of the launch keys, and you wonder what color lies below the "missile launch" key.

Every twenty-four hours, two officers—a crew commander and his deputy—relieve two others who are on duty in the capsule. They will check out the systems and respond to any problems that arise in their equipment, and, if the correctly coded commands are issued, they will simultaneously turn two launch keys.

Down there it's a little bit of everything, and it comes basically as feast or famine. And there's constant pressure. When I'm in the capsule, there's just me and my deputy. Up top there's six security personnel, one facility manager, and a cook. Theoretically I'm in command of them, but my contact with them is minimal. They have their SOPs [standard operating procedures]. I'm responsible for those people, but as far as supervision goes, they are a voice on the end of a telephone. For example, when I have a security alarm, I "declare" a certain security situation to my people topside, and they have their own checklists, their own responsiblities, and their own actions to correct this problem. For example, there are some basic security alarms. There are security alarms around each LF. [An LF is a missile site.] If one were to go off, I simply would declare, "I have a security situation of a certain nature at such and such a time at such and such LF."

Only my deputy and I are in the capsule; everyone else operates topside. Down there you check out the equipment when you come in and make sure everything is uptight, that there are no surprises. Lots of times you process maintenance teams. They check in and then go out to the sites to fix problems. It might be an environmental problem, power problem, or warhead problem. We have checklists or procedures we have to follow to let them on-site.

After you've accomplished your inspections or handled any maintenance you have in the area, you just pretty much react to any status that might occur. In the twenty-four hours that you're out there, it's mainly a two-man team approach, and a good crew partner is worth his weight in gold. He, just like me, was trained at Vandenberg and he's considered to be "mission ready." He then takes some more training here. His first duty is really sobering.

Everything before has been on "simulators," and when he gets out into the field the first time, it's the real thing. So he thinks, hope I don't break this, don't break that.

He hopes he can pick up the system quickly enough to progress in his career. And It's like anything else, I guess, the more he knows about his job, the more comfortable he becomes. The more comfortable he becomes, the better he becomes at that particular job. He gains confidence, and he also gains knowledge in the job.

So it's just a matter of going through the paces with him, and basically everything he sees in the capsule is something he's seen before a number of times in the trainer. If something unusual happens, or if he can't remember how to handle something, I'm there, and my theory is, if I as a commander am busy doing something else and the deputy is unsure of something, he should stop and get me.

The deputy has been through these things over and over and over; now there's just a missile on the end of the wire. He's been over it until it becomes second nature to him; so, hopefully, he doesn't have the nervousness or apprehension that he had when he first started training at Vandenberg. Specifically, when he sees a checklist and he has to run a command or a test to one of his missiles, he knows how to do it, because he's done it a number of times. He touches this switch. Not only does he know that he's supposed to push this switch at this particular point in time, but he knows actually what is occurring within the missile when he does it. Once again that's knowledge, and the more knowledge he gets the more comfortable he becomes.

It's a lot like an air controller. They train and train so that they can deal with these things—like planes coming in—without getting confused or stressed by it. When you're in the field, that's not the time to make a mistake. The time to make a mistake is when you're taking your training.

We all fear making mistakes. The deputy does his best, and he has me, a trained commander, who will take him under his wing and say, "Hey, if you have any problems or doubts, wake me up or come and get me, and I'll help you out." I was in his position about two years ago, and I've gone through everything that he has and had the same apprehensions.

When I became a commander, I was a person the deputy could lean on. The first thing I told my deputy was, "Don't be afraid to ask me any questions. You're not going to appear ignorant to me. There are many pieces of tech data that you are responsible for, and it's hard to absorb it all in the limited amount of time that they give you. It's an ongoing training cycle, and you're going to see new things every month that you haven't seen before.

what's going to happen, you just don't have time to do that. You pretty much don't think about where the missiles might be going.

When it comes right down to it, we will obey the command. That's part of being in the military.

Resident Hall Adviser

I was forced back into the leadership style that I used, and it meshed well with my natural style.

My leadership was one of passages. There was the first phase. The person I replaced had left school, and I was hired at midyear, in December. Since I knew some of the staff and had worked with them, I was concerned about earning their respect, to prove I could do the job. I thought I was a very effective RA [resident assistant] and I wanted to become an effective resident hall adviser.

My basic style of leadership was an informal style, a type of moral persuasion. I wasn't on any kind of an authority trip. Rather I tried to work with and through people, to get them to do things for me out of respect for me, out of friendship. I was very concerned with working hard the first couple of semesters to see if I could do the job, to earn the respect of the staff and the respect of the students. And it turned out to be a good year. Where there had been problems in the hall in the fall, these were greatly diminished. Basically, I just tried to circulate and get to know the students, to treat them with respect, and to treat them as people. I talked with people, and if something came up in conversation, I'd follow up on it.

Phase two. The job was a half-time position. But I'd found it was easy to spend as much as forty hours in some weeks; you talked to students, attended meetings—staff meetings with my staff, staff meetings with the residence-association–level staff and other hall advisers, and meetings with the program advisers and directors—and handled problems, etc. So during the second phase, which began with the fall quarter the second year and pretty much ran through the middle of the last quarter, I tried to cut back the number of hours to twenty, to do a good job, but to limit it. Unfortunately, I wasn't able to pull this off.

In the last phase, I kind of psychologically divorced myself from the job. This was in the last two or three weeks. And I paid the price for doing this. Everything broke loose in the dorms. During the year we had had only one fire alarm. A common prank was for a student to run into another dorm, pull a fire alarm that turned on bells. At this time the hall advisers would hop out of bed and clear all the residents from the hall. But in the last two weeks, we had seven fire alarms, all occurring late at night. In addition, we had a rash of firecrackers being thrown everywhere, bottle rockets, firecrackers, etc., going off everywhere. In fact, there were so many little problems coming up in those weeks that I can't remember but a small percentage.

As students approach the end of the semester, there's just generally a lot of unrest in the dorms because it is a high-tension time. That was my last two weeks, and I was very tried of the job. I had psychologically disengaged myself from the job, didn't talk to students as much, didn't take as much interest in the job, and then I paid the price in those last couple of weeks. My subordinates were very probably doing the same thing; only one of them returned the next year.

Perhaps in here we lost the link between ourselves and the students. We lost that mutual respect, that rapport. A type of equity thing—we hadn't given to them; therefore, they didn't owe us anything. So at the end I was glad to get out of the job. It had been a tough year, full of problems, and I was glad to be out.

My position was one of hall adviser. I was in charge of five resident assistants and approximately two hundred students—about eighty females and the rest males. There were two houses of females and three of males.

I got into the job because there was a half-time assistantship that provided half-time compensation, tuition reduction, an apartment, all utilities, and free food. Also there were some career items involved. I was planning to become a counseling psychologist. I had worked in the dorms two years previously as a resident assistant, and I liked working with people. In sum I guess that's why I took the job, for the experience in working with people and the bucks of compensation. I stayed in the job for five quarters, roughly a year and a half. I quit because I was tired of being responsible for two hundred people and everything they do.

We had to arrive a week before the students to prepare for them, and they had been there just one day when one of my female RA's came down and said she had a problem. She had two new freshman roommates who had never met each other. One roommate had come to her that morning in tears. She, roommate A, said that during the night, roommate B had gotten down out of the top bunk and had made sexual advances to her. And she was very upset about the whole thing.

So the RA and I talked to her and assured her that we would have her moved out of the room by the end of the day. Then this left the question about what to do with the remaining roommate. Wisely, I chose to delegate the problem. After much discussion between the RA and me and between me and my supervisor and my supervisor's supervisor, it was decided that the RA would talk with the person. After a couple of days she did so and found that roommate B had no memory of the situation, or said she didn't. Whether she was walking in her sleep, or roommate A had dreamed it, I don't know.

A couple of months later, the same RA came down and said one of the students, who had been depressed for a number of reasons, had tried to commit suicide by swallowing a bunch of Contac and aspirins. So we took her down to the emergency room and had her stomach pumped. She recovered okay, and as a bonus didn't have any sinus problems for a while.

A couple of months later, I remember it was on December 1st, my wife and I went to supper at the dorm. (I was married then. I remember the first time doing laundry, feeling kind of funny pulling bras and panties out of the washer and dryer as the students filed by.) We had gone to another dorm where we ate our meals, and on the way back we came on the scene where a fight had occurred four or five minutes before in which several international students had been beaten rather severely. I investigated and found out that there had been three football players who had been involved in the altercation. So we took the international students to the health center, and I and two RA's tracked down the football players. One was a tackle about six feet five inches tall and must have weighed about 265 pounds. His two friends were about six foot seven and six foot one and weighed about 190 to 200 pounds. So we went to the tackle's room first. When he opened the door, he looked like a giant, but we confronted him about the fight. I don't recall the details of the conversation, but one quote that does stick in my mind is his comment, "If you want, I'll beat up some more foreign students." Then he slammed the door in our faces. He was still rather upset after the fight, still in a state of arousal.

So that set off a chain of about three hearings and about four court appearances, during which I became very disenchanted with the state and university judicial systems. We booted the tackle out of the dorm, but that took five to six hours over the next two days after the fight. Then there was a criminal court case in which the three football players were charged with assault and battery, convicted, and sentenced. The tackle had been in a fight before, so he was sentenced to twenty days in jail, and the other two were sentenced to ten. However, all three appealed, and their sentences were reduced to a year on probation. The initial trial was a day shot for me. Fortunately, I was subpoenaed but not called for the appeal.

There was also an all-university hearing in which the university considered kicking the football players out. They kicked them out for a quarter. The students appealed and the case was heard by a committee of deans. The university charter said you could either put somebody on probation for a year or kick them out for a quarter. In the judgment of the deans, what the committee intended was to put them on probation for a year, so they did so.

It turned out a couple months later the same three guys became involved in another altercation. The student festival parade had a float in which the driver was totally closed inside the float and could see nothing, and he was communicated with by persons on either side. There was a momentary loss of communication; the float just happened to swerve toward these three football players. So they exchanged some words with one fellow with a walkie-talkie who said, "If you want to, see me at this frat house."

Later the three came over and there was kind of a wrestling match between the tackle and the fellow who had held the walkie-talkie. There wasn't much coming from it, so the other two football players entered in and threw the guy through one of his buddy's windshields. Nothing ever happened as a result of this; they were neither kicked out of school nor put in jail.

Then there was the case of the guy down the hall who was into weight lifting. Occasionally he got into fights. He was fond of and dated a woman who lived upstairs in a women's dorm. When she began seeing another guy, the weight lifter lifted up the guy's car and pulled it around the corner. So these guys wound up getting into a fight. It was a knock-down, drag-out affair in which the weight lifter, surprisingly, lost. So of course, I was brought into the affair. The state attorney's office talked to me about whether charges should be filed. Technically, the weight lifter had stolen the guy's car, so he didn't want to press charges. Of course, all this got me involved because the fight occurred in the parking lot of my dorm.

Then there was our alcoholic. Every Friday night he would go out and get blitzed. Since we had women in the dorm, it was locked at 11:00 P.M., and the students had keycards to get into the dorm. Inevitably he would forget his keycard and kick out the door. Finally we put him on probation such that the next time it happened, he would be kicked out of the dorm. And the surprising thing is that it never happened again. He was uncontrollably drunk until we laid down the rule.

He was an interesting guy. I remember he worked at one of the pizza places downtown. One afternoon, when he was riding his bicycle down to work, he missed a corner, went flying over the handlebars, and landed on his head and shoulders in some bushes. He came walking back into the dorm all stiff, and to anesthetize the pain he went up to his room and drank himself into submission. Four or five hours later I was called to go up to his room to see if he had died of alcohol poisoning.

We had some problems with alcohol. General discipline, noise, stereos played too loud were usually associated with drinking. Students could drink in their rooms, and there was twenty-four-hour visitation, so there was occasionally a roommate problem. Someone would have their girlfriend over and kick the roommate out. And the roommate would get tired of it as time passed on and want to do something about it. I never bothered with these. I'd let the RA's take care of them.

Another thing I'd always delegate was a fight between females. We had two female roommates; both were freshmen and didn't know each other before arriving at the dorm. One was a white girl from a rural area and the other was a black girl from Chicago. They lived together in apparent peace and harmony for six months. Then it all fell apart. They just no longer got along. Each wanted the other to move out so they could have the room to themselves. The black woman in particular caused some problems; on one occasion she packed up her roommate's things and told her to move out. On another occasion, she took the screen off the window and started throwing the white roomate's belongings outside. Finally, she took scissors, pulled out the roommates records, and systematically destroyed each record.

Eventually we resolved this by having both roommates move out. I really have no idea why all that occurred and I never found out. A residence-hall hearing was carried out to see if the black girl should be disciplined. She was very cool about the whole deal; she had done nothing wrong; and she didn't know how the roommate's records had been destroyed. Therefore, our hands were tied and we couldn't do anything to her.

I found, in working with my RA's and students, I had to vary my leadership behavior to fit the situation. In the case of the drunk who kept kicking in the front door, I think that I had to clearly manipulate the rewards and punishments to affect his behavior. When I clearly set up the contingency and punishment such that he would be booted out the next time, then he changed his behavior.

In terms of working with most of the students, the idiosyncratic credits worked for me. I worked through a type of moral persuasion, building credits with the students. They respected me, liked me; therefore, there was little problem with getting them to do what I asked them to. If the student or RA didn't respect me or didn't like me, then there tended to be more problems. Those students I built up many credits with, though the credits were irrelevant to this or that situation, usually would go the extra mile with me. I could just ask them to do what I wanted, whereas those I didn't have credits with really caused problems.

I was a personal friend with all my staff, and I think here the same thing applied. I got along well with each, and I tried to be very supportive of them. So it was a type of tit-for-tat relationship.

It was good that I liked this style because I really didn't have any rewards under my control. I couldn't use financial rewards. And the disciplinary process was such that I didn't have any punishments. I did have threats, but we all knew that it was a long, slow, difficult process to kick someone out of the dorms. You had to give verbal warnings, then written, and then you could kick them out. However, my supervisor was loathe to do this because of the legal implications for the institution. So I was caught in the middle because certain things were expected of me, but I had no power or support from the top. I think the support would have been there, but it was so distant in terms of time and process that it appeared irrelevant. It also was costly to me and my superior to use it.

I was forced back into the leadership style that I used, and it meshed well with my natural style. When I had the opportunity to move into a much larger house with twelve houses—a women's dorm with 350 females plus 40 males—I didn't move because I didn't want to try dealing with this larger situation. That was a much more impersonal situation where I would not have known most of the students. In the samller house, I knew 90 percent of the students, and my style worked well. With 400 and not knowing them, I doubt if it would have.

There were other suprvisors who had very different styles. For example, there was a woman who was in charge of a dorm that had nine or ten men's houses and three women's houses. She had a very directive style—a very task-oriented style, that worked very well for her. She made up for the power void by intimidating people. In an interpersonal confrontation, she could be very intimidating, very loud, and very aggressive.

I don't recall that she kicked out any more people than I did. She and I had some conflicts because of our contrast in styles; she basically felt that I should run my hall as she ran hers—be very directive, have the RA's report back a lot, have assignments. Fortunately my supervisor didn't see any need for us to have the same style. He saw, and I think this is accurate, that your style not only has to be modified to suit the situation, but it also has to be one that is suited to you. You're not going to be very effective with a style if it drives you bonkers to use it.

3

In the Middle

O UR bosses survive helter-skelter days. The skills they possess are best demonstrated when they deal with the conflicting demands that are part of their job. These demands come from above, below, and, occasionally, from the sides. When they are caught in the middle, leaders perform a delicate balancing act in an attempt to play one set of forces against the other and to satisfy both. Many leaders are successful in this; some are not. However, it is plain that the ability to survive in a world of conflicting demands is a necessary precursor to the role of leading.

There is pressure from the bottom. As the abbot says, "The buck stops here." The research director notes that "the crap stops here," meaning that pressure also flows from the top. For the Indian chief, caught between the elders of the tribe and the government's red tape, pressure comes from both directions. The military academy sergeant is caught between the parents and the cadets. The bar owner must protect his barkeepers from the customers. The airline field manager must protect the customers from her irate agents. And our resident hall adviser protected one female student from the sexual advances of another.

Most of these forces are beyond the leader's control. Each demand evokes a countervailing one, and satisfying one demand often necessitates denying the other. Compromise sometimes is impossible, and on occasion it is the worst of all solutions.

In this section, the plights of the Indian chief and military academy sergeant draw on our sympathy. They are snared between two opposing forces. The story of the hospice director evokes both our sympathy and our admiration, because her position resembles that of the hub on a wagon wheel. She is caught between the dying and their relatives, between the relatives and the volunteers, and between the doctors and the volunteers. She proffers an enlightening example of the second predicament:

"In another case, the family said that they did not care for the volunteer, so I took her off the case. To the family I said, 'It's no problem; please don't let it be a problem.' Of course the volunteer had some concerns, and so did I because I didn't want to lose her. So I related to her my discussion with the family. And she goes, 'Oh, I can see my mistakes so perfectly now.' So it ended okay. We both realized that we're all the victims of our own mistakes, and that the family with a dying member is very sensitive to these mistakes, big or little."

Finally in this section, an Olympics official tells the story of being caught between the demands of his co-officials and those of the bureaucrats running the Olympics. The bureaucrats' pettiness handcuffed his effectiveness in dealing with the other officials, and the reactions of these officials, no doubt, complicated his interactions with his bureaucratic superiors.

Indian Chief

I learned early on that consulting with elders was a good idea.

Our reservation is unique in that it is one of the smallest in the United States—seventy-five square miles—yet one of the most valuable per acre, because it lies in one of the fastest growing cities in the Southwest. This situation forces us into doing good planning. We are responsible for land management and water; so we are a mini-municipal-type government. We have to provide all sorts of services. We have to provide fire and police protection and social services to our residents. So as chief, or president, I'm kind of a governor for our tribe [four thousand members]. We have about three hundred employees; we have a public works department, a finance department, a public safety department, a housing department, a maintenance department, a motor pool, etc.

The organizational structure for running the community is a tribal council, a president, and vice president. The council members are elected for four-year terms, staggering terms. The composition of our council now is seven, who are elected from seven districts. The president and vice president also are members of that governing board and are allowed to participate in council meetings and to vote.

This election system and form of government was pretty much forced on us in 1931 by the IRA [Indian Reorganization Act]. The federal government at that time was trying to make tribes flow more into the mainstream of American society, so they thought we had to govern ourselves in this manner.

My people had a system, but it was one that the government didn't understand. But it worked. My people worked together and farmed this entire valley for over a thousand years. They dug irrigation canals and operated under an uncoded law. A lot of it was by peer pressure. Lots of it was by the mores that had been set by the tribe itself and by the customs. And there were certain ways to deal with things without having a law-and-order court, without having to have all these documents. They dealt with them in a different way, whether through tradition, ostracization, or downright rejection.

A lot of that philosophy carries over today. To have economic development, you have to set goals and use management practices to get there. But a lot of this conflicts with the Indian way of doing things. For instance, in our grocery stores the Indian wants us to help all the people and extend credit. But in the business way, if you extend the credit and never recoup it, then the business fails and also there's no business there for the people. The Indian is willing for us to take that risk because he sees that the store is there to help everybody and not to make a profit. His thinking is designed around a cooperative kind of effort rather than having the individual dominating or succeeding. The Indian would prefer for all to come together around that goal.

You can see this tradition coming out a lot in our civil court system. In civil matters we do not allow professional attorneys into our courts. Civil cases are handled by local advocates—local people. These advocates are appointed, and they seek advice from the elders, or they themselves know traditionally how those kinds of disputes are settled. They use those methods to try to resolve the problem. Here and in our lives, we remember the old tradition, and the way we were raised.

We who are in leadership positions still remember our tradition in our decision making and leadership. We consult with elders on a lot of it and follow tradition. I learned early on that consulting with elders was a good idea. One man came by and asked for money to bury his uncle. Well, I gave it to him and started feeling bad so I checked to see where the uncle was so I could send flowers. When I checked with the family I found he wasn't dead.

Or let's say that there are two great-great-grandchildren who are fighting amongst themselves for a piece of property. I wouldn't make the decision or send it to the court; that is not our tradition. I would let the elders resolve it. They—the families or elders—would halve it or something, after they considered the tradition as to how their elders would have solved it. The two heads of the household might resolve the dispute or split the property down the middle, so that everybody is satisfied.

Traditionally the key is not that the problem is resolved correctly but that it is resolved so that everyone is happy. At least they feel that they are happy—they've been treated fairly, given the circumstances. Everybody has been protected and everyone has been fairly treated.

And one aspect of our role as leaders is to see that this happens and that our elders are cared for. In our constitution it says that we will look after the needs of our elders. That's funny, but it is written in the bylaws. When I held up my hand to take the oath as president, I said, "I will uphold the constitution and bylaws of the community." If the elders are being treated unfairly, then I am violating that oath that I took. So in my leadership, decision making, and planning for industrial development, that's always held in the back of my mind. I must look after the welfare of the community.

Not only are the elders cared for; they also are held in reverence. Whatever they say goes, most of the time. So even though I am the leader, I listen to them. They have a lot of power. When they come up with programs, you can just about bet the tribal council will approve it and find the funds to support it. Whatever it is, the council will support it.

So I keep these traditions in mind with my leadership. Elders come straight to me with problems. When I first became president, they would come by my house at any time and knock on my door at night to explain their problems. I learned to be very polite but to tell them I couldn't solve the problem then, but I would first thing the next morning. I keep in mind the way things were done in the past, and I make a strong effort to talk in the old language. I'm not fluent, and I make some mistakes, but it helps us to communicate. Because of my language, the elders know I respect them and our tradition. And they never laugh at my mistakes, because to make fun of someone or to embarrass them is counter to our tradition.

When I keep tradition in mind, I find I get caught between my people and the government. I guess what I'm leading to is that we have to get more and more sophisticated. We have to have more and more bureaucracy. It's an evil necessity, I guess, because we have to respond to whoever gives us funding, and we have to be responsible for financial management. So we set up a bureaucracy to manage things efficiently. As a result, we develop this paperwork and red tape that tends to separate me from my people.

This is the most difficult part in being an Indian leader. The people don't understand what we're doing, what we're trying to accomplish, and how we're operating. Trying to bring the population around to where the council is is difficult. The council deals with it weekly. We go through a whole process of planning, deciding, choosing, but the general residents don't understand this.

Frequently I also get caught between the government and the reality of a situation. Recently we got $1 million from the federal government to build a canal. We had a limited time frame because one of the major utilities that controls the water in the valley dries up the canals for thirty- to forty-day periods. We had to do it in that time frame. We tried to work through the Bureau of Indian Affairs, but they said we had to go out for bids. That takes so many days; then we had to take ten days for advertising. So within their rules there wasn't sufficient time to complete the project. So what we did was to contract it out, and we met the deadline. But if we had to depend on the government and their red tape, there would be no way we could accomplish that. They put pressure on us to meet their rules and regulations but it wasn't feasible.

All that can be so frustrating. Another problem is that there are so many things that I have to do in a day that there's really not sufficient time to do them. And a lot of it too has to do with the vacuum that's created between tribal administration and the people themselves. That's a communication problem. That's always been a problem, and the council recognizes it; so we've tried to resolve that with different methods. We have district meetings every month, where each council member meets with his people. But still some of the people at the lower level feel left out. I'm working as hard as I can for their good, but they don't understand. So I think, What's wrong with them? Why are they complaining? But once I talk to them individually, I overcome all problems.

I think poor communication comes with any form of government, but I feel it more closely because we're small, and I feel responsible to the people. I know the people, so I have to respond. I play different kinds of roles. I wear different hats at different times. I'm the father of children in my family. I'm a church member. I'm involved in sports. I see my people everywhere. I'm such a part of them that I have to be responsive. In other words, when someone calls me and wants a pothole fixed in the road, I can't just sluff it off and say that we'll fix it, because I'm going to see him somewhere and he's going to say, "Hey, I talked to you three weeks ago, and nothing has happened."

I work very hard for my people, but few ever tell me I'm doing a good job. That's just human nature [*laughs*]. But there are times that it happens. And people come in. It's pretty much a one-on-one relationship. Elders come in and talk. Say one wants a waterline to a new home he's going to build, and he doesn't have the foggiest idea as to how that happens. To him it's a simple request, but he doesn't understand that it's a complicated process to fulfill the request.

This one-on-one way of doing things is a source of satisfaction as well as frustrations. I keep close contact with the people, and it allows me to get things done and to see results. I like to work with people and to see positive change come about. I talk with them about their ideas—their dreams—and then I see them happen. That's very satisfying. But when I push for one person's ideas, I always remember that I have to keep harmony with the rest of my people. The elders and people expect it. The council works for it, and it's one of my prime responsibilities.

Military Academy Sergeant

In my first six months here I was nothing but frustrated.

You know, it's hard to take a freshman in high school and put him in a structured environment like this. You see, he's missing out on all the stuff a civilian child gets involved with—running with his buddies, comes home at three o'clock in the afternoon, turns on the boob tube, grabs a sandwich out of the refrigerator.

Here, what he has to do twenty-four hours a day is all structured. He gets up in the morning. He does PT, physical training. He stands formation and marches to every meal. He goes to breakfast. He goes to classes all day long. From 3:00 to 5:00 he has an activity period. At 5:15, 5:20, he eats supper. About 6:30 or 7:00, mandatory evening study begins. It's a structured study hall; he can't study in his room. And he goes through this for two or two and a half hours, and then he's got a certain amount of time he can use to clean up his room or write letters, do whatever, and then the lights go out. This goes on and on and on each day. There are a couple of parades each week. On Saturday there's a parade or preparation for inspection. If he's a high school student, he has to stay on campus on the weekend unless he gets a permit.

That's a very difficult adjustment for the young kids. And it's been a difficult adjustment for me. In my opinion, this place has challenged my leadership more than any other place I have ever been. You might say I'm an authoritarian, and in an army unit I got away with that. And that type of leadership will work as long as you use it wisely. Here, sometimes it'll work, and sometimes it won't. You have to really look down deep inside yourself and decide, How are you going to motivate these young kids? How are you going to keep them motivated, and how are you going to discipline?

When I first came here, I had a couple of cadets who were not the best cadets in the world. So I ruffled my feathers and strutted my stuff. It didn't faze them, did not intimidate them at all. So what? Who are you? That kind of attitude. And that really shocked me. In my first six months here I was nothing but frustrated. That was because I was trying to do too much too quickly. I couldn't understand why they weren't responding the way I wanted them to respond. In the army I would have had their stripes; I would have had them court-martialed; there's no telling what. I might even have run them out of the army. That wasn't possible here, so I did a self-evaluation on my leadership one night. I thought, What are you doing? Everything that you've done in the past does not work here. So what are you going to do? You're going to be here for two and a half more years. You better figure out a system that works.

So I decided, well, I'd join them a little bit. I'd go along with some of their pranks. I'd go along with the way the system works until I got my feet on the ground. I kind of took two steps backwards, did an evaluation of myself and figured how I could transition it in so that it didn't hurt so bad. And they've responded well. I requested an extension of my duty here, and when the army turned it down, about 129 out of 135 cadets signed a petition that they wanted to send to the Department of the Army to keep me here.

This place differs a lot from the army. I have to exercise much, much more leadership and much more diplomacy. In my army company, I had a reasonable amount of control over them under the Uniform Code of Military Justice. Here I don't have that. I have some things—I can reduce cadets, and I can request that they be dismissed from school. But the kids here are not soldiers. A soldier understands. He's got a job to do, he's being paid to do that job, and he's signed a contract. Here, the kids are paying to come to school here, so I got to handle them more with kid gloves. It's very, very enlightening, and as far as I'm concerned it's very educational and very beneficial to be a leader here. I can't just stand there and say, "I don't want to hear it, private, move out."

Here I got to say, "Well, young man, let's evaluate the situation." And then make the right decision. I have to exercise the maximum amount of leadership here, plus I have to deal with the parents. That takes a lot of tact and a lot of diplomacy. Parents call me up or come to see me. They have a lot of undeserved aspirations for their kids. Why isn't Johnny at this rank? Why are his grades so low?

Most of the parents, the bulk of them, are from long distances. So the parents don't just come in every day. But the phone will ring. "Sergeant Jones, you have a phone call."

"Yes?"

"This is Johnny's mother. Johnny told me this and this."

Then I have to engage my brain real quick to think, Which Johnny is she talking about? And what situation took place? Then I smooth it over, and I tell her. I always shoot straight with the parents. "Your son went AWOL, and I'm crucifying him for it, for the following reasons."

Sometimes it doesn't make them happy, but they come back on parents weekend, when I can look them in the eye, and they say, "Sergeant Jones, you know, you were right, and you're really doing well for my son or daughter." That makes me feel good. That makes the parents feel good. And that's what we've got to do to stay in business—we've got to please the parents. It costs roughly $7,500 a year to send a kid here; so we really have to take a close look at a young many before we dismiss him from the school. The parents have a lot of money and a lot of faith invested into us. So we have to really scrutinize each case. Now, there are some cadets who obviously can't be handled at any level. In my opinion those we don't need here, and they will end up in jail, eventually.

The general consensus of the people here in town is that this is a rich man's reform school. Now, that's not necessarily the case. We do have some folks who say, "Look, I can't handle my child, you do something with him." And I tell them, "Okay, no problem, you bring him here, and we'll see what we can do."

We have some folks who are engaged in business that causes them to travel all over the world, and they can't drag their child from here to there. So they send them to a military school. There are some kids here who are in their parents' way, so their parents send them here. And there are a good number of kids who just want to come here. The parents bring the kid by; he likes it and wants to go. We got a crosscut of about everything. We have a kid who wanted to come here so bad that he got on a bus and came, without any money or anything. But then, also, we had some parents come by that were driving down the highway one day; they saw our sign, pulled in, made the tour of the campus, told the son to go down and get himself a hamburger, and they got in the car and left.

Some of these kids come from rich families and are spoiled; therefore, you have to put them in their place. "Okay," I say, "I'm a soldier, I get paid by the army. Your father has nothing to do with my pay except that he pays taxes, the same as I do."

Now, everybody in the corps knows who the cadets are whose parents have the money. I mean *the* money. But it doesn't—yes, it does sometimes have an effect on promotion. I don't get involved in the money; I don't get involved with the politics of the school. There are some things that happen that I am very *un*happy with, but I have to live with because the school is trying to exist, trying to survive.

Sometimes a rich kid gets a promotion because of his money. Now we try to promote them, as much as we can, based on their performance, but there are times that I have to bite the bullet and promote an individual that I've got second thoughts about, because of his money. We have a good working relationship here between the military and the school administration. We try to keep each other happy. We compromise, we talk it over and say, "Okay, is this for your benefit or will it benefit the school?" And that's the key right there—the benefit to the school. See, there's no outside support for this school, government aid or anything. It's all self-sustaining.

I run into my share of other problems. Within the school there is a cadet chain of command just like in an army unit. They handle all the small things, and if they can't handle some then they come to me. Sometimes it gets a little crazy here. For example, let's say they've done everything they can to get a young man to clean his room. Or he's run into alcohol problems or drugs, or he can't adjust to our system. Those types of things come to me. That's when I reach down into my counseling bag and pull out the right things to set the man straight.

And there's no lack of sex here. These kids get out on the weekend. They're not deprived. They're getting about as much as any high school or college kid. Well, maybe not as much during the week or maybe not as much as a college on-campus student, where it's just right across the schoolyard from you. But I guarantee they're not deprived in any way. They're pretty slick operators. The kids who come here are survivors. They figure out the system, and if they think they should be having something, they will figure out some way to get it. Very ingenious, these young men are.

Of course, we have some young women here who are more friendly than we'd like for them to be. I think some of these girls really like being surrounded by so many young men, but I doubt if any of them really wanted to come here. They have their own barracks, but there has been some sneaking in and out. We've got that pretty well settled down now.

You know kids are going to be kids. Everybody talks about a military school; the kids are much more disciplined, much better mannered. They're also cooped up quite a bit more, so they have a tendency to get wilder when they're loose. I have to handle those problems, but my major job here is to run the junior ROTC program and teach junior ROTC. This has been the most enjoyable assignment I've ever had in my career.

I look back at my life. I was born lower middle class, lower lower middle class. You now I had my share of trouble—fights, trouble with the police, and on and on. When I was in high school, I was relatively shy. I played football and baseball and was pretty popular around school, but when I got away from my friends I couldn't communicate. I'd just stand back, listen, and shake my head.

Vietnam changed that, brought out some assertiveness. There I was in the infantry. We did our share of walking through the jungle, fighting, killing, being killed, bearing hardships. We were young. I was nineteen. The average age in the company was probably twenty-one. But like me, they got there and grew up overnight. The first time you got shot at, your first firefight, the first time you were actually satisfied that you took another human being's life. The first time you saw one of your friends get killed. All these things changed you. You changed. You learned or you didn't live.

And I look at how much better my life is now. And I see the improvements I've made because people helped me. And I figure if I can make one person see the light then I have done my job. One person had such an effect on me. I had a sergeant named Red Boxer, from Arkansas. He came to work every day, spit-shined shoes, starched uniforms. You could never tell the hardships—his wife was dying of cancer—he was going through. Good attitude, professional, could crack on you when he had to but didn't like to do it. Just a professional soldier who knew how to motivate people and knew how to deal with people. I was very impressed, and to this day, I know the influence he had on me.

I want to have such an effect on others, and I couldn't have it in the civilian world because I'm not educated or qualified enough to teach in a civilian school. Here I've got a regularly scheduled class. Four days a week I'm teaching leadership development, map reading, oral communication, drill, and ceremony.

Going through the experience in Vietnam gave me confidence as a teacher, in what I teach. There I learned that what I teach works. When I do my teaching, I try to compare the civilian and military worlds. For example, on leadership, I start talking about the platoon sergeant and platoon leader and catch myself staying on the military side. Then I convert over to the foreman, vice president, chairman of the board, and the trustees. And some things I flat tell them, "This is only organic to the military; there's no civilian connection whatsoever." This all helps quite frequently, for then they think, hey, I'm not just here listening to some old army crap. This will work for me in civilian life.

I don't want to see the youth of America go down the tubes. There's a lot of controversy now about the youth of America, but it's a great resource. These are basically good kids, and if they listen to what we teach them, they can be outstanding kids and outstanding leaders [*points to a picture of George Patton that he has framed in the front of his classroom*].

Hospice Director

I try not to assume a higher-level position in talking to people, but more importantly for me, I don't allow them to be on a higher plane than me.

"I'm dying. No one likes to talk about such things. In fact, no one likes to talk about much at all. I am the one who is dying.

I know you feel insecure, don't know what to say, don't know what to do. But please believe me. If you care, you can't go wrong. Just admit that you care. This is what we search for. We may ask for whys and wherefores, but we really don't want answers.

Don't run away. Wait. All I want to know is that there will be someone to hold my hand when I need it. I'm afraid. I've never died before."

These passages, written by a dying child of thirteen, are pinned to the bulletin board in the director's office.

Hospice is a philosophy, not a person, place, or thing, that holds that a person has a right to die with support, affection, and dignity. Really, all we do is provide support for people who are dying, letting them know that someone is there for them during a crucial event in their life. And we let them know that we're not afraid of that person because he or she is dying. We consider that person to be a normal person until they die instead of considering the person a dying person. The person who is dying is a person who has needs that were there before the person started dying, and now they have needs built on these existing needs.

When we have people referred to us, I call the doctor and ask him if the person is knowledgeable: Do they know they're dying? If the answer is yes, then I call the home and set up an appointment. When I go in, I know this person has been told they have a terminal illness, and I bear in mind that they can be in one of the various stages—denial, anger, letting go, etc.—in the dying process. So I first just start up some idle chitchat. Usually we talk about the doctor, and I'll say, "I talked to Doctor So-and-So the other day, told him that I was coming out, and he thought that was a good idea."

That leads us into letting them tell me a little about their last doctor visit. Here I get a description of the patient's perception of their disease. I don't go in there and say, "The doctor told me you've got a primary tumor of the kidney, metastic lung, and it appears to be in your brain also." If I did, I'd be out of the door in a flash. I *do* have to beat around the bush. We don't like to think of "death" as a naughty word, and we do want to get it out of the closet. But we do have to be tactful.

I'll give you an example of how this beating around the bush helps. I was talking to this dying man and his wife. When his wife left for coffee he said, "I don't think she really knows."

I said, "Hasn't she been told, or is she not admitting it right now?"

He said, "She's been told, and she's denying it."

That helped me out a lot, because the next day I called her, and she said, "I've just had some people out here who were picking up an absentee ballot. One of the women said that she'd never heard of hospice, and the other said, 'Oh, well, they're people who pave the way for passing away.' " When the wife relayed this conversation to me, I gulped because I knew she had been denying her husband's death. She said, "To hear that depressed me a lot."

I replied, "Yes, that really depresses me, too." And I said, "Let me give you my explanation as to why we are here. Sometimes when a person is diagnosed with a disease that he probably is not going to survive, then often things come up that they need someone from the outside to help them with. Maybe that's just helping out around the house; maybe that's just listening to them or talking to them, reading a book, or just spending some time with them. That's the only reason we are here." And I asked if that helped to un-depress her. She said, "Yes, it does."

So sometimes it is just the wording. Here, luckily, I had found out in the informal chitchat that she was denying her husband's death, and that helped me subsequently in dealing with her.

When I talk to the family, I also assess the situation and determine whether hospice care will fit in. Sometimes people don't want us, which is okay by me. But most of them say, "When can you have somebody out here?"

Usually during the interview I figure out personality-wise who, of my twenty volunteers, would fit in best for this case. Then I assign two volunteers to every case, when we have enough to do that. In recent months we have not had enough, so I have assigned only one per case.

I call the volunteer and ask her if she'll take it. Then we go out; I introduce the volunteer to the family, and I leave. From that point, I stay in touch with the volunteer on an informal basis—I call up to see how things are going, and they contact me whenever any significant changes occur in the patient's condition.

Then, every other Monday evening, we have a volunteers' support-group meeting. All the volunteers get together, with me there, and ventilate about the cases. This is extremely important for a hospice. Our work can be very stressful and depressing; therefore, we need this mutual support. Eighty percent of the purpose is ventilation, just saying things about the cases. Twenty percent is guidance and supervision. One hundred percent of it is learning.

Support group is so important, because it's there that we deal with issues of reality instead of theory. Each volunteer will recap the past week. For example, last Monday, one said, "I'm still seeing Betty. Her condition is pretty stable. The family went to the doctor last week. He kind of said the same thing. He's upped her morphine a little bit to help with the increase in pain. The family members were able to address that okay, and the doctor responded well. Everything is okay; I've been out there three times this week; I don't need much support."

Then another said, "Well, Joe died last week. I was there for his last eleven hours, throughout the evening. The funeral home came. The family was really upset and one member really fell apart. I had to do this and this. I had to call the head of Social Services. She talked to me."

So here the group is really incredible. They'll say, "Are you okay? How did you feel during all this? You know the family was upset and you helped the family out. Fine. Everybody is okay. We know you're going to follow up on the family and all that, but how are you?"

Usually if a person needs a lot of support, it is obvious, and we spend a lot of time with that person. After the meeting, there's a lot of hugging. The group will just want to hug. A lot of them call themselves "hug therapists."

In the group you do have people relating their past experiences and problems, but they don't get really emotional and cry. They have a detachment that they've learned. Initially, volunteers, I think, get too involved with patients, and then learn to stay a little more detached. If they don't become a little detached, then they burn out and have to quit. That's something I tell each volunteer, but usually they have to learn it on their own.

After the death, we have the volunteer keep in touch with the family on a bereavement follow-up. This is a fundamental principle of ths hospice. The philosophy here is that the dying person was a real, live person who had real needs until death. The family was involved in that care through the dying experience and continues to have special needs. Therefore, we follow through after the death. The grieving process, we know, easily goes to two years, so we continue the hospice care to help the family in the grieving process. It's also a grieving process for the volunteer, who has gone through a lot of this and has gotten rather heavily involved. For the volunteer to keep in touch and to pass through the grieving in a healthy way (as opposed to just breaking the relationship and going on with her life) is very important. Also it's very rewarding because you can see the family's intense grief in the beginning, then it dissipates over time.

Helping some people to die and others to deal with the death of a loved one is a tough job for our volunteers. Fortunately, we have people who are willing to do that and who will devote a lot of time to others. I've never had to recruit volunteers; enough of them come to us. Most of them are women. On occasion I think this causes some problems for the patients. Female patients enjoy having a male volunteer and/or a female volunteer. On the other hand, a male patient many times would really enjoy some male companionship, as opposed to, "Oh my, here come some more women. They're just going to pour over me." Having another male around can be a real psychological boost.

For example, I was talking to one of our male patients, and I asked him what he did during the day to make his day go by. "Not too much," he said. So I asked him if he went to the Elder Berries' Center, and he said, "I went down there once and they were all playing euchre!" He wanted to play some other card game. Well, I've been around a lot of men and I've played a lot of card games, so I felt I could relate to him. I said, "Wow, I've never heard about that one," and I asked him to tell me a little bit about it. He did, and I could see that he just wanted to get together with some fellows to play that game.

In managing these volunteers, I have to keep in mind that it's a lot different from managing employees. Consider what I should do if I disapprove of what a person did as a volunteer. They're telling the support group what they did, and I disapprove. Do I talk to that person and tell them they should have done this, this, or this? That would be okay for an employee, but volunteers could say, "Boy, I'm out of here." So you're at a kind of disadvantage in having to manage volunteers. I have to use kid gloves, principally because (a) many of them have more experience than I do, and (b) they can leave if they don't like the way I treat them.

I feel my role in managing volunteers is very ill-defined. Therefore, I'm not sure what my limits are and what the organization expects from me. But the organization does expect me to manage these volunteers. This crunch gave the director before me some real problems. She didn't know exactly what she could or couldn't do in managing the volunteers; however, the board expected her to get the job accomplished and in a certain way. I see that as a potential problem, but I've not been caught in that bind yet.

That's probably because of my managerial style. I handle people pretty well. I have a pretty decent ear, and I try not to impose myself on people in any given situation, but I may end up doing that in order to get the job done. You might say I'm assertive but not aggressive.

I try not to assume a higher-level position in talking to people, but more importantly for me, I don't allow them to be on a higher plane than me. Most people I deal with in this organization have a higher status than I do in society. So I try very hard to be their peer, and I let that be known in my dealings with them. I don't play up to their level. By my demeanor, I let them know that I consider myself to be their peer, and I want them to treat me as a peer.

Yet I strive hard not to be aggressive. I'm energetic but not aggressive. Between you and me, I don't care for all this assertiveness-training stuff. I can identify people who've been through assertiveness training, and I really get strung out with that type of person. Some of our volunteers are like that. I think, if that helps them go through life better, then that's okay. I think it helps men, especially doctors and administrators. But I don't like that type person, and I won't behave like one. I like people who are natural and who have some instinctive insights; therefore, that's the approach I take.

To get volunteers to do something, I just ask them if they will take a case. They usually do, and then I touch base with them each week on what they're doing. The support group substitutes for a lot of my leadership because here the volunteers interact and get direction and support. I also need the support that the group gives me because I am in contact with the patients; I need a pat on the back once in a while; I can use some support. They know that and are real sensitive to it. The support group also helps me to monitor my managerial behavior. I have to watch myself because I'd just as soon do the work myself. But I can't, and here the support group helps a lot.

As the director, I, like the volunteers, feel a lot of stress and pressure. To reduce it I talk to my husband, to the services director, and to the support group. I *find* support for myself. I never expected this much stress and depression, not as much as has hit me. I knew I was going to be working with people who were going to die. What I have found is that I'm working with *people*, who happen to be dying. I have about two or three die every month, and that's hard. Some of them hit close to home, because I really like them. So that's depressing, and some people say, "If you didn't act this way I'd be worried about you." It's nice to have those people to lean on when I have to say, "My God, these people are dying, and there's no solution."

I can't cope like doctors. They detach themselves because they know being attached is dysfunctional to their performance. For me, it's the opposite—the detachment from a dying person would be dysfunctional to my performance, I *don't* want to be detached, and I don't want to lose my sensitivity to these people. Another factor with doctors is that they have the fortunate experience of curing people and making people well. That sort of balances out their day. But that doesn't happen for me. I lose all my patients. So I miss out on that balance.

Because of that, this probably won't be my career. I may leave sooner than I think because of burnout. But when I think of burnout, I say, "Big deal, what are my problems? This woman's husband just died. Someone else has a lot bigger problems than I do, and they're hurt more than I am by them." I try to think about the help we gave to the person who was in pain—his case was hopeless—and who died. Also I think about how we helped the family and how the wife hugged me tenderly at the funeral.

I just try to keep my head about me so that I can be a good manager. Never do I have to motivate my people. That comes from the job they're doing. It's so rewarding to them in so many different ways. When they feel like quitting, they do; then they come back. For example, one of my former volunteers called in two weeks ago and asked for a case. He said, "I really need to take a case; I just feel empty without it."

Unfortunately, I can't just trust in the volunteer's enthusiasm. I also have to be sensitive as to whether or not a volunteer is doing a good job. For instance, I had this woman that I called to see how her case was going. She said, "I feel bad because I haven't been out there as much as I should."

I said, "Well, what's going on?" She and her husband have only one car; she gets it only on Friday; and then she has to do all her chores. So I asked, "Do you think you can fit it on Friday?"

She said, "Well, it'll be only for fifteen minutes." Then she said, "You may want to put someone else on the case, because I'm not really holding up my end."

I said, "I don't have anyone else, and I want you to stay on the case if you can." Then I encouraged her, and I suggested that she use some phone calls to let them know she was thinking of them. That sort of thing. And I told her to talk to the other volunteer, to find out when he goes out, and to find what she could do in the interim to help out, even though she couldn't get out there but fifteen minutes.

In another case, the family said that they did not care for the volunteer, so I took her off the case. To the family I said, "It's no problem; please don't let it be a problem." Of course the volunteer had some concerns, and so did I because I didn't want to lose her. So I related to her my discussion with the family. And she goes, "Oh, I can see my mistakes so perfectly now." So it ended okay. We both realized that we're all the victims of our own mistakes, and that the family with a dying member is very sensitive to these mistakes, big or little.

This last example is a rare one, because I make it a point not to go around my volunteers to the family. The dying person and the family are the volunteer's responsibility. I don't have time to work with each patient, his family, and twenty volunteers. The director before me tried that and got too close to the families. Consequently, she got overloaded, too attached, depressed, and then finally suffered burnout.

Before you go, I think there is a very important point that needs to be recorded. My volunteers are better than other volunteers. I think a lot of volunteers are volunteers because they've got extra time, and they don't want to have too many hassles. They just want to be doing something and hopefully for a worthwhile organization. Our volunteers, on the other hand, are people who don't have the time but they make the time. They have a commitment to others and to our philosophy. And they're doing the frontline work.

This is *not* a social organization that also manages to do something worthwhile. It isn't fun, for me or for the volunteers. Dying isn't any fun. And when we come together as a group, it's not to have a good time. We *need* our interaction for support, direction, and learning so that we can be effective in the next week.

L.A. Olympics Officials' Referee

Getting the job done right was my number one priority. Number two was to keep people happy.

In the track and field events for the 1984 Olympics, 202 officials were used. They were given no travel funds, no per diem, and no housing; all of this came out of their own pockets, so that the average official had to pay between $1,500 and $2,000 to officiate in the games. To my knowledge, this was the first Olympics in which track and field officials did not receive housing, meals, and probably some type of transportation. I know in Montreal they did receive these. We worked ten to eleven days in the Olympics, not counting our training days, and we put in some long hours.

We had to be in the officials' room two hours prior to an event. Since most of the events started about 9:00 A.M., that meant we had to be in the room by 7:00. Usually we were out of bed between 5:30 and 6:00; we didn't eat much breakfast, and we'd walk or ride the bus to the stadium, getting there about 6:45. We left about 10:00 at night.

Since track and field officiating in this country is one area in which no one ever gets paid, we expected some sacrifices out of these people. Why did they give so much? Because they love the sport, and the Olympics is the zenith for a track and field official—the highest goal that any of them could achieve. This was *the* Olympics. Looking back on it, it seems like it wasn't a real situation. I'd just be sitting there watching an event, and I'd say to myself, this is the Olympics. All of a sudden, it occurred to me. When I was doing it, it felt like any other track meet, but every once in a while you'd just pinch yourself and say, this is the Olympics. I look back on it, and it's not like a real thing that happened. It's almost like something I read about or saw in a movie. It was like being in a different world, and once you're out of it, you're not even sure it happened. It was so intense and I was so involved. I had to remind myself every night to call home or to go eat, because I just forgot everything else. We were all like that.

We were selected as officials by a committee appointed by The Athletic Congress [TAC], who invited any certified TAC official—local, masters, national—to apply, although they pretty well made it clear that only masters and national levels would be considered. So I, along with about 600 others, applied and 202 were selected.

The selection process generated some problems for those of us who were the leaders. The Los Angeles Olympic Organizing Committee [LAOOC] originally wanted to have only Southern California officials, but the TAC said no and more or less took it away from the LAOOC. Prior to this, there was a parallel planning going on. The LAOOC was planning how many officials they needed, and the TAC was doing the same thing; each didn't know the other was doing it. Well, the LAOOC came up with 150 officials, and the TAC said they needed 202. This argument went on for six months and wasn't resolved until a month before the games.

The TAC won out by going to the IAAF [International Amateur Athletic Federation] and saying, "Hey, we're running the meet, so tell the LAOOC that we're running it." They did. TAC won, but the LAOOC was upset about it, and on a lot of subtle things they got back at the officials. For example, they provided only 150 tickets to the opening and closing ceremonies; therefore, we had to decide who was to go and who wasn't. That provided sufficient friction between us and our officials. Also, the LAOOC had originally planned a brunch for the track and field officials, and they canceled it. More importantly for a hot L.A., the officials were supposed to get two of everything—two pairs of pants, two shirts, two jackets—but when we arrived, we were given only one. The reason was that they had only planned for 150 of us.

I'm mentioning these incidents because they sort of handcuffed us as leaders. They led to a lot of hard feelings and a lot of grumbling on the part of the officials, and for several days it affected our performance. For example, there were officials going around saying, "The fencing officials have three coats, and so and so; we're being treated as second class." Also some officials were threatening a boycott.

It took a while to get over that, it never was resolved, but by the end it became a joke. With some of the officials it was really really a sore point, but for most, it was turned from a sore point into a joke.

While these problems were caused by the LAOOC-TAC flap, it was up to us, who were serving as leaders, to cope with them. Another problem we had to cope with was that we didn't know until *very* late who was going to be the leaders [referees]. No one knew they were selected as officials until January [The Olympics were in July]; the actual assignments weren't made until spring. So I didn't know until spring that I was to be a referee. There was a referee of each area; one for the throwing events, one for the jumping events, one for the walks, and one for the marathons. I was selected to be the referee for the throwing events—the shot, discus, hammer, and javelin.

So I wasn't given quite enough time to get prepared. I kept asking the head official, "What is my job?" and he kept saying, "I don't know." We had five days of training once we got there, before the athletics started. So I asked, "What's going to happen in this training?"

He said, "Well, they're going to take care of it."

"How are we going to organize this or that?" I'd ask.

"They're going to take care of it."

"When will this be done?" I'd wonder.

"Don't worry, they'll take care of it."

I never knew who "they" was. Right before we started the training, I found out that *I* was they. All of a sudden, I was in charge of training the officials for the events. So that made for a short night; I had to do a lot of planning. Here I found myself leading a lot of people I didn't know; they were older than I; and many weren't very happy.

The training itself went rather well. But in it and in the Olympics, I did seem to run up against two problems as a leader. First, people in California think that track doesn't exist anywhere but there. So all of a sudden they got this guy—me—who's not from California telling them what to do. The second problem was age. I was younger than almost all of them. Many of the officials were selected because of their long service in track and field. On the interpersonal level I just tried to ignore the age issue and run my show.

Age turned out to be a problem in other ways. On occasion we had to shift people around because they just weren't capable of doing the job. Here I had to be very careful that I didn't injure any egos. We had some people who were unable to move fast; because of this we had to hide them. We had to put them in positions where there was the least chance of them messing up. For example, in each event, there was a sector judge who was to judge if an implement landed on a line or outside it. That was a good place to hide someone because, first of all, in any one competition you're going to run into a close throw only once or twice. Second, the person judging the landing would also be right there so that the sector judge had help. So we could hide people in these positions if we needed to. For the most part, though, people who were not agile did not want to be in a position where they could make a mistake; therefore, we had a type of self-selection.

To keep from hurting any feelings, I never broached this problem directly. Rather, I made it real plain, up front, that we were going to try a lot of people in different positions and then make our selections. So usually I would not make the final assignments until we had cleared these things up.

There were two examples where this thinking ahead paid off. We had one fellow assigned to run an event. He was a neat person, great person, but he was soft, very quiet, very capable in certain jobs, but he wasn't a "take charge" person. And we found out in the Olympic trials—this is where we sorted a lot of things out—that people were just standing around wondering what they were supposed to do now. So we did some switching there.

Another was a gentleman who was quite a bit overweight and was a heavy smoker. He was assigned as a judge, which meant that prior to the event he had to march around the track to that position. The march was scheduled to take seven minutes, so we had to march along rather briskly. He unfortunately couldn't keep up; we were marching along as a group when this gap all of a sudden opened up, and I said, "Let's try to close it up a little bit."

He said, "Oh, I will, but I won't be able to stay up." So he trotted to catch up and then fell back again. Well, I met with some of the other officials, and we were able to switch him into a position where he was a timer and a lap counter. Actually, he was happier with that, because he had wanted to do that all along.

After the Olympics got under way I found I had a problem of trying to lead eighty chiefs. The people selected by the TAC were those from around the country who traditionally have been the leaders in different events. These were people who normally in a dual-university meet would be the head of something. Now all of a sudden, most of them were being asked to do some mundane tasks. That led to some hard feelings, where someone might say, "I'm normally the head of the discus where I come from, and I'm just as good as this guy who's appointed above me." Eventually, I think, everybody took the attitude, "Well this is the way it is; this is a chance of a lifetime so let's make the best of it."

But at first there were quite a number of these problems. I actually had one head official who came to me and said, "I can't work with this guy; get me somewhere else or take him off." Usually I would just wait until they had cooled down a little. I'd say, "Let's wait until the event is over, and then we'll talk about it." So usually there would be a half-hour delay. That was good because many times they would sit down and talk about it. Otherwise I might talk to each one individually and say, "We've got a little problem here. So and so seems to think that you're overstepping your bounds in this area." By talking to each one individually and letting them talk together, we, in every case I know of, worked out the problem.

My objective here was to get the job done without any problems and at the same time not to offend any more people than was necessary. There were times when I did step on people's toes, but I did it only when I thought it was necessary to keep the operation running. I guess I was goal- or job-oriented; I wanted to get the job done right. That was my number one priority—getting the job done right—and my number two priority was to keep people happy.

In dealing with the athletes I had the same attitude. As a referee I was in charge of each throwing event—shot, javelin, discus, and hammer—and each event had about twenty officials running it. Above me was a three-person rules committee for the IAAF which we jokingly called the Red Coats, because they wore red coats and the chairman was from Great Britain. They observed us and answered questions, and they had the power to remove an official. They didn't have that much of an impact because of my approach—do the job right. I felt if we did a good job, then there'd be no reason for them to do anything. So it became a contest for us; we didn't want to give them anything they would have to overrule us on. It was a contest, a friendly contest, that if we did a good job then they wouldn't have anything to do. It wasn't like they were hanging over us all the time, but we knew if we did anything which was controversial, they were going to review it.

It never did happen. Rather, they took the position, you make the decisions and we'll back you. For example, consider one of my tape incidents. There are very specific rules as to when a thrower can put tape on his hands. In all throwing events, except the hammer, the athletes are allowed no tape on their hands, except to cover an open wound. One javelin thrower wanted tape on his forefinger, and I said, "You can't have tape because it's not covering an open wound."

So he goes over to his bag, takes out a razor blade and slices, superficially, the top of his finger so that it bleeds. Then he came back and said, "Now can I have tape?"

I said, "Yes, that's an open wound, so now you can have tape." That was in the qualifying round, and my decision bothered me because I knew he was using that to get around the rule. So I went to an LAOOC physician and said that I wanted someone with me for the next round of the men's javelin. When the rules committee heard about this, one of them pulled me aside and asked, "Why are you wanting this?"

I said, "I want help in making this decision."

He said, "You don't need help; that is your decision."

I said, "I'm seeking a medical opinion."

He said, "You make the decision, and if they don't like it, then they can appeal it. What's your decision?"

"He can't tape the finger because he has a small cut on the back," I said.

"Fine! That's your decision. We back you."

I was trying to avoid the decision, and he was saying to go ahead and make it. Make the decision and don't try to be spreading it out. The buck stops with you. Make the decision, and if you don't like it, then we'll get involved. I think, in a way, I was trying to escape the buck by bringing in a doctor. By the same token, I felt like I was seeking a medical opinion, not a rules interpretation, as to what kind of bandaging a type of cut required. The doctor did give me an opinion. We agreed, and then the athlete came out and said, "Your fancy-pants doctor looked at my finger and said that I don't need tape. Guess I don't."

At about the same time I had a shot-putter with tape on all five fingers. When I asked to see his hand, he gave me a prescription from his team doctor which he said prescribed tape for his fingers. I told him that the prescription didn't matter and that he had to take off the tape since I saw it didn't cover any open wounds. He didn't like that, and he argued. He also was a lot bigger than me. To make a long story short, he took off the tape and won the gold medal.

So after the throws were over, I shook his hand and told him he'd won. I laughed and said, "See, you didn't need your silly tape after all." He laughed, grabbed me, and gave me a *big* bear hug. I'm not sure if he was being friendly or if he was trying to punish me [*laughs*].

Looking back, I see that my attitude or philosophy as an Olympic referee differed substantially from my philosophy as a coach. As a coach, I put the person first, and the goal of winning second. I try to help each athlete to achieve his or her potential. In other words, when I go to a meet, I get a lot more excited about PR's—personal records—than I do about wins and losses. As a coach my emphasis is toward the person and their PR's. If they continually achieve those, then they obviously are going to achieve victories.

At the beginning of my coaching career, I would call each athlete in and we would put down, in writing, his goal for the year, and then we would plot his progress toward the goal. Now I still do it, but it's more informal. In conversations, I'll say, "This year I think you're capable of a certain time or distance." When the athlete says, "What do you think I can do in this meet?", we'll discuss it and set out this short-run objective. When an athlete fails, I try to treat failure as a step back, but it's not a permanent thing. Okay, you had a bad meet; here's what you did wrong. Correct it and you'll do better next time. I see performance as part ability, part motivation, and the athlete can work to correct shortfalls in either area.

In the Olympics we couldn't treat failures that way, so we did everything to avoid them. To my knowledge, we didn't have any in my events. We trained, trained, and trained for five days. Then I had everyone sit around to brainstorm. We'd say, "What would you do if this happens?" Then we'd bring up other problems and ask what we'd do then. We planned for every contingency, and no problem came up that we hadn't discussed. If personal problems had come up—say there had been a boycott—I would have replaced the officials. If an official was making mistakes on the field or was uncooperative, I would have first gotten him off the field and then disciplined or fired him. But I would have avoided a shouting match at all costs.

Another referee gave a good example of how to do this. All officials were strictly told they were not to cheer, take pictures, or anything like that. There was a guy working as an umpire, seated on a stool at a curve. He had really been a jerk and done a lot of screwy things. (We were very specific that all officials were to wear black socks. He wore white socks, and when the head official jumped him about it, he said he didn't have any black socks.) On the track that day, there was an event in which an American was running. Every time the runners would come by, this guy would get up off his stool and yell encouragement. When the referee saw this, he immediately picked somebody who was not officiating to go over to him and say, "The referee wants to see you." Then once he was off the track, they unloaded on him.

I was ready for problems like that, but none occurred. I was working with eighty mature individuals who had invested their time and money to be there. To them, it was the Olympics, just like it was to the athletes; it required the ultimate performance. This was *the* Olympics, and they didn't screw up. At first they did get a little bent out of shape because they didn't get some perks. They had donated time, effort, and money, so that they wanted the little rewards they felt should go with it. There were some frustrations there, but once the Olympics got rolling, most got over that.

Two gentlemen, in particular, got over it very fast. They were responsible for escorting the athletes off the field to the control tent, and between the events of the heptathalon they were performing their usual escort for two Scandinavian women. Now, participants in the heptathalon are very attractive women. They generally are tall; they're not very thin like the distance runners, nor are they very muscular like the throwers. These two ladies were extremely good-looking; they looked like models. Between the events, the escorts took them to the control center—a tent. This was close to where they had a place to lie down; there was shade, a warm-up track, and lockers. Well, many of the athletes would go to the locker room and change uniforms between events because it was so hot. One of these girls, instead of going into the locker room to change, did so in the control tent. She just took everything off and put on dry clothes, in front of these fellows. These older gentlemen came back and couldn't believe what they had seen. They almost fainted, and the next day we had two hundred volunteers to take their place.

4

Stress

S TRESS. Prostitutes, test pilots, missile commanders, nurses, air controllers, prison guards, and most other leaders interviewed for this book suffer from it. Yet the hit man does not. Why not? Two reasons—he keeps a "positive" attitude toward what he is doing, and he controls the source of stress:

"It's hard work, but I like work. It keeps your health up. And there's no stress. There's no stress in what you're doing if you like it. . . . And I don't get overloaded. That's something you never let yourself get into. A good businessman or organizing man never lets that happen. When you get overloaded, you recruit more people. Like if I got this project that I figured I could do with six people, and something comes up or they start dragging their feet, then I go on out and find me a couple more people and ease them in it, with the plan."

The hit man controls stress, meeting one of the major challenges facing leaders today. They must control their own stress and that of their subordinates. As we all know, stress has multiple causes. Overload, time pressures, constant changes, insufficient time, conflicting demands, constant evaluation, and the suffering of others all contribute to our level of stress. The need for precision, the high cost of error, the unreliability of superiors, and fear for one's life are several other sources.

Since stress is so prevalent in jobs today, the importance of managing it cannot be overly emphasized. How good are our leaders in handling it? Most of them—the air controller supervisor, head nurse, prison supervisor, and hit man are representative—do an excellent job of it.

For the air controller supervisor, the major keys are structuring the task and training for stress. As he notes, the day-to-day operations are set, for the planes and the controllers: the airspace is defined, the operational procedures are defined, and the plane flies in a designated airspace at a designated speed behind the plane in front of it. Everything is proceduralized as much as possible, and the supervisor enforces the procedures. His controllers need not worry about errors, the cost of errors, or their awesome responsibilities if they stick to the procedures. When overload threatens their sanity, they can relax and rely on procedures.

Then there is the training. As the controllers learn the procedures, they are educated toward stress. First, there is academy training; then they are trained to handle the least busy position. Then it is back to school and a return to on-the-job training. The procedure serves as a confidence course—each step somewhat harder but yielding an increment of confidence—for the "developmental" controller.

The controllers' supervisor adds another stress-reducing ingredient—one-liners. He breaks the tension with his own and allows (encourages) others to sally theirs.

The head nurse must take a different tack, for she cannot structure the life and death of her nurses' patients. Nor does she have significant control over the patients' needs—pain relief, correct blood pressure, bandage changes, medications, psychological problems—that her nurses must meet. Likewise, the doctors seem to defy structure.

Complicating the problems of the head nurse is the absence of stress training for nurses; they are trained to heal, not to cope with stress. So the head nurse realizes she must deal with stress on a very personal plane:

"I do a lot of counseling to eliminate any stresses that don't have to be there. Sometimes I'll just sit down with a nurse and say, 'Look, it's been a bad day. Let's just sit down now and go through it all again and see where you could have done some things better—delegated a little more, taken fewer of the tough cases.' And I discuss stress with her. Not theory, but the nuts and bolts: 'You are under stress; here is the way it starts at the beginning of the day. This is the way it works during the day, and this is what you can to reduce it.' "

Her approach reveals her perceptiveness; yet the balancing of stress reduction against high standards reveals her superiority as a leader:

"I've got to be a counselor, but I'm also responsible for keeping the standards high. I can't just stroke feelings. If I had a nurse come in and say, 'I really did a bad job; this, this, and this happened,' I can't afford to say, 'Oh, don't worry about it; it'll be okay.' When everyone else also thinks she did a bad job, I've got

to say, 'Your behavior was inappropriate and had some bad consequences. Next time, I would do the following things differently.' I listen a lot, think about it, and then give the feedback that's appropriate.''

Like the air controller and head nurse, the prison supervisor leads subordinates in a high-stress world. There are bloody killings, overload is the order of the day, and the inmates delight in scaring the guards. The supervisor's solution for his guards is one part "follow the rules" mixed with one part "tolerate the rest." The garniture is a combination of discussion and humor.

His comments, like those of the head nurse, reveal an oft-forgotten fact: people can tolerate stress. Our jobs are stressful, and we can, with proper assistance, function well under stress.

As the prison supervisor assists the guards, he manages his own stress. No doubt he does what he preaches. And he hoes in his garden.

Unfortunately, the director of the women's crisis center has not developed the stress-management knack. Her clients' problems become her own. She feels that she is batting her head against the wall, that she is not getting anything done. The bureaucracy has her caught in the middle. "If I work with my clients," she says, "I can't get the supervisory work done, and if I do the supervisory work, then I don't get my client work done." Daily, she searches the newspapers for her failures—the suicides.

Ironically, the hit man is better at coping with stress. Not only does he relax and take time off, but as the overload intensifies, he hires new personnel. His approach is rather representative of criminal leaders. They realize that their jobs—killing, robbing, bombing, drug dealing—are stressful (as the heroin dealer notes, "life's rough, killing's rough"); therefore, they consciously control stress. They stay cool, never allowing stress to sneak up on them. Very seldom do they concern themselves with the stress of their subordinates. Subordinates who cannot cope voluntarily withdraw from the alliance. And if they mention that they are fearful, the criminal leader seldom will involve them in the next project.

About 60 percent of the criminal leaders interviewed in this book stated that they use drugs and alcohol to provide a release from stress. For most of the remainder, the thrill of the conquest and the sense of achievement compensate for or neutralize the stress. Accentuating the thrill of committing the crime is the thrill of leading the operation. Together, the two produce an endorphin high that counterbalances stress. The hit man is quite right when he says he just runs on a natural high."

Hit Man

There's no stress in what you're doing if you like it.

I do my straight work—landscaping—as a cover-up for my money. Most all businesses are cover-ups for different illegal incomes. It's a good legal business. I do insurance killings; that's what I mainly do. The beneficiaries come to me, and I take care of it.

After the insurance company pays off, I get my cut. They usually collect over $100,000. I get about $35,000, $45,000, or $50,000. If it's a woman, I usually collect about $50,000. If it's a man I collect anywhere from $30,000 to $40,000. Women have a better understanding about giving money to get rid of their old man than a dude has about getting rid of his old lady. Dudes feel guiltier about dusting the old lady and pay more.

And I have other people doing things for me, like arson. I always have people I can go to. I say, "Go burn this one," and I don't have no problem.

In 1968 I's going nowhere, and I learned how to do landscaping from this guy. I seen how easy it was, and I said, "This ain't nothing." Then I got the money to start up the company off of killings. Buying my machinery and stuff like that. That stuff costs money, trucks and things like that. Took more killings than you'd think.

I started my company; now I am a businessman. Gives me a cover-up for my money. Like, a landscaping job gives me $10,000, and I go to the bank and put in $20,000. If I didn't have this business, people'd be saying, "Where's this sucker get all that money? He don't never work." But they see my trucks with my name on them. I got a big banking account; there's nothing to it. they don't ask no questions then.

Hey, as long as you're not doing nothing conspicuous . . . the working man can put down the worst schemes in the world. His name is on the truck, and everybody just presumes that he is a working man. There ain't no questions. Even if you don't do any work. As long as you got your trucks driving around with your name on it, and they think you're a businessman, and if you always got money, then they presume you're working somewheres.

Sure I get more respect too, but I don't get off on the respect I get. It's mainly the cover. I've never been a publicity-type person. Publicity can kill you.

I've financed a few robberies for people I know. I'll have my boys go out and get them cars to do it and give them guns to do it with. But robbery isn't all that good. Sooner or later one of them will take a fall, and when he does he'll roll over on you. No matter how good you been to him, he rolls over on you. Also I got some women working for me running prostitutes; that takes a lot of money up front.

But I make most of my money killing. I do some, then others do some for me. I know most of the other hit men. Here's the way it is. Most hit men know each other, and there's honor among hit men. So I know about a dozen, and if I got a killing—say I meet the people who want the killing in Michigan, but the person they wants killed lives in Texas, Arizona, or anywhere. So I just call up one of the dudes, say the Grim Reaper, in that area, and I say, "Hey, I got one out there, blah, blah, blah."

And he might say, "I got one back that way. You take care of him for me, and I'll take care of this one for you." That way it's less conspicuous. If I had to drive out there or fly out there, then anything could happen. They could pick up on it. And it don't make no difference how the money is going. He's getting $50,000 and me $35,000; a few thousand dollars don't make me no difference. So we'll exchange, photos, names, addresses; then we do the jobs.

I just work with the high-quality people. A guy knows his business if he's going to be a hit man. The ones I always mess with, they appear to me to be good, and I never do see them get busted so I assume they's okay dudes. So I call him. He dusts the fellow. Whenever the beneficiaries get the money, they put it in the bank and let it lay anywheres from ten to fourteen days. Then they get it all in cash and take it to another bank. But they first pay me off. I just put it in a box and put his address on it. It's his money.

Never had anybody contract with me and not pay me off. There's honor. I can beat them, and they can beat me. They know I'll come down on them, and I presume they'll come down on me. That's the way I see it. If the dude's going to kill somebody, he don't mind killing me too. I'm not crazy, you know.

But the organized crime—the Mafia and all that—I've never messed with. I've always been leery of them. Because if you start to do things for them and start to knowing too much, then eventually it's going to be your day. And they ain't going to kill me.

Sometimes I will handle their excess baggage. But they're cheap, anyhow. They don't like to pay hardly nothing. Their going price is about $3,000. That's all they want to pay, because that's what their flunkies will do it for. I told them, "Not me. I won't kill nobody for less than $10,000; that's my starting fee." And the way inflation's going, pretty soon, I won't do one for less than $25,000. You just can't come out ahead.

There's a lot of misperceptions about hit men. The biggest one is that we're out to really dust the world [*gestures as if he is mowing down people with an automatic weapon*], but it's not like that. I never, ever, took a life or will ever take a life unless someone personally bothers me—causes me to do it—or somebody pays me some money. That's the way most hit men are. They do not go out and dust people just for kicks. They's crazy people that does that. But a hit man kills as a business. It's a business just like you do what you do. Hit men kills people. The closest thing I've seen to a hit man that was any reality at all was the movie *The Farmer*. Burt Lancaster played in it. It's a whole lot true.

My weapons are a 12-gauge—a pump 12—a .44 Magnum, and of course knives and piano wire. You can dehead a person with piano wire that quick [*snaps fingers*]. Just as quick as I snap my fingers, you can take a person's head off. Just say, "Whee," and his head says, "whip," and it's gone. It's real simple to do; it's quick, easy [*demonstrates in the air*].

It all depends on what job you're doing. You use different things. Now if you're in the subdivision, and you got to kill somebody, it's got to be quiet, because you got so many people. Or if you got somebody at a distance and they're moving (like in a car), the 12-gauge is the thing. Or a .44 Magnum; that'll blow up anything or go through most anything.

After the hit, the shotgun is cool, because they can trace nothing. But a pistol—when you use a pistol, you gotta change barrels. Take the hot one and melt it down or do away with it or put it in a vat of acid. Anything to do away with it to make sure it's never found. And knives, course they can't tell nothing about knives. One knife is a knife.

Now, hey, I don't go out killing every day. Not that type of demand. On an average day, I'll get up about seven o'clock of a morning, and my wife'll fix breakfast and get the little boy off to school. Then I'll call my men up and say, "Hey, we got these jobs [landscaping] to do today."

I always use dopers and hippies and winoes, mostly. That's what I work; the underprivileged people that can't get no work nowheres else. I work them. Pay them $10 an hour, and they'll work as long as I want them to work and never say nothing about it. I buy them all some wine. Buy all of them some weed and say, "Let's hit it, boys." And they'll work.

The winoes, the hippies, the dopers, they like someone to pay them attention. Everybody in the world—I don't care who it is—needs to be needed for something, and that's what it is mainly for them. They need somebody. And I put money in their pockets, where they don't have to be so humiliated by the public. They like that.

We work eight to ten hours a day. I lead by example. I show them what to do and how to do it. They like that, and they work their tails off. They're all good boys; they're just discriminated against by society. And I work blacks and whites. I don't have no racial barriers, I work them all; it don't make me no difference.

I tell them what I need done. After a few jobs they know what to do. I say, "Okay, boys, get this done, blah, blah, blah, and I'll get the equipment and grade this and that while you do this. It'll take me a couple of hours, so have it nice when I get back." And they'll do it.

I never have come back and found they did a bad job. You could look at any job I done and ask anybody I done a job for, and they'll tell you, "Hey, the man done a superb job." Just ol' winoes and hippies do it.

I give them a bag of weed of a morning—ounce of weed. And I buy five or six bottles of wine and give it to them. The winoes need a drink and hippies need a hit. That keeps their heads right all day. Then of a Friday evening I add up their hours and pay them cash.

I got me the same leadership style on the legal and illegal sides of my operations. First you got to cop people's minds by your conversation and get them to believe in you; that's the main thing. You got to believe in what you're doing and get them to believe in what you're doing. You got to explain it to them, and you got to do your best. Then you have to perform, and you see how they do. You put the basic rules down—what we all need to do and then if we all do this then we'll all make money.

And I put the pieces together. Like when we're going to burn some buildings, I tell this fellow to have his insurance up to par. And he's an upstanding citizen; nobody's going to investigate it. Then I'll get him relaxed and tell him I've got the man who'll do the burning, and he'll not need to know who he is. That don't concern them. I pull the big puzzle together.

I drive a lot and think up these scams. Then I lay back and think what people would be good to use in them. Then I get the people together, explain things. Get them motivated. I get an idea, and then I start talking it over with someone. Then they start to think they're helping with an idea or if they start thinking it's part their idea, then they get enthusiastic. Then that gives me a turn-on, a natural high. They're fired up about helping me do something. It's a good feeling.

It's hard work, but I like hard work. It keeps your health up. And there's no stress. There's no stress in what you're doing if you like it. You got to like it. There's no stress in this; I like it. There's no stress in killing people. It's just like killing a cockroach. That's nothing. To me it's not. To other people it might be stressful.

And I don't get overloaded. That's something you never let yourself get into. A good businessman or organizing man never lets that happen. When you get overloaded, you recruit more people. Like if I got this project that I figured I could do with six people, and something comes up or they start dragging their feet, then I go on out and find me a couple more people and ease them in with it, with the plan. "Now look here, here's the plan. We could use you if you want to make a lot of money."

Then you put the same scam on them that you done put on the others. Fit them right on in and tell them what they'll be doing. Then I can sit back and watch and plan. Yeah, everything is cool and going according to plan.

I'm never under stress because I got me a positive outlook. And every once in a while I'll go down and see my girls, of an evening. That gives relaxation. Like, I'm doing something, it's all over, and it's three o'clock, I'll say, "Maybe I'll just see some of my women." I get in may car and drive out there. They know who I am and that I've got a piece of that bar. They want to please me. I come into the bar, have a few drinks, sit around and talk to them, talk to the managers, and get into some relaxing.

If I see something I don't like, I draw the manager's attention to it. Then I explain to him why it shouldn't be. I take him in the back room and talk to him, explain to him. Never get rough. You don't never get rough with your employees. It's bad business, and then they start thinking of ways to retaliate against you.

You make sure your employees are always happy. A happy employee is a good employee; that's a fact. If more business people would do that, then they'd have a lot better businesses. That's the way with everybody. A happy person does more because they just feel good about themselves. They're excited. They know they've got money in their pockets, and they're doing good. That makes them take care of their jobs good. That's the way the human race is.

I just look around. Explain things. Make sure everybody's happy. And I look at the receipts to see how good the take is. I ain't looking at the records to see if there's stealing. I don't care if people are stealing a few dollars, like one of the women's turning a trick and holding out some. That's the least of my worries. I just look at the overall. I'm making money, and if they're taking a little then it's okay. But I doubt if they are. I take care of the madam, and she takes care of me.

You see it's always better to use your head than your muscle. Use muscle when it's needed. That's the object of any organization. You got to have discipline in an organization, but the *best* thing in an organization is understanding. If a bunch of people have got good understandings, and everybody has their mind on their business, then there's not much that the business can't do.

When you're in charge, you explain your ideas and show people. Sometimes you do have to hard-muscle people. If you got a hard-muscle person then you keep him back and hard-muscle him in return. He's satisfied with that because he gets off on it. I decide who I can talk to and who I need to hard-muscle. I can pick people by talking to them. I know how to work men and how to talk to them.

I know people. See, I read people well. It's just a gift I've got. I don't have a good education. I can't read or spell too good. But I don't need that. I run this company, I do my thing, and I pull down a half to a quarter million a year. That's because what I do I do well and because people will work for me.

Most people have inferiority complexes. Most of your people need someone to organize them. For some reason they all revolve around one person. They could do everything they're doing in the organization on their own and make good money but they can't get that momentum without a leader. They don't actually put 100 percent in it.

I use conversation to get them up to that 100 percent. I was born with a gift for gab. I can talk. When I's seventeen I'd axed a few people and done this or that. Finally I got smart and said, "I got to do something about this. I ain't going nowheres. And I can't read or write." So I listened to intelligent people, and I learned to talk. I talked with this one fellow. Forget his name. He got busted with a machine gun. Was an English teacher and smart. Then I talked a lot with Robert Stone; he's real smart. Taught me the murder gig. Oh, Robert. . . .

So I use what I've picked up. When I'm running a killing, arson, burglary, or prostitution I get people interested by telling them how much money they could make. Basically they're all crooks anyway, and it takes me a while to spot them and get with them. I'll say, "Look here, we're going to do this." Then I explain to them how easy it is.

Then I have to get them fired up. That's not hard. Most people are basically greedy, and the greed will make them dishonest. That's why you see a scam that gets people busted up in the White House all the time. Somebody has got to them with a gift of gab. That's all it is. They just pulled that little greedy spot out of them. Your politicians are the greediest people in the world. And they're all basically dishonest. If they wasn't dishonest they wouldn't get on the TV and lie like they do. They know they're not going to do any of that stuff that they're saying.

Just like Reagan. He knows he ain't going to do any of them promises, but he's the best we got right now. I don't knock the president. I'd like to cop his mind for a while. I could straighten that guy up. I could make a good country out of this country. I *really* could! You can bet one thing. There wouldn't be nothing going overseas to them foreigners. I'd cut that off. I'd look after the United States. Like Bruce Springstein says, "I was born in the U.S.A."

I learned the right things. Don't do no killing unless there's money in it. Set you up a business to cover your money. Invest your money. Put yourself together an organization. Get a bunch of people all doing their parts. I get off on that; a natural high. I don't drink or dope. Just run on a natural high.

Air Controller Supervisor

When two airplanes are moving at each other at over eight hundred miles per hour, you can't be making excuses.

The airspace surrounding the airport is divided into two parts. The first is most easily perceived as a large cylinder sitting upright on the ground with the runway as a point in the middle. The radius of the cyclinder is 10 miles, and the height, 12,000 feet. Surrounding this cylinder is a doughnut of airspace 22 miles thick and 12,000 feet high.

Planes within the airspace fall under the direction of two separate sets of air controllers. One set, located in the control tower, supervises the planes on the ground and within 10 miles from the facility. Controllers for the planes in the doughnut— that is, 10 to 32 miles out from the runway—are housed in a bunker at the bottom of the control tower and never see a plane. Rather, a plane to them is a one-quarter-inch blip accompanied by its flight number—for example, TWA 555.

Surprisingly, when you enter the bunker, there is an air of familiarity. You feel you've been there dozens of times because it resembles a video arcade in both sight and sound. Located around the periphery, six to eight figures are focusing intently on video screens, punching numbers, rolling cursors, and speaking into microphones. Two men, a supervisor and his assistant, prowl the center of the room, tearing off slips of paper about the size of a four-inch-long cash-register ribbon and arranging them on the desk of each controller. These slips indicate which planes are soon to enter the controller's sector.

There are six sectors, one for each controller. Each controller's radar screen, and likewise the doughnut, is severed by a line, representing the runway, that runs from northwest to southeast through the middle of the screen. All planes in the airspace are either arriving, departing, or at low altitude. So this two-by-three delineation neatly carves the planes into six sectors—N (north-arriving); S (south-arriving);

E (north-departing); W (south-departing); B (north–low altitude); and D (south–low altitude)—one for each team member.

The white slips passed to the controller by his supervisor cue the controller that a plane is to enter his sector, and as the blip enters the screen, he communicates with the plane, rolls his cursor up to touch the blip, thereby accepting the handoff, makes sure the blip is labeled correctly, and then directs the plane toward or away from the runway along a zone—a funnel-shaped designation or his scope—of which he is in charge. As the plane is about to enter the airspace of the control tower, that is, 10 miles out, the controller clears it for a visual or instrument landing and tells it to open communication with the tower.

In introducing themselves, explaining their responsibilities, and conversing among themselves, all the controllers sound like Chuck Yeager, slow and easy. But when they cut in the mike to direct a pilot, who also sounds like Yeager, they resemble disc jockeys vying to determine who can speak the fastest. Most of the conversations to the pilot are quick, pleasant, polite, and formal, closing with the controller saying, "good night, sir," and the pilot responding, "Thanks. Have a good night."

But occasionally you hear a controller saying, "Where did you come from, buster?"

"No, you can't come in from a different direction. Do what I tell you!"

"Come in on instruments, if you can remember how."

And behind you someone yells, "Breaks?"

"My turn."

"No, you didn't say, 'May I?' "

"Break? What the . . . I was supposed to go home at 7:30."

"Notarize that for me."

A mumbled hush returns, and you concentrate on the N controller who is bringing in fifteen flights from the north.

After jotting down the fifteen plane numbers, you go over to the terminal to watch some of them unload; three to five thousand people is a good estimate of the people in the fifteen blips. All of these people were the responsibility of the controller at one point in time.

What is stress? When was the last time you went to an International House of Pancakes on Sunday morning and saw the after-church rush come in? The cook's got thirty-five slips of paper there, and there ain't two meals alike. And he has to perform in such a manner that the people don't get up and leave. *That* is stress.

We have the stress built in procedurally. But we educate toward that. We're not taking John Doe off the street who's never been educated and plugging him into a microphone and saying, "Here. Talk to this airplane." We're sending him to sixteen weeks of academy. We're bringing him in for six weeks here. We're putting him in the least busiest position, letting him get certified on that. Then we send him back to school. It's a little like a confidence course but with one major difference. In the military you don't fail a confidence course; here we fail you. There, if you fail a confidence course, you fall in the mud. Fail here, and you join the unemployment line.

Initially we screen very thoroughly, and that's what the first year is, a screening process. Initially the first-line supervisor is not in that screening process. But once the person is assigned to his team and starts his on-the-job training, the supervisor *is* the screening process, and I take that job very seriously. There's a knack for doing this job. Some people have it. It has nothing to do with personality; it has to do with the ability of the person. I guess it's like being a professional golfer. Some people can play golf very well, and others, like myself, sacrifice $35 worth of Titlests to the gods.

Sometimes we get people in here who simply don't have this knack. This is Pebble Beach, not some putt-putt course. In terms of traffic, we're running right now at about sixth in the nation. So they come in here and they're just overwhelmed by it. It's like they're out at Pebble Beach, and the first hole is 525 yard par five, and he says, "Which club do I use?"

If they come here and their effort is good and they are willing but do not make the program because of the sheer inundation of traffic, then we farm them out to a lower-level facility to gain that experience. There they can grasp this at their pace and not ours. Then they can be recycled through here.

We use controllers in a team, and normally there are six or seven controllers on a team. And the "pressure" comes mainly from this team. Air control *is* a pressure job, but the pressure in this business is mainly peer pressure. You have to do a good job. You cannot make mistakes.

As a first-line supervisor, my responsibility is to ensure these pressures are not over demanding. I want team pressure to be high enough that I have high-quality performance but not so high that it gets dysfunctional. We can take our shots, and we do. And you'll probably find among air traffic controllers that their sense of humor is fantastic, like the British. It's one-liners. It's strictly dry one-liners. Here's a perfect example. To release pressure, a man that's working fifteen airplanes may key the mike and say, "TWA 497, turn right heading 270, descend and maintain 5000," unkey the mike and say, "If you think you have those capabilities, Captain."

Just things like that, one-line shots. If they become a distraction, I control them. But if they don't, I let that release go. And I have to tone that release so that (a) I don't have six wise guys, but (b) I do have six people who know they can release their tension without their first-line correcting them all along. And sometimes I come in with *my* one-liners to break the tension. Plus I've got to be *good* when I work a position. I set an example.

But my main job as a leader is to ensure a continuity of leadership in the control personnel. Basically I do that by working with the six-man team and reinforcing SOPs [standard operating procedures]. As a typical government agency, we have 355 ways of telling you how to do one job. We have a new program now; we wrap the planes up with red tape, weight them down with paper, and defy them to get off the ground.

I say that in jest. As any organization, we are not in the business of making mistakes. So we attempt to proceduralize things to the extent possible. Then we state that if you must deviate from this, common sense must be the factor. As a supervisor, the way I enforce the procedure is over-the-shoulder monitoring. In other words, I'll plug in and monitor a controller. I'll tape his talks when he's not aware of it and determine if he's applying the procedures. We have these spot checks, and every three months I sit down with each controller and discuss his performance. I see what I can do either to improve it or to encourage it, if the gentleman is doing a good job.

I invest a lot in training controllers. Here the day-to-day operations and standard procedures are set. The airspace is defined; the operational procedure is defined; the plane flies in this airspace at this speed behind this guy at this distance. We have the most problems in teaching these standards. It's like anything else. If you, I, and forty other people were asked to scramble eggs, we could do it forty-two different ways. In air traffic control, it's the same thing; we *could* do it a lot of different ways, but we have to do it *one* way. That's probably the first-line's most difficult job when it comes to training of the developmentals [new people]. We do it *one* way only.

If there was a word for my managerial style, it's "informal," the reason being that we have all the formality in the job. We're not the U.S. Marine Corps. The structure there is rigid—and the leadership style was rigid—you will do this. But here we have people who have volunteered for this job, and they know what they are to do. So if I use a rigid managerial style, the man feels no more than a robot. He must do this. He must say "Yes, sir." He must say "No excuse, sir." That makes him feel very uncomfortable.

I feel that management in this system has only one prerequisite, and that is to make sure that the controller is comfortable doing what he is paid for. Don't get me wrong. I'm not running a good ol' boy operation. It's not like we're a bunch of buddies who're sitting around trying to get the job done and if we make some mistakes, then it's okay. We can't afford that luxury. We approach the job with pride, professionalism, and humanistic values. We do the job perfectly, and we try to be comfortable as we do it.

The problem that we had before, that led us up to the PATCO strike, was that the human factor was always the lowest. Now the pendulum is in the process of swinging totally in the opposite direction. But we have to stop it at the happy medium. If you go too far to the humanistic side, then you find you get into the excuse mode, and we can't afford that. When you look at the radar scope, you see an aircraft as a one-quarter-inch blip, but when the blips are moving at each other at over eight hundred miles an hour, you can't be making excuses.

When I run into problems, I handle them. The first thing I try to do, quite naturally, is to counsel a problem case. The counsel ranges from a "talk down" to the individual to a discussion with him. I prefer the discussion aspect the first time. There may be things at home that bother him—a gentleman could be going through a divorce, his kid may be sick—and those things can affect his wherewithal when he's making a living with his voice.

Then I try analysis. Let's talk analysis. Is it that he knows better and doesn't care? Is it that he doesn't know better? Or is it that he knows better and thinks he can get by with it? If you can identify the category, then you're better able to cope with the problem. That will affect your conversation. Very seldom do we see a problem occurring more than once.

Once I analyze the situation, it so tones my discussion that from that point on I usually have the problem resolved, for the most part. I'm dealing with professional people, not with kids that throw temper tantrums. If a reoccurrence should happen, I use an oral or written reprimand, and nobody wants that on their record because their pay is accordingly adjusted.

There's a lot of learning here. And it helps us to avoid the burnout factor. The job here, I'll be truthful, it's not the pressure you think it is, because we define it. We have to; we run a half-million plane operation. Our airspace is divided, cut up, defined such that if you keep your planes in your airspace and do the same thing every time, then you'll never get hurt. Do that and speak rapidly.

Listen to the controllers; then listen to the pilots. The pilots speak slowly. We don't have that luxury. If I were making $100,000 a year being a senior captain of a Lockheed 1011, and all I had to do was worry about flying an airplane, I'd take my sweet time too. But if I were a $30,000-a-year controller charged with twenty of them and keeping them from running into each other, and they're trying to get to the same airport, my speech rate and the sincerity of my occupation would be a lot more."

The director notes that controllers in the tower operate under the same pressures as those in the bunker. The job of the former group of controllers is to handle the planes on and within ten miles of the runway. In this operation the controllers seem to work together in a modified assembly line, instead of each performing similar tasks. On the far right, facing the runway complex, a male controller punches away quietly on a computer. To his left a rotund female pulls pieces of paper out of a computer, tears them, puts them on boards, and hands them to her left to a controller who is handling the sequence and intervals for planes taxiing to and from the gates.

On the far left is Tom, facing a screen that indicates which planes are soon to land. He's a smiling, bespectacled fifty-year-old who calmly ushes planes in and clears others to take off intermittently across the paths of the in-comers. He does so with grace, concomitantly explaining his procedures to a "developmental."

As he does so, planes take off and land. Every five minutes or so, a light appears about two miles out in the gray fog, grows into two, three, or four lights, forms into a plane, and lands, crossing in front of the tower.

No one talks very much. Two people are eating fried chicken in the back. A junior officer from some airline has come up for a chat. The aroma from the coffee machine nearly permeats the air but is defeated by the smoke from five or six cigarettes. Everyone, including the supervisor, smokes and drinks coffee. Like a mute precision drill team, the whole system runs without anyone mentioning their actions to anyone else. But they are talking about everything else.

"Look at that fat navy plane sitting there."

"Hey, take it easy on the squid."

"Find its base [looks through binoculars]. *Isn't that where* An Officer and a Gentleman *was filmed?"*

"Hey, squid, are you the officer or the gentleman?"

"Who cares?"

"Hey! I can't find my headset."

"I'm getting out of this hole. Who wants some chicken?"

"Okay, American, get off the runway."

"United coming in. Where are you, boy? Oh, finally thought you'd turn on your lights. Good boy."

"Good boy, John Boy."

"Get off the runway. Get off the runway. This guy was ten miles out when I cleared you for takeoff. Oh geeeezzzzz!"

It's quiet for a while; then the supervisor belts out a few lines of "They Call the Wind Mariah" and "Me and Bobby McGee." He doesn't sound like the Kingston Trio or Janis Joplin. He then takes over the director's slot as Tom eats some chicken. Then he switches some people.

Someone's mistake is revealed by the comment "I'm sorry, Pete, I crossed you up on that."

A question comes up concerning whether a plane can cross the takeoff runway at a certain point. Permission is given. The cross is made. Another query surfaces as to whether more planes can be gotten off by some procedure.

The supervisor frowns and shakes his head no. He then asks a developmental if he wants to take over the takoff and landing slot. The developmental does so while the controller stands at his side.

All goes well for thirty minutes; then the controller overrides the developmental's radio and tells a plane to abort a landing and circle. Subsequently, the controller quickly takes over the position and during a slack period tersely explains to the developmental that he didn't keep the proper interval between his planes. The wind turbulence from the lead plane could have caused the following plane to crash.

The atmosphere is tense; the tower, quiet. Then from the rear comes "Oh, Lord, won't you buy me a Mercedez Benz. 'Dialing for Dollars' is trying to reach me . . ."

Head Nurse

If the leader doesn't set high standards, then there is no peer pressure.

My nurses have one of the most stressful jobs in the world. You hear nurses say this and you think they're just saying that. However, it is that stressful. Each has a certain number of patients that are totally dependent on her for pain relief, to get their wounds healed, to ensure that they get the right diet, to control their blood pressure, to monitor their health, to make sure they don't die, and to make critical decisions all day about their health.

Nurses are under this stress because they deal with life-and-death situations or with ones that have long-run effects. For example, if a nurse puts a dressing on a person's arm that's too tight, then it can damage the nerve. That could be it—the person might not be able to use that hand again, ever. So my nurses are dealing with those types of tasks, plus they are under pressure to get things done on time and correctly.

They work within this very structured framework, and the bombardment from the environment is unbelievable. The most stressful event is when they come on a team and a patient is about to die. It's not a terminal patient who you're letting die and who's not in pain. Rather, it's a patient who is borderline. They've got all kinds of medications running in all kinds of lines. You're titrating a medication to keep the blood pressure at a certain level. The pressure goes up, so you have to turn this medicine off and then turn that one on. You're hard at work, concentrating, and you wonder, What if I make a mistake? If I do, then this person will die. You're there just waiting and hoping that it doesn't happen on your shift.

A nurse cannot predict what is going to be required of her during the day. For instance, she can't predict that a patient with a pressure of 120/80 will have it all of a sudden bottom out at 60/40 and the patient will be unresponsive. She's constantly monitoring patients, wondering if each is getting worse, and asking herself, I'm taking vital signs and blood pressures; should I call the doctor now, or should I wait a while? So it's a constantly changing environment because of the people you're serving. These are life-and-death situations. If a nurse makes a mistake; if she gives the wrong medication; if she doesn't turn them; something pretty disastrous could happen with the person's life.

Some days nurses think they can get all of their tasks done and get in some extras, like discussing the psychological problems a person is having with dying, or sitting down and talking with a person about their pain or their financial problems. But a problem with one patient will put her hours behind. And these problems don't come one at a time; they come in bunches. So the nurse has this schedule of all the things she must do on time and correctly, and then she's constantly bombarded with all these other problems—important ones—that she has to handle.

They're dealing with a lot of pain. You've taken a patient through a surgical procedure; you've cut on them, and the patient is in pain. We deal with it and help to relieve it. A nurse can do a lot of things for pain, and choosing the right one for the patient is very important. It can mean the right medication or the right position . A lot of times she doesn't have to give a patient a narcotic to make them more comfortable. For example, she can look at them if they're an orthopedic patient and find their traction is not quite right. So she corrects it.

And since this is a trauma floor, the nurses deal with fairly extensive dressings. They deal with fairly intricate, large wounds that have to be dressed; some take up to two hours to dress. For example, it would take a nurse and her assistant that long to change the dressing on a person who has had their whole pelvis crushed and has a severe puncture wound—four inches long, four inches deep and open to the hip. This wound is usually infected; you open someone up, and the bacteria from their own skin is going to invade that wound. Here they have to dress the wound and pack it. When you pack the wound and pull out the gauze, then some of the bacteria and dead skin come with it. The dressing takes an extensive amount of time, and the nurse simply cannot leave the room. So she has that to deal with plus demands that arise from doctors, other patients, etc. Also this patient is in a *great* deal of discomfort; therefore, she has to give a great deal of emotional support to the patient as she does her job.

My nurses have to deal with all this—high demands, interruptions, pain—plus there's always infections. And on this floor, more than on other floors, we also have a lot of disruptive patients. We have a lot of head-injured patients who really have no idea of what they're doing. They're disoriented toward persons, time, and place. They have no idea who they are, they don't know what year it is, they don't know who the president of the United States is. These people tend to wander off, so we have to guard them from injuring themselves.

My nurses deal with these problems, plus they try to free up time for personal patient-care items. A patient might find his doctor won't talk to him, and he doesn't know what's going on. Or the patient has cancer, is dying, and doesn't know what to do. Doesn't know how to handle it. A patient can be on Medicare and is told she has to leave the hospital, but she doesn't know how she's going to get home or who'll take care of her at home. All of these are problems that nurses want to help with. They try to be of some assistance in these matters. There is pressure from the patients to help here, but so many things come up that interfere.

A lot of my job involves helping my nurses to deal with all this stress. As a head nurse I have 20 RN's [registered nurses] reporting to me, 18 LPN's [licensed practical nurses], 15 technicians, ward secretaries . . . in total, there are 50 full-time employees and 20 part-time. This is one floor, a wing with 50 beds.

At one time we did not help nurses cope with stress. It was accepted that stress was a part of life on this type of wing, and if a nurse couldn't take it, then they weren't much of a nurse, and they went to another floor. Now we realize that these other floors can be just as stressful. The nurses there are still in life-and-death situations, and they have to do a lot of things in a limited amount of time.

I do a lot of counseling to eliminate any stresses that don't have to be there. Sometimes I'll just sit down with a nurse and say, "Look, it's been a bad day. Let's just sit down now and go through it all again and see where you could have done some things better—delegated a little more, taken fewer of the tough cases." And I discuss stress with her. Not theory, but the nuts and bolts: "You are under stress; here is the way it starts at the beginning of the day. This is the way it works during the day, and this is what you can do to reduce it."

Death. This contributes a lot of stress, but it may sound strange that it all depends. It depends on the patient, on how long the nurse has known him, and what the nurse did. It is traumatizing afterwards if she feels that she made a mistake that caused the death. Then she probably will go home and have more than one sleepless night. She can be six months down the road and it will come back into her mind, if I had just called Dr. So-and-So when the blood pressure dropped ten points instead of waiting, or if I'd gone in that room fifteen minutes earlier, then this wouldn't have happened. She sees the faces of the patient's family.

But if she did everything she could—she did it immediately, and she was right on top of the situation, and she called the team in to resuscitate the patient—she feels sad but not overly stressed.

On my floor, it is more stressful than usual. On most floors, the patient comes in; the nurses see the patient on rounds that day, and then they hear that Mr. Jones died on the evening shift. They're sad and feel bad. But it isn't as much a stressor as it is for us, because we get to know the patient for a long term. So I have to deal with my staff differently than do most staff nurses, because mine become very attached to the patients. For my nurses it's more of a guilt trip. Sometimes I initially don't know where they're coming from. It's like, "I should have done this."

"But you weren't even in the room; you couldn't have done that."

Or a lot of times I'm used as a sounding board. They'll say, "We did this, and it was really smooth," or "It didn't go so great. We did this and that; what do you think?" I'm the ultimate authority for them, and I set their standards of care. If I say, "You did fine," that's very important to them. If I say, "I don't want that to happen again," then that also has a strong impact. I know that my feedback sets the standards for the staff, so I talk a lot with them, and we talk about death a lot.

As a leader, I don't just talk; I also try to be a good listener. If it's a problem with a patient dying or a nurse can't stand working with another one, I always listen to the whole story, gather the facts, and then talk with others. For example, if a nurse is upset at the death of a patient, then I'll talk to the doctor to get his input. I've learned from experience that you gather the whole picture before you advise anyone or anything.

I've got to be a counselor, but I'm also responsible for keeping the standards high. I can't just stroke feelings. If I had a nurse come in and say, "I really did a bad job; this, this, and this happened," I can't afford to say, "Oh, don't worry about it; it'll be okay." When everyone else also thinks she did a bad job, I've got to say, "Your behavior was inappropriate and had some bad consequences. Next time, I would do the following things differently." I listen a lot, think about it, and then give the feedback that's appropriate.

Also I react to the way the nurse is behaving. I've had nurses come to me and say, "Hey, it was a little mistake." She doesn't realize it may be a little medication or a little bit of a time lapse in which she didn't give something, but it was not a little mistake. There are no little mistakes when someone dies. If a nurse says, "Dr. Jones is going to come in here and say that his patient died because I gave him too much insulin. But hey, there was a lot of other things going on at the same time," then I say, "sit down. This is a bad problem and your attitude, to begin with, is awful. Our service is to get these people home and to a normal life, and you're falling down on the job."

On the other hand, if a nurse comes in and just falls apart, is devastated, I'll ask a physician to prescribe a tranquilizer to calm her down. You can't discuss problems with a person in that condition. But after she has calmed down, I would still gather facts and give her an accurate evaluation. I might have to go back and say, "From the looks of it, this problem did originate with some action you did or didn't take. I can't have that happen again! This is what went wrong. This is what you should have done." And I'll do this even if she's been devastated by the death. Sure, I'll wait until she's calmed down. But I've got to give her feedback so that she doesn't make those mistakes again.

I always set high standards for my nurses, even as I counsel. Some people think that peer pressure or professionalism leads to high performance. I disagree. If the leader doesn't set high standards, then there is no peer pressure. Once the standards are set, then people will buy into them. Nurses are funny about confronting each other; therefore, they need those standards. It's like, "Gee, I don't want to step on her toes, because, God, she's supposed to know what she's doing."

But once the leader sets the standards, they will step on toes. They will exert peer pressure because they can say, "The head nurse said . . ." Since I set high standards, I've been able to have a floor with tremendous peer pressure, but it doesn't evolve naturally. People will tolerate the poor performance of others. They'll think that the person will change or that they're overloaded right now. There's a natural reluctance for nurses to confront each other and say, "I think what you did was just awful!" Rather, they like to dump those problems up one to me.

At times this puts me in the middle between my nurses, but that doesn't give me any problems. I just monitor the behavior of the nurse who has performance problems and enforce my standards. When I get caught between other departments, or doctors, and my patients and nurses, it's not so easy. A lot of other departments demand a piece and a part of our patient's time. The patient is scheduled for x-ray, but he is taking a bath or becomes nauseated; therefore, we have to reschedule that. The physician comes to make rounds, and he wants the nurse, right then, to talk with him about how the patient is doing or to explain something in his chart.

The major conflicts come between nurses and physicians, and the head nurse usually is caught right between the two. Doctors plan the care that the patient is going to get. Nurses challenge a lot. They say, "This is going on—the pressure is this, the pulse is this; I think we should do such and such"; the doctor will respond, "I'm the doctor, you're the nurse, and this is what we'll do."

The doctor comes in for rounds twice a day, but the nurse is with the patient eight hours a day, and therefore thinks she really knows the patient. So she'll say, "I know this patient. This is important to her; therefore, we should do the following." Or she'll challenge an order: "I think this is kind of more morphine than I've ever seen given in an order. Did you really mean 25 milligrams, or 15?"

The nurse sees herself as a patient advocate or a safety valve for the patient's treatment. She feels she is totally responsible for the patient eight hours of the day, while the doctor just comes in and out. Physical therapy comes in and out. Occupational therapy comes in and out. The x-ray machine man comes in and out. Residents come in and out. But the nurse is there all day with Mrs. B, with her problems and her concerns. The nurse sees trends, problems that are building up, so she'll say, "Dr., consider this. It's important, and do this, not what you think is correct."

So this generates a lot of heat. The doctors will come to me and say that they're trying to get something accomplished and the nurse keeps butting in. Then the nurse will come to me, almost in tears, and say, "This doctor is being a real horse's rear end. He won't answer his beeper. I can't get hold of him, and this is going on. Then he came to the desk and really worked me over in front of everybody."

Then I have to get in there, between these people, and deal with these issues. I get the nurse's side of the story, see if anyone else saw it, get the story, and then go to the doctor and say, "Don't ever do this again." Or, "My nurse said this happened. We're having some problems with the patient, and you're obviously having some trouble responding to our needs. This has got to change or I'll have to do something about it."

Doctors take criticism *very* poorly from their peers, let alone from a nurse; therefore, I have to be a liaison. I always have to deal with these problems, because nurses will not go back and confront the doctor. Or when he's sitting in the chart room, they won't go in and say, "This morning was really unfortuante. I wish it hadn't happened. Here's what I think about it." The nurse has already been put down so much that she won't confront the doctor.

These conflicts can come to a head when the patient is dying. The nurse gets to know the patient. She knows the pain he's in, and he tells her, "I want to die. It's all over; there's nothing more they can do. I just wish they would let me go, let me die." The nurse knows the patient and doesn't want to let go of him; yet she sees moment to moment how uncomfortable he is and that the quality of his life is nil.

On the other hand, the physicians are trained to prolong life as much as possible, and to them death is a failure. They almost set themselves up to be God-like in that they don't want anyone to die, when we all have to die. The patient is totally riddled with cancer, and the doctor says, "Let's do one more thing. Let's ship him off to California where we hear Dr. So-and-So has done five experiments on a limited number of patients and one of them worked. Let's go with it." And you think, "Just give this man a break. Just let him die."

Here again this conflict comes because the nurse is an advocate; she knows the patient as a total person. She hears his emotional problems in the middle of the night. She hears the moans from the pain; she sees the tears and grimaces that the pain brings. She has the empathy for that.

The doctor just looks at it differently. He says, "If I can just get this patient built up to this point, I can do another surgery and just possibly I can save him." The doctor can't give that hope up. That's probably very good. But the nurse hears, "I can't go through another night of pain, another procedure, another day of this type of life. If the doctor does this type of surgery, my body will be mutilated."

My biggest conflict comes when a person is on the respirator with severe brain damage and will never come out of it. My nurses come to me and say, "Why is the doctor continuing to do that?" I'll go to the doctor and he'll say that the family is pressuring him, saying to do everything he can. So that's what he's going to do.

If you step back, you'll see that our floor is a little transient community in which I'm kind of the mayor. Patients come in, we give them a service, and they move on. At times there's a lot of stress on my nurses, there's conflict to be handled, but it's an upbeat environment.

Whenever the student nurses—young, inexperienced, and cute—are scheduled to come through, we tell the patients to behave themselves and not to pick on the poor girls, don't do anything rude. But one of the patients will usually hold his breath while a student nurse is learning to take his respirations. He'll also close his eyes real slowly, and the student nurse will come out shaking. Then the nurse leaves, and the patients are rolling on the floor saying, "Can you believe she asked this. Let me tell you what this one did. Guess where she tried to put her hand."

One day my staff gave a surprise party for me. They called a "code blue" on me, which means that a patient has died, and we're calling the whole team there to resuscitate the patient. I was to be there because I can start IV's well. (It's very hard to start an IV when the patient has died and the veins have collapsed). The call came. I had been very busy and very irritable all day long with everybody. So they called the "blue"; I went running in, and they all laughed.

We have birthday parties for patients, or the staff will smuggle in wine for the patients when I'm not aware that it's going on. They will also pick on me. For some time, I'd been riding the staff to conserve supplies, to be cost-efficient; so one patient got some surgical gloves, blew them up, put my name on them and wrote some other verses on them that I won't mention.

I make my staff wear nursing caps, and they just hate it. So one of them stole my cap and drew some pictures we won't mention on it. And they put some salutations—that'll go unmentioned—on it. As a result, I couldn't wear a cap that day. They had me; I always want to be the role model and lead by example, but that day I was in the embarrassing situation of having to say "do what I say, not what I do."

My leadership style is a mix of all styles. On some things I'm a dictator; I tell subordinates what to do. I'm a role model; I lead by example. In this environment I normally let people participate. I'll guide decisions, maybe manipulate them. In staff meetings I'll say, "Here's a problem. If it were me, and I were out there as the staff nurse, here's what I'd do. What do you think?" My nurses usually buy into my ideas. Perhaps it's a plan I've been working on for a couple of weeks. They'd accept it and think it was theirs.

I very much like the participatory idea, but in a code blue situation where a patient is dying I automatically become very autocratic: "You do this; you do that; you, out of the room; you all better be quiet; you, get Dr. Mansfield." The staff tell me that's the only time they see me like that. In an emergency like that, you don't have time to vote, talk a lot, or yell at each other. It's time for someone to set up the order.

I remember one time, one person saying, "Wait a minute, I want to do this." He wanted to do the mouth-to-mouth resuscitation. I knew the person behind him did it better, so I said, "No, he does it." This fellow told me later that I hurt him so badly to yell that in front of all the staff and doctors. It was like he wasn't good enough. So I explained it to him: that's the way it is. A life was on the line. I couldn't give you warm fuzzies. I couldn't make you look good because you didn't have the skills to give the very best to that patient who wasn't breathing anymore.

If anyone ever tells me that they're a democratic type of leader, I don't want them. In an emergency, if you're a democratic leader, I wouldn't want you leading the team. There come times when you can't stop, vote, or have participation on what's to be done. If you're doing that all the time, then you aren't a leader.

Supervisor, Maximum Security Prison

This job, you'd have to like it or you just couldn't stand it.

Trying to get guards to follow orders is my biggest problem. The new employees are the worst because they fail to realize what they're gettin' into. We have a big turnover. I suspect 50 to 60 percent of the people we hire stay less than a year.

They have three weeks' schoolin' and there's no possible way that anybody can teach a man in three weeks what it's like here. You should have three or four months' training. Lot of people, when they go through a training program, they let it go in one ear and out the other. They don't listen or they think you're putting 'em on. They don't take it serious. They even break a lot of little rules that to them ain't that serious; but it is *that* serious. For example, we had one man—an inmate—come in from work and wanted to go on another floor and get a pack of cigarettes. Now that don't sound too bad, so the guard says, "Okay, go up there and come right back."

Well, he went up there and killed somebody. So you have reasons for all these rules, and a lot of guards fail to realize why we have them. Even the inmates in this same example would understand why we got the rule. They might say, "Why can't I go up there and get a pack of cigarettes?" But they understand why not: somebody on that floor has had his cell robbed that day, you know that, so if an inmate is allowed to go up there—maybe near the time of the robbery—someone on that floor sees him, thinks he did the robbin', and stabs him. The guard is a part of it; if he hadn't let the inmate run up there, the inmate wouldn't of had the heat on him, and it would of all been over. If we could get guards, and the inmates, too, to just see the rules and carry them out as they was wrote and as they was intended to be carried out, we'd be in a lot better shape.

The guards also need to remember how to give orders. For instance, if I say to an inmate, "Hey, do this and that, and when you get through, do it again but do it right," that's wrong. He's going to resent that. On the other hand, if I was to say, "Hey, stud, give us a little help here and clean this up," sure he's going to help. You can see that sometimes if an inmate is told something in a little better tone of voice, the guard would get on better with him. Inmates have bad days the same as we do, and they have good days. If they're approached wrong on a bad day, then sure they're going to blow up. That's human nature. Whereas if the guard used a little more finesse in the way he told the inmate what to do, then the problem probably could have been avoided.

A lot of it is the way you talk, and I try to get that over to my guards by telling them, setting examples, giving them feedback. For example, if an inmate violates a rule and he says, "I'm innocent"—they all plead they're innocent—then that's a good time to use a proper approach. You sit down, you read the violations, you get witnesses, you find him guilty, you tell him why, you tell him what you're going to do to him—throw him in the hole for ten days. Then there's no problem. 'Course you could act like a fool and say, "You're lying, you bastard, and you're going to the hole." Then you deserve the problems you get.

The type of people—they've committed every crime you can think of—you're working with here is different than the ones working in the factory. On the outside they want to work; They need to make a living; They're easier to get along with; Their attendance is better. But with inmates it's different. They don't have to work; they can quit when they want to; Many of them never had a job.

It's so hard to get people to understand the seriousness of this place. We've got people here as bad as any place in the world, and guards usually just fail to understand who they are working with. On the other hand, some come in and fall apart. I had a guard come up to me in the dining room on his first day and ask me to escort him out. He was afraid to walk out by himself. See, these inmates know a new guard, and a lot of them don't mean nothing by it, but they try to scare him. They're going to try to scare him out, and they succeed a lot of times. They do things to set him up, to get him trapped or get him fired. This is all told to the guards before they go to work, but somehow or another they don't grasp it.

There's no way to prevent the inmates from doing something like that. We've got about 4,000 inmates and 600 guards, but that's on three shifts and guards got days off and all that; therefore, we got a ratio of about 25 to 1. And one man, especially a green one, can't watch 25 inmates. No one can, especially since the people in here want to be somewheres else.

It's a serious business here—bad people, high ratio—and they're trying to make life miserable for the guards. They put a lot of stress on him. And there's some guards that just can't stand to see people locked up; it bothers them. So there's a lot of tension and all that; but if a man stays here for a year or year and a half, you can pretty well figure on him staying. They get adjusted and don't worry about it; stress don't bother them. And if they see a stabbing or killing, they don't get bothered.

So I try to get people through the first year. I tell them, "It's a serious place, but you'll do okay. You'll adjust if you just follow the rules. Don't worry. Don't get too scared. Just follow the rules." I lead them by example. Talk to the men about their fears and problems. Try to get them to laugh once in a while. There's a lot of stress here and they just got to learn to tolerate it, to adapt. Of course, stabbings bother you anytime, but not to the point that it shakes you up where you quit. One day a guy was killed right here. It was pretty bloody and the guard who saw it fainted. Well, you don't need him here; I had to do something with him before I hauled the corpse off [*laughs*].

There's a lot of humor around here. It takes a different kind of person to work at a place like this and stay. You're not all hard. You've got to be hard at times, then you got to be sympathetic at times.

I think supervising in a place like this is probably, in my way of thinking, harder than any other supervisor's job. You've got to supervise over guards who carry out your orders, and you've got to make sure that they at least care for people. You got to think about the inmate's welfare—for people who might not care about their own welfare, or for the other inmates, and they want to kill you—and still keep him in line. It's a whale of a job.

I can see why some people wouldn't like it, but it's a challenge. You really feel like you're doing the government a justice by being here. You feel like you're helping others, and I guess you shouldn't never feel this way, but you wonder what would happen if you were to leave—who would get your job. Believe me, a lot of these inmates who've been around for a number of years feel the same way. Some say, "Oh, man, don't go. Who's going to take over?"

You feel wanted, and you feel along the line you've helped some people that society has put down. Some of them leave and never come back. Of course,

I've had some young ones come in who say I was the guard for their fathers. It's quite a challenge, and if you go through life and help at least a few people that society has put down—locked up—then you have done something.

There's been a lot of changes since I come here. Now I encourage my guards to think about the inmates' welfare but not to get too familiar with the inmates; that's a fine line to point out. Used to be that you weren't allowed to talk to an inmate unless it was strictly business. He would walk up approximately six feet from you, take his hat off, and ask permission to talk to you. There was several reasons for this. In the first place, if he'd come any closer, he'd probably get the club over the head, so he didn't want to get close to you. Second reason was that standing that far, he can be heard by all the other inmates, so they know he's not snitching to you. Also the other guards in there can hear that you ain't settin' up a deal, trying to blame him or something. Today it's different. You know so many by name. I go on vacation and they want to see snapshots of the vacation.

So in a situation like this, it's tough to lay down the line to the guards. You don't tell them to club the inmates for gettin' too close, but you don't want them to let the inmates get too close. I tell them that the inmates don't care how strict you are—they prefer it that way—but they want to know how you are to work with. They want you to be predictable. If they know you won't tolerate this, they won't do it; if they think you will tolerate it, they'll test you. They're not dummies, by far. Sometimes I think they're a lot smarter than we are.

Looking out for the welfare of the inmates includes more than just talking "nice" to them. When you find a prisoner is in danger or is being picked on, then you move him or give him a job change. Maybe you put him with an older inmate who's a fatherly type and will look after him.

Sometimes you put an officer in a position that he just don't fit because his personality clashes with the inmates. So an inmate comes in and tells you he don't like the man. That clash ain't doing no good for the inmates or for you and the guards, so you move him to another job. You have personality conflicts everywhere, but *this* is the worst place to have it. But after I get my guards placed, I let them handle the problems.

I try to keep the stress off of them as best I can. Some I don't get along with, and some don't like me, but even those what don't like me know that I care. I care for them because their job, like mine, is a tough one. They can get stabbed. That's in everybody's mind, but that's remote. We've had only a few officers get killed here. A lot get hurt breaking up fights, but few are intentionally hurt. I've had some pretty hairy times, and I wondered then why I am here.

The stress on us is awful, and there's nothing you can do about it while you're in the prison. It's a mental strain all the time, and I don't know what a man would do—I think he'd go crazy—if he didn't have something away from here to release that on. I got many, many hobbies. I Like to stay at home at night, change my clothes, go out and hoe my garden or do something to forget it. You couldn't like this all the time. If I didn't have something to do to get my mind off this, I don't think I could stand it. It's too many pressures. Some days you leave and don't think you've done everything you should, but you got to get rid of it.

This job, you'd have to like it or you just couldn't stand it.

Women's Crisis Center Director

My failures show up in the newspaper headlines.

Fifty percent of my job I like. The other 50 percent I hate. This job is a 50–50 appointment in which I am supposed to spend 50 percent of my time counseling and 50 percent in supervisory duties. I really love the counseling and dislike the management part.

I spend my counseling in direct client contact—talking with women in residence here or else those who come in with a crisis. Usually women don't know where we're at—we try to keep it that way so that abusive husbands can't track down their wives—so they call in first, and we direct them here.

When we get people on the phone, we get them to discuss their crisis. We know that it goes back four to six weeks, so we try to go back to find what is the problem. Once we have the problem figured out, we work on alternatives, what you want the solution to be and how you want to get there. Then we tell them what we can do to help—what services we can provide. If they want to come in, that's fine, because we do outpatient counseling. Or they can become a resident if they fit our guidelines.

We can take up to twelve people here. If they just want a place to stay, that doesn't fit because our population includes only battered women, minor children, rape victims, and abused children, referred to us by Family Services, who have been pulled from homes. If the caller has a drug or alcohol problem, or if they have mental disorders, then they aren't appropriate.

In addition, we have the crisis hotline. For this I can't train people to handle every problem that comes up. All I can do is train for the major areas I think they'll encounter. Others, of course, spring up. Even though we're here for women, we've had men call in on the phone who've been raped. It's the same basic feelings that the victim has, but you've got to change your thinking around completely for a man calling in. And men call in afraid that they're going to abuse their children. Potential suicides call in, which we're not set up for, but we try to help. When someone has just lost their job or got a divorce, and is talking about suicide, you can't just hang up.

When I counsel I prefer counseling the rape victims, because the battered women seem to get into a cycle of abuse and it's hard to get them to break out of it. You feel like you're batting your head against the wall all the time, because it seems like they're always going back to their husbands. Or they take up with someone else who batters them. It just seems like you aren't getting anywhere. Sometimes a woman comes in and she really wants to start a new life, and that makes up for the other times.

With a battered woman, it's hard to realize that one person will do that to another or that a woman will stand it for eight years, being beaten every day. That's hard for me to understand; in a sense, I can because I know that love overpowers all, and love is blind; that sort of thing.

Even though I prefer counseling rape victims, it's hard to listen to someone who's been raped. Your stomach reacts real strong and you get extremely angry and you want to go out and find him and hurt him, castrate him. You just want to put your first through a wall.

We try not to ask for any specific details about the rape—the color of the man's hair and so forth—because if the woman does prosecute, then we can be subpoenaed. So if she wants to tell us a lot of specifics, that's okay, but we won't ask for them. If we are subpoenaed, we won't go, because we consider our relationship to the victim to be a privileged one. We focus in on the feelings that the victim is going through—the hate, fear, humiliation, anger, embarrassment, etc.

A rape victim may call us and talk over the phone. She can come in for counseling, and if she likes she can stay here. When she stays as a resident and then leaves, we try to make outpatient appointments right there because she's been in this protective environment and now she's going out with a new job and a new home, so she is likely to experience a little mini-crisis right there.

We don't really set a time for the stay here. Operationally I guess it would be six months, but the average we're seeing for a single woman is about a month, and for women with kids, about six weeks. If they start to stay too long, we say, "You know, you've been here for four months. You haven't been out for even more than two job interviews; you haven't looked for housing.

You know you need to get in gear this next week or we'll have to ask you to split." Usually they agree with us, so it's a semimutual decision.

Sometimes when people stay here, you get really attached to them, especially when it's a little kid. You see them going back to their parents. A child is helpless. Unless someone sees them being beaten, they can be abused for three to four months before anything is being done.

If it's a woman that you get attached to and she goes back home—seems like all the women I've gotten attached to have all gone back—to be beaten up some more, then that's really distressing. But we've got to take heart in the fact that maybe she's a little more assertive now and that she knows she doesn't deserve to be beaten. When they come in here a lot of times they say that they deserved it, that they were responsible for the beatings. Maybe they won't take the beatings; they'll walk away.

On the management side of my job, my problems come partly from my superiors' expectations of me. They expected me to come in here and know what to do. They threw me in here and told me what to do but not how to do it. When I first came in, this was stuff I'd never done before, and for me it was trial and error. They don't believe in trial and error because it was a new shelter and it had to be run right the first time or we'd lose the volunteers and the community support. So it had to be done right, right then.

Another problem is that I take my ideas to my supervisor to get approval. He has to take them to the executive. The executive has to take them to the advisory board. After the advisory board approves them, the corporate board gets them. And if any one of those vetoes an idea, even though the rest think it's wonderful, then there it goes.

And the pecking order comes down the same way. Corporate board to advisory board to . . . and I really don't have anybody to peck. I can't give it to the volunteers. So trying to get anything done is real frustrating. I get an idea and I work on it and then my superior comes in with this *top priority* item. "Drop what you're doing right now and get your people on this." We had this nice flow chart made up last week on who was going to do what and when. Then my supervisor came in and blew that out the window. We thought it was a good idea. We'd been working on it for a week, and then my superior changes the whole structure of what we're supposed to be doing.

When I first took the job I liked the responsibility, but that was quickly ruined by the bureaucracy. From my boss and from up the line I hear "This is what you're to do," and "This is what you did wrong," never "This is what you did right." That comes only from the volunteers. Everyone up the line is concerned about their own heads and their own responsibilities. That's frustrating, and there's frustration caused by the overload on me—so much to be done. I have to recruit volunteers. On paper we've got about fifty volunteers, and of these we've got about ten coming in to do in-house coverage. On the hotline we have a call-forwarding system that transfers the call to someone's home so that they can take care of it there—the hotline's got to be covered twenty-four hours. There are about fifteen volunteers. I recruit them by putting out fliers. People around in the different agencies also pass the word around that we need volunteers.

I screen every volunteer that comes in and talk to them about what they want and try to get an idea about where their head is. A lot of women we get were abused themselves, and if it was real recent they might not be ready to help someone else because they're still in it so much themselves. After I talk to each volunteer, I decide who we will use and put them in a training program, which takes about a month. It goes through all the areas that we think are relevant, like domestic violence, child abuse and how to report it, incest, and varying skills in working with the kids.

After the training, the volunteers have twelve hours of on-the-job [OJT] training alongside another staff person. I don't just train them and push them out there. In OJT they can get some idea as to where things are, what a normal shift is like, what kinds of questions you ask, how you ask them. Then after the twelve hours of on-the-job training, if I feel that they're ready, they take a shift by themselves.

Once they're working for me, I have trouble managing them. When I came here, I always had jobs in which I was supervised. I had never been a supervisor. I was real scared, and I wasn't sure I could handle it. I knew it would be hard, and it really has been for me.

I also have a lot of trouble telling volunteers that they're not panning out, and I have problems with telling them what they're doing wrong, because in my other jobs I haven't had to tell people what they're doing wrong. And here we *do* have guidelines we need to follow, like you can't write with a pencil; you have to use a pen. Confidentiality is very important. When the volunteers go home, they want to relieve some of their anxiety by talking with someone else: "A woman came in today and she had been raped and beaten, and she started describing it and . . ." They just can't do that.

My volunteers, about half of them are good. They went through our training; they came in and did their shifts and they are good. They have been qualified on the hotline, and we can leave them here by themselves and know everything will be okay. The other half had some of the training, didn't finish the other, and are very hesitant even to answer the hotline. You can't leave them [on their own].

This job is so stressful because it seems sometimes like I'm not getting anything done. If I work with my clients, I can't get the supervisory work done, and if I do the supervisory work, then I don't get my 50 percent client work done. But most of the pressure comes from inside. It's the pressure you put on yourself worrying about whether or not you've done everything you could. With the residents that go back to their husbands, it's a real disappointment. We're not advocating that they leave their husbands and get a divorce, but when they go back and fall in that same cycle, you question whether you've done everything possible.

When you get on the phone with a suicide call and the caller doesn't sound better—calmer, more in control, less inclined toward suicide—that gets scary, because you never know. Like when I get off a suicide call, I just start checking the papers for the next few days to see what happened.

5

Flak Catching

W HEN caught in a firefight, the standard operating procedure is to protect the troops. Likewise, a basic rule for leaders is to protect the
subordinates. Because leadership boils down to getting things done through
people, it is not surprising that leaders place high priority upon shielding their
people—those who do the work—from interruptions, danger, stress, and other
distractions. The research director put it this way:

*"I try very hard to serve as a screen for my people, because they're the ones who
have to do the research. (I know I'm not going to do it, because I don't have the
time.) It saves them time, it raises their morale, and it saves their energy."*

It can also save their lives. In stating the obvious, "Don't nobody want to
work for you if he's going to end up dead," the heroin dealer pinpoints a basic
requirement of leadership: protect your people. This is a common-sense precept
that is seldom taught in MBA or executive programs but is very apparent in
the comments of leaders interviewed here. The heroin dealer catches flak—
bullets, actually—from his competitors, because failure to do so would scatter
his personnel:

*"You got to think and protect yourself and your people. You got to kill, because
if you don't, then the other dude's going to kill your people. And nobody wants
to work for you if you can't protect him. . . . It's simple as this. Sometimes I get
them, or they get me and my people. Surviving. If you got something going and
somebody come and try to take it from you, then you can't let them take it. . . .
You can't let dudes come in hitting on your people. I got to protect them."*

Like the heroin dealer, the collection agency owner-manager and airline
field manager perceive the abuses coming from the outside. Both step in

when the heat becomes excessive. The collection agency owner-manager notes that his collectors make sixty to one hundred calls a day to unreceptive debtors. So in the best of times their jobs are stressful. When the hotheads get on the line, the manager steps in, takes a lot of profanity, and then draws upon his experience to solve the problem. Unlike the heroin dealer, he does not attack or fend off the antagonist; rather, he positions himself strategically and tries to reason the problem through. His approach differs from that of the strong-arm collector, who is somewhat more aggressive.

While the airline field manager's tactics are the same as the licit collector's, her motives are more varied. On the one hand, she knows that handling the "hot potato" reduces the pressure on her people:

"Whenever there's a problem, I'm always there to deal with it. If an agent calls to say 'I've got a passenger I can't deal with,' then I'll go right out and deal with him. I know I can handle any problem they have, I can answer any question, and therefore I take pressure off my people. My subordinates have to take the pressure for eight hours; so it's really helpful if I can take it off them once in a while."

Protecting people also motivates her troops. By "taking the abuse with them" she demonstrates that she cares, that she is competent, and that she is tough enough to take the heat; as her subordinates say, "She's not just standing there looking cute."

While catching flak allows the airline field manager to lead by example, it prevents the research director from doing so. His pressures come from within the organization, mostly from his superiors but also from every bureaucrat with a bright idea. His boss's superiors, the fire department, security, safety, contractors, affirmative action, and a few others try to direct his Ph.D.s to do this, that, and whatever. He does what he has to do to protect them and then finds himself frustrated that he has no time to participate in the work he is supervising. The good news is that his people are self-motivated. The bad news is that he has fallen victim to the obverse of the Peter Principle (call it the Paul Principle): "You're promoted to the point that the administrative crap doesn't let you use the competence you have."

Heroin Dealer

You don't ever use fear in working with your people.

I used to live with my grandmother sometimes. I'd come out of the house and sit up on the porch where I could look down in the street and see pimps and prostitutes, all kinds of criminals. And I got to looking at it, and it looked exciting to me. I said, "When I get big, I'm going to be just like that." Cats riding in Cadillacs, jumping out, looking sharp every day. Never going anywhere. I see them cats twenty-four hours a day.

And then I look at my father. He go to work and come home dirty, mad. The paycheck ain't right, and he's got to pay out on bills. I said, "Man, I ain't going to do that." My mama says to me—I never forgot—"When you get older you gonna have to do the same thing." And here I look around me. The man's out working hard every day, and the woman? As soon as her man goes out the door, then another one comes in the back door. (Now, this didn't never happen with my mama.) I said, "No." My mama said, "You gonna have to bring your paycheck home to your woman." I say, "No way."

I seen these things out on the street when I's young, and I heard different stories. Another thing, I look at TV a lot. They tell you about that TV thing. It's true; it's very harmful to a child. I'd always be angry at Eliot Ness [of the TV show, "The Untouchables"]. I couldn't never understand; the TV don't never make the police get killed. I always said, "Police ain't going to do me like that. They ain't going to take me in. They gonna have to kill me right there. Kill me there."

My father was a weakly type dude. He worked for the city. He weren't no man as far as I was concerned. I loved him so deeply, but he neglected me. He broke up with my mother. Never talked to me. Never knew that much about him. He always when I's young told me he was going to whip me. I said when I get big he better never put his hands on me. And I meant that. I would have killed him.

Now my mother could whip me. I honored her up to today. When I's growing up, she's the manager of an apartment complex. Had four floors of the apartments. I used to help her clean the areas up around the apartment buildings. She took rent. Called the plumber.

She's a good lady; everybody that knows her loves her. Like I got my outlook on life—the motherly approach—from her. She's honest. She not going to use nobody. Not going to mess nobody around. I'm the same way. I ain't going to misuse nobody.

She don't smoke, don't drink, don't go to nightclubs. She handles all the neighbor problems. Whatever she asks people to do, they'll do. If anything needs to be kept for them they'll always come to her. That's where I get my leadership qualities; they come from my mother.

She's little, short. She get upset now when people get rowdy. If they thinks she's upset, they'll quit doing what they're doing. Once when I's young, she shot someone. She had a permit. My aunt and her husband got into it or something. Mom shot at him and shot the wrong person. She's easy going, but she'd crack down. Never got too mad.

I lived around there and then went in [to a juvenile institution] for armed robbery when I's sixteen. I's pretty much a number one guy there. About everywhere I've been, people look up to me. I can think pretty good, and I sing good.

Got out, and I went out and robbed again. Went to prison for four years. Knew most of the guys in the prison from my area. These guys knew people across town and in Chicago and New York City. They talk about me—I got a good business sense. Then everybody said, "Man, when you get out, come and stay with me. I'm doing this and that. Come get with me, man, and we'll get rich together."

But I wanted to be my own man. Didn't want to think someone is taking care of me. So I put my own group together. But I had to go to another place to see how it's done first—how you pay the police off, how you get judges, how you get prosecutors, how to cut the stuff, how to distribute. Didn't take me long, then I's on my own. But I could manage people better than they could. I taught them how to manage people.

Lot of times, I think, What is it about me that makes people come to me, makes me a leader? I haven't quite pinpointed it. I don't know. It's a God-given talent. Some of it I picked up from my mother. Rest of it is just a God-given gift. I watched her and saw how she dealt with people, but I built on that.

I got six people working for me, and I don't never have more than six. Don't want to put myself too thin. It's stressful. You got these other dudes muscling in on you. Cops on you. Working with the suppliers. I have to think for everybody under me. That's a lot of pressure. They can't think too well. You got to sleep all the time with a pistol on you. Never know when the police might kick in on you. Or somebody playing the police game, kick in on you and kill you. It's a do-or-die situation. Only the strong survive. So you got to be thinking twenty-five hours a day.

For my people I got to get the stuff, show them how to put it together, make the stuff up, how to cut it. And you got to watch them. They turn on me, not to kill me but to get me sent up. They can work for me now, but they'll start to work for the police someday. My enemies aren't the people around the corners; they're the ones that sleep with me, eat with me, walk with me. Those are the ones I got to watch.

There's always people—them that does the same thing I do—getting jealous of me. If I won't help them or hook up with them, then they're mad at me.

If I'm not with them, then I'm against them. That gets rough. The game of life is rough; killing rough. They're trying to kill me and my people.

A lot of times I lose, because I try to deal with that competition in a gentlemanly type fashion. Anything that's associated with me, they try to kill. I don't try to kill anyone associated with them. Any killing I do it's just to protect myself. When you're surviving, you do what you need to survive. And you got to develop instincts.

One time, I knew some guys who wanted in on our action and was going to try to kill me. I woke up that morning and told my sister, "Something is going to happen today. I visualize it." Every time before I've almost got killed I've visualized it. So I'm thinking it through. Hurt is hurt, but death, you can't get it back from there.

I went out. If they's going to kill me I didn't want them to do it in front of my kid, so I got me a .45 and a sawed-off shotgun and walked around the streets. If they want to ride up on me and shoot me down then the best man just wins.

That night it got dark, and I say, "Maybe I got the wrong feeling." Phone rang. The man called and said, "Man, you going to see your baby at the hospital tonight?" My mind went tilt, bing, "This is it—set-up time." He come, pick me up, take me to the hospital. Now it would have been better to kill me coming out of the house, but no, they take me to the hospital.

I see my wife and the new baby. Then the cat calls at the hospital, "Man, I can't come get you because the car done broke down." And it's raining. Every time I've been shot up or hurt it's been raining. So I come to the hospital door. A lot of light there. I called me a cab. So I think if the cat's thinking like I'm thinking he's going to hit me with a 30–06 in the light.

But they don't try that. So I'm in the cab and I tell him where to drive, because I don't want him taking me somewhere to get killed. It don't go like I'm thinking, but the cat what set me up knows I had to go to my mom's house to get some money; I'm broke.

So I have the cab pull up where it's dark, and I get out of the cab, and my gun, I cock it. But I try to get out without turning my back to the driver, because I know he's going to shoot me in the back of the head. I see this car coming around the corner and it slows down. I see one guy rise up in the back and aim at me. I'm diving into a puddle of water. When I dive, the first guy shoots and hits me along here [along the outside of the left ribs]. Next bullet hits me in the back and comes out the top of my shoulder. And my whole side burns. I think they got me with a shotgun.

I fall into a wall, and lay beside it. I say, "I'm hit, I want to take somebody with me." So I cock the gun, and the first person I'm gonna kill is the driver. Then the car can't move. I shoot—pow! I see the driver's head fall over, and the car runs into the back of the cab. I got him. So I jump up and run straight toward them. The cats see me. Two jump out of the car, run, throw down the guns, and run. Then the car starts rolling backwards down the street. Now I'm shooting, but I don't know how long I'm gonna be on my feet before I drop dead. The next one I get, I want to have him in my hands so I know I shot his brains out.

There was four of them. The driver is dead, and I saw two run. The other guy's in the car hiding, laid down. I sneak up. He must sense I'm coming. Up he jumps and shoots. Runs—pow! I get him.

I go over and get my mother to let me in. I come walking in, blood running out my shoes. I call the operator and tell her to get me an ambulance. Then I get real weak and think I'm dead. Come to find out I wasn't hurt that bad.

Competitors are always giving me trouble, but I don't have trouble with the people above me—the suppliers; they like me. They want me to be with them because I don't have no habits. I don't smoke, drink, shoot drugs. Nothing mixes with business. Business is by itself. If you put things with it, then you're defeating your purpose.

Now I do a little pimping. I don't turn no women out. If I run across a woman that's in the game—she's making money and needs me for help to do her thing—then I help her out. I protect her. She's with me then like cool.

I like to match wits with the boys above. It ain't always how good you can read a book. I demonstrate it from scratch—street sense—out of the ghetto. All you got to do is apply common sense, and common sense will beat book sense out any day. That's how I survive.

And when you do that, people like you. Suppliers like me. They ask me what I want. I name it and get anything I want. I can pay them later, or if I mess it up, that's okay—that's dead. I can get some more. They always want to keep me happy than to see me mad. Sometimes I think they're a little afraid of me.

I'm not scared of them. I never met no man who can do no more to me. We all got to die one day. It ain't the man with the fastest gun that wins, but it's the smartest. Like these cats never are no problem, don't put no pressure on me.

If I could swallow my pride and not feel like it's them taking care of me, I can be rich, filthy rich. I could go with them, lay with them, help them think. I wouldn't have to put a gun in my hand, not cut nothing. But I can't swallow my pride and let someone else take care of me. Can't let them take care of me like I'm a child.

I want to carry my own weight. If I make a mistake, then the mistake be on me and not on nobody else. I do my own thing. I'm a little guy, and I got a complex about being little. I'm a little guy in a world of big men, but I want to be looked up to. I can move them. I got to think more better. I ain't as tough as them and I ain't going to fight anybody too quick. But ain't nobody going to push me around or treat me like a child. I'm tough. Like there's this story what went around that I'm so tough I decided to shoot my own self.

I's up all night and I's smoking strong—I mean strong—grass. I's high and I take a bath and I dry off. Now I got my .38 in my pants pocket. Usually, when I'm in my right mind, I take my pistol out of my pocket first and then my money. This particular time, I'm high and not thinking. So I'm taking out my money, the pocket tilts, and the gun falls out, shoots me in the knee.

When it hits me, it knocks me clear across the room. I'm so high that I think somebody done sneaked in the room and hit me in the jaw. I fall back into the wall and I jump up ready to fight. My leg's flopping around. My mom knowed I done killed myself. I'm sitting on the floor laughing. Somebody called the cops and they come in and bust my partner. And the police say, "What? Who that done shot him?" My partner say, "Man, ain't nobody shot him. Man, he so tough, he wanted to feel what it's like to get shot. He shot himself."

Being a dealer ain't no picnic. I never buy myself too much of nothing, because everything in the life deals with numbers. I always got to think about that. If I buy a car or a home, the car got to have a license number, the house got an address. Then they can find the numbers and get you.

I've been a hit man, and I know that any man who's got numbers, you can get. And he works; so, eight hours a day, he's got to come to that job. He got a certain routine he got to do. You can get him there.

I ain't ever going to stay in one spot too long. That's what they want me to do. Can't do that and stay alive. You got to think and protect yourself and your people. You got to kill, because if you don't, then the other dude's going to kill your people. And nobody wants to work for you if you can't protect him. Don't want to work for you if he's going to end up dead.

It's simple as this. Sometimes I get them, or they get me and my people. Surviving. If you got something going and somebody come and try to take it from you, then you can't let them take it. If they take it they not only take it but they take your life with it.

Like one time I's at home and this dude said, "Man, come and meet me. I got something going, and I need to see you." Now in the process he done told somebody else he was going to get me. He done talked with a bunch of women around. There be this woman on my side, and she call me and say, "Don't come because they plotting over here to kill you."

So I get this dude that called me and I said, "Man, I can't make it now. I'm coming, but I need you to come help me to do this here." He don't think I know already what he got in mind. Then he come on over and I killed him. He intended to take my life. I'm a firm believer you got only one life to lead. You can make a million mistakes, but you only live one time. They can't kill you and say, "Sorry, I made a mistake," and then bring you back. So when a man tries to take your life from you, he intends to take the only thing you got valuable to you.

Same thing about your men. You can't let dudes come in hitting on your people. I got to protect them. I treat them good too. Like I see how they work for others and that they get only 30–70 or 40–60. I don't like that. And they get a lot of problems with it so they can't have no peace of mind with what they do.

You get better action from a person when you give them a piece of the action so they can be their own boss. My main thing is that the best way to motivate a man is through his kids. I give a man a 50–50 split basis so he can take care of his kids. I always got this psychological thing with the child. I say, "Call me Uncle." I always make them get good grades in school. I stop by the house and let them come see me. At Christmas, they got just as much presents as my kids. They got to go to school every day, clean. I don't want to see no raggedy shoes on them. People that's stole clothes, I get the shoes and clothes from them for the kids. I make sure they get taken care of. And if a man sees you're taking care of his kids, he's going to be taking care of you. He's your man, and he'll be out there making money for you.

I always let them know they ain't just working for me. They're also working for themselves, because I give them a 50–50 break. It's as much yours as it is mine, and if you lose mine then you lose yours too.

Mostly I pick people what's been recommended to me by people here on the street. Like I see people around me and they say a man's good at his bag; then I consider he can work for me.

Most of the time I got me good people. And it ain't so much that I have to motivate them, because I be generous and nobody wants to see me mad.

I ain't going to mess over nobody, but I ain't going to stand for no messing over me, no petty games. We going to do it one way—my way. They can speak their opinions on some situations and if the money don't come up wrong then we're cool.

You don't ever use fear in working with your people. Like this dude asked me one time, "If a guy owed you some money, would you kill him or would you make him pay you the money?" It all depends; there's principles involved. If he took my money and talked about it then I'm going to kill him. If he took it, and something accidentally happened—he had to throw it away— then he don't owe me nothing.

Now this dude said, "You can be slicker than that. You can play a man."

I said, "If you leave a man alive and make him scared of you, then there's no telling what he'll do to you. But if you kill him then you can start all over new with somebody else. You got him out of the way, and every day when there's one dead you got two or three more to take his place. But if you leave him alive and you keep putting that fear in him, then somewhere down the line he's going to get you."

And it happened to him. I told him, but he didn't like it becaue he wanted to be right and me to be wrong. I was with him when it happened. He brought a man in the house who owed him money. Talked bad to him, pistol-whipped him, made him get in a woman's dress, put lipstick on him. Shot him up around the face.

I said, "Man, kill him or let it go." I went downstairs because I didn't want to see this. And I didn't want the guy seeing me there.

He said, "Okay, man."

I said, "Okay, don't get mad at me because you got to do your business."

So he don't kill the guy. He beats up on the guy and then gives him more business. And this guy came back and got this dude and his wife.

I'm a firm believer that you don't do people just any kind of way. You do it to them what you want done to you. And to be a good leader you got to listen to people. Try to understand the people you're dealing with. He got a like and a dislike too. You got to get into the person. If he got an opinion, get him to speak it. It might be right or wrong, but listen to what he say.

But it's on you; you got to be able to weigh and judge. If you make the wrong decision, then you got to pay the price. You're the man calling the shots. I don't have ulcers, and I still got good sense, but I wonder how I make it. Guess I'm just young, wild; nothing can stop me.

Collection Agency Owner-Manager

Here we've got a relaxed atmosphere, on my demand!

Very seldom do I ever see a new situation. I have gone through the period of time in which I could say, "Oh boy, this is something that's never happened before. What will I do now?" I have probably faced that situation before and made the decision, whether it was right or wrong. Now I can play back on my past experiences and utilize them in the current problem. Very seldom do I have a new decision to come up where I don't have the past to guide me or that I don't know what is the best area to take.

That experience makes me the best person to handle our hot potatoes. That's a big portion of my job—being a flak catcher for my people. For example, a collector gets a real hothead who wants to make somebody's life miserable. I can talk to him and say, "Hey, you didn't like the other guy, so he called me in. Well, he's got rules he's got to go by. I'm the owner, if we talk then maybe I can work with you. But if we can't talk then we can't make a deal!"

If he starts cussin', saying what I can do with some parts of my body, where we could put the bill, or is uncomplimentary about my mother's sexual habits, I just sit there and say, "Uh, uh-hum, uh-hum, yes, no," and wait until he winds down and ask him, "Have you pretty well got everything you wanted to say done?"

"No."

"Well, keep talking. . . . Through?"

"Yes."

"Well, now we can talk about the problem now that you've cooled down a little. Now be honest with me and don't start chewing me out again or cussing me out, because we're not going to get any further than you did with the other one."

If I listen, then I can find out what his big problem was to start out with. Maybe one of the collectors said his name wrong. And it happens. They get off on the wrong foot. He can't get along with them. For example, one fellow—Tommy Joe Clifford—called in raving mad, and when I got to the core of it, it seems it all started out by the collector calling him Tom. And he don't like Tom and goes by Joe. It's weird what can happen and what the real problems are. He says, "This guy calls me up, keeps calling me Tom, and I don't like that."

We have about seven to ten people working here in this collection agency. Four people work directly on the phone all the time—they're the collectors.

I have an outside salesman, two clerks, and a bookkeeper. The salesman's job is knocking on the door of potential clients like hospitals, doctors' offices, retail outlets, utility companies, and so forth. He's on the road, because the odds of good clients coming in on their own are 1,000 to 1. You've got to sell this service.

The four people on the phone are the central core of the business. We work accounts two ways. First, when the account comes in, it is made up on our computer, and the computer prints the notices. The first notice is then mailed to the debtor. If he or she doesn't pay, then in ten days it goes to the collector, on the phone. They check all directories to get a phone number. They reach the person to talk to them because if the debtor has to answer why they haven't paid, it's tougher for them to refuse. It's a lot easier to just throw a notice in the trash can.

So first it's one-way communication and then it's two-way, because if they have to answer, it's a lot harder to turn you down. By law there is a section on our notice that says if there's any trouble with this account, please contact us within X number of days and explain your position. So they've gotten the notice, they should have hollered, they didn't, and now we can go to work on them.

We *want* to talk to people because we collect twice as many accounts as we will by sending them mail. One phone call is worth two pieces of mail, and a phone call on the job is worth two calls at home. The collector then gives a regular line: "This is John Doe, of the collection agency. I'm calling for the account that we have listed at City Hospital. We haven't received your check. You got that notice in the mail, didn't you?" They're always affirmative; it's an affirmative pitch. I always tell my people, "Sell the steak, not the sizzle." It's like when you pull in the gas station, they say, "Fill it up?," not "How much do you want?" In other words, be positive! The guy at the gas station is trying to sell a full tank of gas, and we're trying to collect the account in full.

On the phone you're working with individual circumstances. We like to think of ourselves as being in a business of *helping* people pay their debts. Now there are some poor situations—some people we can't cooperate with, they won't cooperate with us. But 75 percent of the accounts we collect, we collect through cooperation. We find out why they didn't pay it, how they can pay it, or how we can help them find a way to pay it. A lot of times people don't realize they have income available to them. They can borrow from their credit union; a guy's in the Guard, and he gets a Guard check every so often.

My collectors' lives are rough ones because they have to make sixty to one hundred telephone calls a day, and they know over half the time they're going to be dealing with people who don't want to deal with them. The debtors aren't all bad, but man, let me tell you, you get some real ding-a-lings sometimes—they're really horses' rear ends.

The collectors deal with these fellows in one call, and in the next, they've got to decide if a person has problems paying or if they're just stalling or lying—giving the same story three or four times down the road. So it's a rough life out there, and once I get a good collector, I like to keep him. You could hire twenty-five people and find only one good collector. So once you get them, you try to keep them.

I had a girl quit me last month and I had to hire a new collector. I don't like to do that for two reasons. One, monetarily, while I'm training a new collector, I've got a unit down $2,000 to $3,000 a month, so that's $1,000 to $1,500 per month I'm losing in commissions. Two, I'm having to spend a lot of time and effort training the person.

So in running this agency I do the hiring and training; otherwise, I guess you'd say I'm just a glorified gopher [*laughs*]. I pick up the mail, I go to the attorney's office, I go pick up checks. If a client calls in with a problem and the salesman's not around, then I smooth it over. A lot of problems that I handle never become big problems, but if I'm not around to handle them, then they drag on for a day or so and become real problems.

I'm here to handle big and little problems; that is part of my managerial job. Another responsibility is to set the right relationships and atmosphere. Most of my employees are young; most of them, if they have problems, would not hesitate to come to my house and talk to me at night. Problem is that you can get too big for that, and I don't want that. I care for my people. I had a girl who had to leave because she has a little girl who has kidney problems, so she has to measure her intake and outflow for a period of three months—you can't get a babysitter to do that. After that time she thinks the little girl will be okay. So I told her she'd have a job waiting for her. We had to hire someone to fill her position, but we'll hopefully get enough new business in here that when she's ready to come back in here we'll have the spot for her.

I give my people responsibility and let them make decisions on their own. I found there was a cost to that. I lost a girl who had worked for me for five years. I'd let her make a lot of decisions, to the point that she thought she owned the place. And then it came to a point where I had to say, "Hey, babe, this is a decision I have to make." Probably I let her have a little too much responsibility and lost her because of it. That don't happen too often.

I tell my employees that if they can't get along with the other people in this office, then they can't get along with me, because we work in a hard business. Every time you get on that phone, you're apt to run into an argument with somebody, so I don't want *any* employee friction. If you're the kind of person that creates friction with other employees, or you can't take a ribbing, then I don't need you.

Here we've got a really relaxed atmosphere, on my demand. I had a girl come over from this other collection agency and said she left because they were always fighting over there. And I told her if she couldn't get along with my people, then I didn't want her, because we fight hard to do our job, and we just can't fight with each other. It's as simple as that. I'm lenient, probably a little too much so with my employees, but I think it makes for a conducive atmosphere around here as far as the work is concerned. And we need that—we're small; the work is rough; so we've got to hang together. It's got to be a relaxed atmosphere.

Whether I was in a collection agency, or being a basketball coach or whatever, I think I would have risen to some sort of management position. I, like any manager, don't like to find that the buck stops here; you know, when you're the manager you have to make the decision—that's it. Maybe there's some fear and anxiety of not making the right decision, but time usually takes care of that.

I really want to avoid ruffling the feathers of a debtor. We serve a very vital function to everyone when we collect the bill. People don't usually realize that. Let's say a patient owes a doctor money. Now as long as he owes the doctor money, he probably won't come back. But once his account is paid, if it's done right then he'll filter back in. Now the doctor might not want him on a charge basis, but he can get him on a cash basis. But if I rough him up in the process, then some of his anger will fall back on the doctor and he'll say, "I'm not going to that Dr. So-and-So. He gave me to that collection agency, and they roughed me up. There's no way I'm ever going back to him." Maybe it was only a $10 to $20 account, and the guy potentially could be the doctor's patient for twenty years.

So if I can do it in a tasteful manner, that serves a useful purpose. If I call him and say, "Mr. Jones, the doctor needs his money. He needs his money just like you do. If you go out and work a week, then you want your paycheck. Now he's been fair; he treated you; he gave you four or five months to pay the bill. Don't you think it's time you paid him?" Then the patient'll usually pay and, more important, he'll go back. So we've done a good job.

The collection business has been good to me. Sure, you have bad days. There's days when I ask, "Why the devil did I get into this?" You get hold of a bad debtor, and you could talk reason all you wanted to, and there's no way he's going to pay. Or you have problems with employees. But I know I couldn't make this much money working for someone else. So I'm making it here.

Guess I don't really want to retire for a while. Sure it would be nice to retire but . . . I'd like to increase this business to the point where I'd have an offic manager and I could come and go as I please. Guess what you could say right now is that I'm trying to manage myself out of a job.

Strong-arm Collector

I'm like an atom, and all the energy comes from me.

Technically, it's right on the borderline between being legal and illegal. It's legal to collect, but the methods we use is illegal. What we do is we get 50 percent of the debt plus the $7.00 for the returned check.

My lieutenants go talk to them. They're good PR [public relations] guys who can speak, talk, communicate with somebody. We tell them, "Hey look, you're getting stuck with these bad checks. You got to take bad checks because you're in a large-volume business. And I can guarantee you that if you give us your accounts, that you will have your money within three weeks." Now usually if they give them to a collection agency, they got to wait six months to a year for their money.

Then—to the debtor—what we do is send in the PR guy. He goes in and says, "You got a $50 bad check out." We say, "Now look, you know you're wrong to have a $50 check out. You could be prosecuted on it. We're not interested in that BS. All we're interested in is the $50. If we can set it up on payments of $2.50 a month, maybe $2.50 a week, that's all we want. You sell pop bottles, aluminum cans, we don't care, just as long as the money comes in. But when the payments are due, we don't want to hear the aspect of the rent is due or the kids have snotty noses, dirty diapers, and excuses. We want our money."

Seldom do people buck or slip and slide. We got a reputation. But still you got your bums. So first what we do is hire a consultant for $25. He comes in and smashes the car windows. Well, the car windshields have a deductible of $50. So now they got the broken windshields. They got to pay $50 there. The $25 we had to pay for the consultant we tack onto the $50 they owe us. So now it's $75.

Then if they still want to buck or slow pay, we have a small shooting incident. We shoot into the house, into the upper parts. No one gets hurt. By this time, the bill is $175. The consultant who shoots up the house charges $100, so we tack that on.

By this time, the guy is saying, "These guys are crazy. All this complication over a $50 check." So they go out and borrow it from their family or whatever, even though it's now $175. They pay off and they're happy to.

Once this example is performed, everybody else knows. You, your clique, and your army—two PR people, two to do leg work, and four consultants—got the job done and you got the reputation.

I got to have these people working for me. You got to be a leader in this field; can't work alone. There is nobody that can continuously keep doing this themselves without getting busted. I don't care how slick you are or how sophisticated your techniques are. The odds are you are going to get busted. If you're doing it, you're caught. Hire it done, safest way.

Now if you're not smart, your employees will roll over on you. But if I give a PR man or lieutenant an order and he turns around and gives it to someone else, then you're safe. It's the layering. So if this guy gets busted he can say, "this guy hired me," and then that guy can say that this other guy hired him, but it's all hearsay. That'll never hold up in court. So layer as needed; keep the protection in front of you.

But usually there's not much trouble with stooling. I don't worry about people keeping their mouth shut. I'll kill them. And technically they're professionals in their own field. I use them over and over and over. They work for me; it's an annuity, employment for life. They work for me and I look out after them forever.

I use maybe one or two guys, and I'll keep using them. Once they stay at that job over and over, they get good at it. Then they can think on their own, and realize they're making money. Plus there's the excitement, the women and drugs they can get from this.

That's why I became a leader. It's safer this way. And I think anybody becomes a leader because they want excitement. They're wanting people to look up to them. They want to impress people. In any organization, Kiwanis Club, Jaycees, whatever, the idea, the goal is to be the leader, to climb to the top. There everyone knows your name. It's a high itself.

Money. It's down at the bottom. I give a lot of that away. I'll go in stores and see little kids who can't afford toys looking at them. I'll buy them for them. I like making the money and being Robin Hood, but I don't crave it.

I like the high of being a leader. I'm like an atom, and all the energy comes from me. I radiate to my group. If it's positive radiation, then everyone feels good. I keep a positive stream of energy flowing the people around me can feel it. They know I'm in control. I'm doing the thinking and I got the charisma. I radiate the positive vibes. Never let people get no negative thoughts in their heads!

They know when they're with me they're going to do okay. I got the vibes. I protect them. All they got to do is do their job and I look after them. I'm the big umbrella. They're under it just doing their job. They don't have to worry or think. They just do their little part. I keep it simple for them.

And I find what motivates each man, what excites him, what makes him tick. Like I take a guy to dinner, watch his eye contact when I say things. I have a couple of good-looking broads come by. Or I'll invite him to a party and have a woman turn on to him and hustle him with no absolutes. I find the weakness, and I capitalize on it.

Then I dialogue people, build them to a high plateau that they've never been to before. Most of my people have been dumped on all their life. Never had anyone to look out for them, to give them money. When you give them that then they respect you for it.

Some want to hustle broads. Give them that. Some want drugs. Everybody wants to be rich. Give it to them and turn them loose. Everyone wants their family to look up to them. To drive the new car. If you can find and fuel a person's fantasy then you can control them.

And when you get people who screw up, even then give them positive strokes. Always positive. You can't scold them like a two-year-old child. For instance, I had these two consultants—two blacks. I gave them $50 a piece, a bottle of wine and a half ounce of dope. I says, "Here's the address, here's the car license number, the color of the car, the make, etc., etc., etc. I want you to go and break out the windshield."

They're to do it Friday night. So on Saturday morning I drove by this address. I think it was 810 Chesterfield. I swear to you, every car on the block had its windshield broken out.

I went to Joey that afternoon and he came up to me. I said, "Joey, what happened?" He says, "I know you might be mad, but after smoking that dope and drinking that wine we lost the address. We knew it was the 800 block. So we figured that we know we got to do the job. So to make sure we got the car, we broke out every windshield in the whole block."

So I said, "Joey, look, I'm glad you showed the initiative to go ahead and do that. Most people wouldn't do that. I like that. Be aggressive." Note: I give positive strokes. "But next time don't hesitate to call, and I'll meet you somewhere. I like that aggressive behavior. You got potential."

Airline Field Manager

Agents will work harder for me if they see me out there taking the abuse with them.

She's a walking, talking whirlwind, in about her mid-thirties, somewhat shorter than average and perhaps a little heavier. Decked out in a professional mustif—an outfit that is sufficiently professional but not a uniform—she darts from one region of her turf to another in one of the nation's busiest airports. She is a field manager for a major airline, and she is currently responsible for her company's ticket counter, security, and sky captains in the airport. That's a lot of responsibility, especially when it's coupled with serving as the airline's number-one flak catcher and occasional overseer of the lost bags, or "bag heaven," operation.

What makes this job, shall we say, "interesting," is that I get pressure from the top and the bottom. Now that's not unusual; you expect that. But I don't have much control over either side. This comes from the top [*she pulls out a computer sheet*]. I'm judged on delays—Do the passengers get there late and delay the plane? For another field manager it's, are the bags late so that the plane is delayed? Somewhere high up in the bureaucracy someone has set up a standard. I have no input into that, but I've got to meet it. And this is the first place it hits. If there's a delay, they call me on the carpet and say, "Your loading times are too late. What's wrong? Don't you have proper staffing? What is it?"

Whenever there's a delay, the tower decides who is responsible. I'm judged on my delay. It is a big deal. All airlines do this. Time is money to airlines. There is scheduling of aircraft, and if there's one delay it backs up all the way down the line. The ideal is to have everything on time.

From the top it's "rule by exception." If I don't meet the standard, the pressure comes rolling down. My boss sits down with me and goes through my computerized charts for every month to see how I'm doing, and then gives me feedback. Most of my "upper stress," however, comes from keeping up with my paperwork. I feel that it's more important for me to be out there, especially when things are going bad, than to be back here writing up reports or evaluations or writing letters back to passengers. However, someone in the bureaucracy says, "Fill out the paperwork!"

And the pressure that can come up from below is intense, especially here at the ticket counter. At the counter, the pressure is speed. Here the pressure is to make sure that my passenger lines move as fast as feasible; therefore, I have to get enough staffing so we can handle passengers for that particular time of day. On a full day, that's sixteen positions. The counter handles most customers, but at times I do too. Anyone out there can call me when a customer wants to speak with management. In fact, when it's really bad—I mean a really bad night, weather delays, people missing connections—then I will be out on the counter as a visible member of management. I always try to be up front, visible, when I think I will be needed. You don't hide in this job.

Some of the men, especially the older ones working under me, are MCPs; they just can't handle being supervised by a woman. But I try not to come on with the woman boss image. I try to treat them in a fair manner. I try to let them know my job is to make their job easier, and I'm not there to punish or to make them look bad.

I'll deal with them one-on-one and say something like, "This is what I expect from you, and this is what you can expect from me." A man, say fifty-five years old, sometimes won't respond to that. So my problem is to find out how I'm going to get him motivated. The only thing I can do is say, "You have to spend eight hours a day here. You can spend the eight hours a day being miserable, or you can spend it doing your job, trying to look at this with a different attitude."

When I first took this position, I think that I was pretty successful right away because of my quick reaction to a problem: a baggage belt broke, and we had bags up the yeenee. So I just jumped in there and started throwing bags around. That made them say, "Well, she's not just standing there looking cute. She's in there humping just like we are."

My passenger problems can bring on the major headaches. If we—the company—miss connections, if it's our fault that we've missed connections and if there is no other flight to get the passengers to their destination, then we must put the passengers up in a hotel and get them out on the next flight. One night I stayed until 3:30 in the morning because Las Vegas had a mechanical problem that delayed them, and they still sent the plane here— eight hours late! With connecting passengers on it! Of course, when they got in at 2:30 in the morning, there's nothing going out. So we had to get hotel rooms for all these people. What happened was that Las Vegas shifted *their* problem to us. And when the people got here, they were very tired and bitchy, plus we had to handle them. Not only did the people in Las Vegas screw us; they also were totally uncooperative. I asked them to give me the names of all the people who were connecting—they had the tickets and knew who the passengers were. They wouldn't tell me, so I asked them at least to tell me how many people they had so I would know how many rooms to book. But they wouldn't do that either, so I had to guess. I guessed about 40. So I booked 40 rooms, and it turned out that we needed 50.

As you can see, I have no control over a lot of the problems I face in this position. Other stations shift problems. There are mechanical problems. And if another station doesn't handle it well or chooses not to handle it, I know it's my problem.

Baggage loss is also uncontrollable. I don't lose the bags, but I have to help customers locate them. And people are always so sensitive about their bags. They have to find them *now*, and the contents are always *so* valuable. I work very hard to find a bag, but after a month, if we don't locate the bag we consider that it's gone to "bag heaven," and New York settles with the customer. But in that time we really work hard to find the bag. One nice thing about working baggage is that you get to see the results of your work. When you see a bag that's been missing a long time is found, then there's a good feeling.

I'm under a lot of stress, and to cope with it, I get out on the firing line. I'm visible. I try to ease situations, try to be visible to the agents so that they can come to me. And I release nervous energy. Somebody asked me if I was a workaholic. I'm not, but when I see a counter with lines, I want them down. So whatever I can do to help them, I do. Now I don't just say, "You've got a line out there." I help. When I see there's a line, I walk around behind the counter so people can call on me if there are problems. Then I move out into the lines to see what I can do.

My philosophy of management? I don't want to be a big buddy to people. I'm their boss, not their buddy. Plus I think you should lead by example. When my people ask a question, I come back and give them an answer. If I don't have the answer, then I find it out for them. Whenever there's a problem, I'm always there to deal with it. If an agent calls to say "I've got a passenger I can't deal with," then I'll go right out and deal with him. I know I can handle any problem they have, I can answer any question, and therefore I take pressure off my people. My subordinates have to take the pressure for eight hours; so it's really helpful if I can take it off them once in a while.

When I deal with the problem, say an irate passenger—and the agent's been right—then I'm sure to tell the customer that the agent was correct, and I tell the agent she was right. If the agent's wrong, I apologize for the agent's behavior and then talk to the agent later.

Sometimes I'm in a position to do something for the customer that the agent can't because I've got more authority. For example, I can handle money adjustments. A lot of times I have to do some things to break the tension. If the agent's having a real hard time I say, "Let's go to the back room and say all the bad dirty words that we want." Then I tell them to go back out there. Or I'll say, "Go back out there and when it gets tough, come back in here and beat on something besides the passenger."

My feeling is that the agents will work harder for me if they see me out there taking the abuse with them. Leadership by example is the way I see it. That's the way I do it. Not everybody does. I do. I was in their place. I know at the end of the day they can be mentally and physically exhausted. If they see me out there in bad times, they know, one, I'm there to help them and two, they know I'm working. If I'm here in the office, they don't know what I'm doing.

But you don't *just* work alongside your people. Sometimes you have to be forceful and step in. Like I say, if there's trouble between the agent and a customer, the agent can call me. And I handle any frictions among my people. For example, there's friction sometimes between the skycaps and the passenger assistants. The assistants are responsible for the wheelchairs and making sure that people in them get to the planes. Sometimes an assistant will tell a skycap to push a passenger to a plane. The skycaps don't like that because they want to be out front or downstairs where they can get tips. The assistant has the authority to tell a skycap to take a passenger, but he also can do it himself. So a lot of times there is friction. Here I step in, rule, and arbitrate. Or if a skycap and a passenger have a problem, I listen and make a decision. Being assertive with people doesn't trouble me; it's just one part of working with people.

I feel one area that the airline is falling down in is training in the airport. Some of our people are not well trained; therefore, they're not sure of themselves. They're unsure of their technological skills. Therefore, they have an overbearing attitude toward passengers and put them down.

Since a competent agent is more effective and courteous, I work very hard to make sure they know their job. But I don't want them just efficient and cold. I want them efficient and courteous. When you're dealing with a large public sector, you're going to have a tendency to be cold. And you tend to be cold to the public when the company is cold to you.

We at this end have to make sure that the company's push for cold efficiency doesn't filter down to us. Sure, I've got to process a lot of people and get them out without delays. But I can't let all that make me a cold supervisor or a cold-fish company representative. I'll be a failure if I'm cold and hard on my people, and they're going to fail if they act that way toward the passengers.

Research Director

My people need to be on their own but not alone.

There's a classic story: The general wants to inspect the battalion, and he's going to inspect at 9:00 on Saturday morning. The battalion commander says he wants to have the troops out by 8:30 so he can check them out himself. The company commander gets hold of each of his platoon leaders and says, "Guys, I want you out there at 8:00 in the morning, because I want to make sure everything is okay." The platoon leaders . . . Well, by the time it gets done, the poor jerks at the bottom are up at 5:00 in the morning and standing at attention at 6:00.

It's that kind of philosophy that is so prevalent here, and it takes a lot of effort to stop the pressure from just rolling down on your people. Truman talked about the buck stopping with him; well, I make sure the crap stops with me. I don't keep shoveling it down.

We have all sorts of pressure from the top. I have the fire department, security, safety, contractors, the whole group. I doubt if it's too different anywhere else. It's a little different here because we're handling exotic and poisonous chemicals, which adds to the normal administrative pressure. Some of it is important, but it can get absurd as more and more people along the line add their bright ideas. Take this requirement: each and every payday, I put down and names of the people that work for me and how many hours per day they work with chemicals. Now that doesn't sound like very much to do. But what it means is now I have to ask each individual his hours—how many hours did they spend on Monday, Tuesday, etc., working with chemicals. So they make up numbers, and I understand that. And sometimes I get only three guys out of twelve who turn in papers at the end of three weeks. I say, "Who cares?" I don't really care. I turn in the cards.

And there's so much of this. This was Safety and Industrial Hygiene's bright idea. They want to know how many hours people work with chemicals so that down the road, if there's a problem with them physiologically, you can say, "Aha, he worked with chemicals." That would be okay if we worked with the *same* chemicals all the time. But, good Lord, we work with all sorts of chemicals. This is useless. But, got to do it. Working with chemicals; got to fill out the cards.

I can make up the numbers, but I say, "No, as long as they're asking for it, I'll play the game as straight as I can." But I try to eliminate as much of that stuff as I can. And my boss—he's not bad—also tries to eliminate as much of that stuff as he can. But a lot of it he can't because a lot of people putting the pressures on us don't have to come through him. They just make an end run to us.

I try very hard to serve as a screen for my people, because they're the ones who have to do the research. (I know I'm not going to do it, because I don't have the time.) It saves them time, it raises their morale, and it saves their energy.

My subordinates are Ph.D.s, and Ph.D.s are a strange lot. They're very individualistic, and they like to accomplish something. The fellow I get, the new graduate, has been almost totally on his own when he was working on his thesis. When he comes here, he still is pretty much the same way. Here I can assign him one of these subtasks and let him have the responsibility to work on his own but not be alone, because he can have support from the other fellows here.

I don't assign people to little groups—that I see too much of in other places—because that just creates little cliques. So if I can keep them working both individually and together, I feel that I generate more of a team effort. You know, you get the "we did this this week" as opposed to "I did this this week." I try to cultivate this team spirit because we are such a small group—there's ten to twelve of us. We have a couple of guys who are professors from somewhere. We bring them in here, give them a salary to live on, let them learn a little bit on their sabbatical, on equipment we've got and colleges don't normally have, and let them get their hands and their feet wet for a year. So we have a couple of those floating through.

But with such a small group, I just have to keep them working together as a small team, or else there's too many times that one person would get stymied. In the field of pyrotechnics, which is what we're working with, it involves physics, and it involves radiation laws and things for the most part that a person won't pick up in physical chemistry. They might touch on it, but unless they happen in their research to do something in that area, they're not going to know very much. A person has to learn outside his discipline when he comes in here, and that's where the team concept really trains people, because there are no books you can pull off the shelf that will help you from a research standpoint.

Most of our work has to do with research and development in pyrotechnics, and that's 90-plus percent of our efforts. I organize the guys in and around specific work. A job comes in and I match it up with a person's interests and skills. Then other people in the branch support that person. One of those "associate" investigators might be a primary investigator on another job. We have this mutual assistance, but for the most part, it's individual times and efforts. That is, one man on a project or two, and he spends most of his time working on that project or two, occasionally supporting another person working on their job.

I operate this way because it's the nature of the beast. My subordinates' work is individual and it's their job to do. I give very little advice. I give them overall objectives—where I expect them to be at the end of this year, at the end of next year.

It's applied research in that there's always a specific end point that we're heading for—it may be a new composition, like infrared energy, UV energy. It's a very specific end point. Usually those jobs last at least two years, and normally three to four years. So there's a significant amount of time, calendar time, for the work to get done.

When I came here, we had three major tasks. Underneath each of those there were two to three tasks broken out, and so we were ending up with as many subtasks as you had people, almost. And my feeling was, rather than select two or three people and say, "I'm going to make you a team leader and you work with him; you're a leader and you work with him" . . . If you do that, sure as shootin' you're going to need the guys on this team to be on the team over here. When you do that you've set up artificial boundaries and created constraints on people's thinking. With no larger group than we've got, we don't need that structure.

We've got about the perfect-sized group right now. Ten to twelve in the group is a good, nice size. I can do things socially; it's not so large that I can't have everybody over to my house. We can get together easily and informally.

Sometimes I do find that people get so caught up in their own project that they have trouble tearing themselves away to help others. To avoid or overcome this I casually suggest to the guys—and I don't have any problems doing that—when I think another person might be able to help them, and I work with the groups to get this needed cross-fertilization.

Once a week I have each of the principal investigators put together what they have accomplished that week. This lets them stop and think what they did that week, to see what they did accomplish. Too often in the research world you can work for a year and not really think you've accomplished anything. If you write it down, it makes you think you've done something, and you realize what you did do, or didn't do.

Then I put together this information in a very short, one-page status report that I send up the line to my boss. I also put the report on the board so that the individuals can go to the board and see what's happening in other areas. If one group for some reason, didn't get much done last week, I never have to tell them they didn't get much done. It's on the board, and it's a kind of quiet encouragement to perform. In a more positive vein, it can serve as a form of praise.

That helps motivate people. In research you can praise a person for the work they're doing, and they may appreciate that. But what really counts is when they know they have done something that they consider significant. It really doesn't matter if I think it's significant or not. If I don't praise them when they do something significant, most of them tell me [*laughs*]—that's no problem.

I get a lot of feedback because we are informal and unstructured. If there's anybody that's unhappy at me or anyone else, I'll know it in twenty-four hours. And problems are not an exception in this line of work. I spend about 20 percent of my time on personality problems, either listening to, trying to solve or cope with one kind of problem or another. A classic example, which is not abnormal, was the last one. Things were going along well in our work and I had to travel, so I left another guy in charge. While I was gone, he and a technician got into an argument about overtime. Now they handled the problem okay—they shouted, but they handled the problem themselves. While they were arguing the technician was cleaning his fingernails with a knife. Now another Ph.D. standing in the background starts the story around that the technician was threatening the acting director with a knife. He has a weird sense of humor. Now if it were a tight little group and nothing left it, you might look at it as a slightly sick joke. But when you know those things always leave the group and you know there will be people who will hear it and blow it up, which was done, then you can't tolerate it. So by the time I returned, we had this story circulating about the knife fights among our Ph.D.s.

So I put my foot down by dredging up this nice little government reg that says malicious comments are grounds for disciplining of one kind or another. So I got my people together. I didn't mention names; I just said, "There'll be no more malicious comments, period." What happened was that it got extremely quiet for six or eight weeks. And one individual got tempered considerably.

Those are the only types of problems I have with my people. Fortunately, I don't have any problems with any individual as far as his work performance or technical capability. Luckily most of my people are self-motivated. Again, that's the nature of a Ph.D., for the most part. No one *makes* him get a Ph.D., and no one *makes* him work. He's self-motivated and he loves to work.

So actually I don't have many problems from my own people. The problems and time wasting mainly comes from the top. That is my biggest complaint. I love the work here. In the 1970s, because of the work I did, I worked myself to a supervisory slot. Now I've been assigned to "supervise" a group of people in an R and D area. So now I "supervise" instead of doing the technical work I like. I was promoted out of what I like to do. The only way I can get any technical satisfaction is to raise aesthetically nice questions—I wonder what would happen if. . . If I can fix a guy's ears, he may pursue my question and then the answer will be interesting. It's *his* work and *he* does it and *he* gets credit for it. But *I* get my answer. I love that. That's the only technical satisfaction I get for my contribution.

I think two weeks ago I worked for two hours in the lab, and that's the first time that I've done anything directly in the way of research, simply because I don't have time. I simply don't have time. We have supervisory meetings, then we have supervisory safety meetings. Then we have EEO affirmative action meetings we all have to go to. Those sorts of things. You may or may not be put on an employee-safety group. They try to get us to volunteer for quality circles—which I have done. It's endless. I spend probably half of my time involved in administrative details, time cards, leave slips, committees, etc. And we have quarterly technical reports to our customers reporting our progress. That comes every three months; you can count on it. And then they do an extra-special one every six months. And you've got five-year plans that are updated yearly. Now that's the type of thing I'm spending a lot of my time on. When these reports are due, I must go in and talk to the sponsors about those technical reports, how the job is coming along, where we're at and why.

The Peter Principle holds that people get promoted to the point that the demands of the job exceed their capabilities. Here the opposite is true. You're promoted to the point that administrative crap doesn't let you use the competence you have.

6

Sticks and Carrots

OTIVATION is a simple topic that we have managed to complicate. Basically, a person's performance is determined by his or her ability and motivation. If a person does not have the ability to handle a job, the leader must see to it that he or she is educated. People are motivated to work hard (a) when they understand what they should do and (b) when they are fairly confident that they will be rewarded. The job itself can provide intrinsic rewards, such as the satisfaction that goes along with task completion, a job well done, or work on an important task. The rewards can also originate outside the task itself. Examples of these extrinsic rewards are pay, advancement, compliments, and vacations in Hawaii.

In motivating people, the leader must provide both intrinsic and extrinsic rewards. At times, this boils down to giving people a pat on the back, even though the job itself is motivating. As the heart transplant surgeon notes:

"I can't rely just on professionalism—that my people do a good job, know they did a good job, and are motivated by a job well done. They have a strong professional motive, but I can't let that suffice. I tell them that they did a good job. Such positive feedback is very important to all of us."

On other occasions, a leader can raise the payoffs from the job. There is a common misperception that leaders are tied to the use of extrinsic rewards. The surgeon lays that notion to rest:

"Motivating the team, as I said before, is a very important leadership function. I give them personal feedback. More importantly, I have the patients do so. When I see the patients after the operation, I find they are now healthy, happy people. So I encourage them to go by and visit (a) the people in the intensive care unit,

(b) the people from the operating room, (c) the physicians, and (d) profusionists so that the team members can see how well the patients are doing. Unfortunately, we don't usually spend a lot of time with patients who have done well. They have their operation, get well, go home, and we never see them again. We spend a lot more time dwelling on how to make the system better and how to correct our mistakes."

The body builder's comments are almost a carbon copy of the surgeon's:

"In motivating my staff and keeping their quality up, it seems that intrinsic motivation is most important. Everyone wants to make enough money to live on, and they like bonuses, but I think most people here are doing a good job because they take pride in what they do. Also, they're competitive, so they want to be the best and work hard at it.

"My staff just want to be considered good people, so I play on this. I tell them they're good, and I suggest if they do this or that then they'll be better at what they're doing. 'Maybe you could even do this, and that would make you much better.' Being up in front of people also helps. They know they're being watched, and the customers provide them with a lot of strokes by saying things like, 'Hey, that was really great.' "

The same theme surfaces in the antisubmarine mission commander's report: Provide rewards for your crew; be sure that the job does likewise; and enhance the importance of the job:

"I think the most important thing a mission commander does is to let people know why they're flying out. . . . You can say, 'This isn't just another training flight that we're going on. There is a Soviet sub out there. It is one that's of high interest.' And within the limits of classification, you let them know why you're going out there."

Punishment. The last two leaders in this section—hospital director and robber—broach this topic. Like most leaders, they find they must use it on occasion. When leaders do punish, they should follow the "hot stove" approach—be (a) immediate, (b) intense, (c) consistent, and (d) impersonal. The director of the drug and alcohol hospital follows the first two precepts to the letter. She is immediate:

"With disciplining it's good to get the cards on the table quickly. My employees get nervous when they have to come see me; especially when I close the door, they get really paranoid. So I hit it right off—'This is my concern with you; let's talk about it.' "

And intense:

"What I don't do is tell the person some good things about their work and then also point out the bad. I don't sandwich the feedback. I break the bad news to people, especially if I'm going to fire them, right up front. I don't pussyfoot around. I just say, 'Your work is poor,' or 'I'm going to terminate you.' Then I explain it to them and don't let it take a long time."

The criminal leaders' approach toward reward and punishment was the most surprising result of my interviews. Without exception, they use immediate, continuous rewards. That I expected. The unexpected? Of the thirty or so that I interviewed, over 75 percent *avoided* punishment as a means for controlling behavior. The comments of the hit man and heroin dealer are quite representative. You will recall the remarks of the hit man:

"Never get rough. You don't never get rough with your employees. It's bad business, and then they start thinking of ways to retaliate against you."

And the dealer states firmly:

"If you leave a man alive and make him scared of you, then there's no telling what he'll do to you. But if you kill him then you can start all over new with somebody else. You got him out of the way, and every day when there's one dead you got two or three more to take his place. But if you leave him alive and you keep putting that fear in him, then somewhere down the line he's going to get you."

Unlike leaders on this side of the law, criminal leaders do not switch gradually from rewards to punishment. Most licit leaders initially use rewards to motivate subordinates; if this approach fails, they withhold the rewards. Then they threaten punishment; they punish; and finally they terminate the subordinate. The criminal leaders' escalation is more abrupt. Like other leaders, they prefer to use rewards; however, if these fail, the next step taken by criminal leaders is generally to terminate the relationship by one means or another. As the robber notes:

"You don't use fear. If you make somebody afraid of you, then they're going to shoot you. Plain and simple. You scare someone bad enough then he's saying, 'I got to kill him.'

"Who wants this? Not me. What I want them to realize is this: If he rolls on me I'm going to kill him. That's all. I realize if I scare you then I got to start

looking in my garbage can when I go up the steps so you don't jump out of there and blow me away.

"I don't want people scared. I don't want them to think I'll go around hurting them, but I want them to know I'll kill them if they do anything that makes me have to. See what I mean?

"That's the reason, too, you don't go around punishing and threatening people. Right or wrong you stay with what you got. If a guy screws up, you pay him off and ease him out. Don't ask him back on the next score. You don't want to make him so mad that he drops down on you. It's just 'Hey, there's nothing happening. I ain't got nothing.'

"You got to put them off like that. If you tell them, 'Hey man, you can't work with me,' he's going to burn you. Keep him happy as long as possible. If I'm really scared of him, put him in the bushes."

Heart Transplant Surgeon

During my training as a surgeon, I not only picked up surgical skills,
I also picked up leadership techniques that appeared to work.

Last year, about two hundred heart transplants were performed in the United States, and experts estimate that thousands more of us could have benefited from the operation. In addition to performing transplants, cardiac surgeons routinely replace defective valves, patch holes in the heart, bypass clogged arteries, and undertake a variety of operations that not only save lives but improve the lives of those suffering from heart ailments.

The team that undertakes a heart operation is led by a head surgeon, who directs between one and three assistant surgeons; two cardiac anesthesiologists; a profusionist, who operates the heart-lung machine; a scrub nurse; a circulating nurse; and a team of intensive care physicians and nurses. The track record for this surgeon's team is good—about 98 percent of their patients have been made better and about 85 percent have been cured.

I try to impress upon patients and their relatives that our surgical team is an assemblage of people that is doing the best they can to help the patient. Physicians can do a lot for patients but they hold no magical force. They are human beings who are trying to do a good job with the information they have.

Prior to coming to us, a patient has been seeing a cardiologist who has performed tests to ensure that certain diagnoses are correct. Once the diagnosis is established, the patient will contact me.

In the initial phase I meet the patient and the relatives. There is a fairly lengthy discussion about what the problem is, what would happen if it was not corrected, what could happen if it is corrected, what the different risks are in the two options, and, finally, what problems might potentially come up in either course. This is a period of persuasion and education: I try to persuade the patient and relatives to take the course of action that is preferable for the patient, and I try to let them understand what ultimately will be happening.

After they've decided for the surgery—and it is the right step—an agreement is made as to when the operation should take place. It's usually two weeks or even a few months away, so that the notion of the operation can be lived with by the patient and relatives—so that they can accept their decision and live with it. It isn't done hastily. That's important; the delay is intentional so that they have the time to go home, think about it, mull it over a while, and be sure that they want to do it.

When it's scheduled for the operating room, I inform the circulating nurse, the scrub nurse, the profusionist, and the anesthesiologists as to what the operation is going to be. I'll have several conferences with them and the surgeons, the cardiologist, and the people in the intensive care unit who will be taking care of the patient after the operation. These conferences serve as a forum for the education of all concerned. We discuss what the problem is, how it's going to be treated, what the potential unexpected problems will be, and how they will be treated.

The patient usually comes in two days before the operation, and I discuss again with the patient and the family all the variables we talked about previously. This is to see if there's any misconception about what is to take place. What people hear in the first discussion can be widely divergent from what you try to communicate to them. I prefer to go over everything three times—once as an outpatient, again when they're first admitted, and then I'll touch on a few points about half an hour before the patient is to go to the operation. Thus I have three opportunities to eliminate any misunderstanding and to give the patient information that makes him feel more comfortable about the operation.

We also do a series of tests to make sure there are no contraindications—e.g., infections—for doing the operation. Then the patient is taken to the operating room, put to sleep, and a series of catheters are placed to give various medications and fluids to the body and to monitor pressures.

After the lines are established—which can take anywhere from one-half hour to two and one-half hours, depending on the size of the patient—the patient is placed on the operating table and a sterile field is created. An incision is made and the heart is exposed.

The way I've set up my team is that I oversee the placement of the catheters, and I make the opening. In some institutions, the first or second assistant will do the opening, exposing of the heart, and putting the patient on the heart-lung machine. Then the head surgeon comes in, performs the critical part of the operation.

I prefer to take it from the beginning because there are some logistics problems with changing the position of people around the table once the operation has started. And the opening takes only about ten to fifteen minutes; so you don't save much time or energy for the surgeon.

After putting catheters into various chambers and vessels, the patient is put on the heart-lung machine. Here the blood is taken from the body, the machine performs the functions of the heart and lung, and then the blood is reinfused into the body. This is done under my direction, with the assistance of the profusionist.

Even though the heart is not getting blood, it will continue to beat. To stop it we cool it, and this also provides some protection for the patient during the operation. If cooling doesn't stop the heart, we can use some medicines or a short electric current. After we've stopped the heart, we measure pressure, oxygen delivery, oxygen utilization, and so forth. When we're sure the pump is operating properly, we begin the procedure on the heart. It is opened or removed.

There are a lot of things that happen during the operation that I have to watch out for. I constantly monitor what's happening in the operating field, what's happening at the head of the table with the anesthesiologists, what's happening over by the pump. In addition, the scrub nurse and the circulating nurse need direction. I monitor all of these, and if I perceive that something is not functioning properly, I intervene and direct the correction. I've also got to ensure that the stress level isn't getting too high and that all the team members are well coordinated in their activities.

I have to be perceptive of subtle changes that occur within the room. I've seen circumstances in which a surgeon was so engrossed with performing the technical aspects of the operation that he was not aware of other things happening in the room. As a result there were some real problems with the operation. I also have to anticipate the next moves and make sure that the people who are helping are ready for what's coming next. Without a doubt, this is the most intense time for me as a surgeon.

Usually things go along very smoothly—the problem is corrected, the heart is closed—and I direct the profusionist to do various things to have the heart warm up and be ready to come off bypass. The heart is made to start again if it doesn't beat by itself. It commonly will start to beat again by itself, once rewarming is undertaken.

Then I, or the first assistant, take some maneuvers to make sure that any air that is left in the heart is removed. After rewarming the heart and observing satisfactory beating, the anesthesiologists start to breathe again for the patient, and the patient is allowed to take over his own circulation. Once he does that—his blood is being pumped by the heart, and the lungs are performing properly—the heart-lung machine can be stopped and, eventually, the catheters that had been put in can be removed. If all bleeding is stopped, the patient is then closed.

After the operation is completed and the wound has been closed, the patient remains under anesthetic and is taken over to the intensive care unit, where he is allowed to recover from one to ten days. While he's in intensive care, there's another group of nurses and physicians that helps with the patient. They're under my direction until the patient comes out of that unit.

After the operation, I go immediately to the relatives. Their questions are pretty much a function of how well prepared they are before the operation. If they've been adequately prepared and know what's going to take place, I can usually just say, "We found what we expected to find. We did what we expected to do, and everything is going fine."

They relax a little, but usually I don't until I see that everything is working fine in intensive care—namely, there hasn't been a stroke and that the heart is working well. Gradually my intensity subsides. For me, the intensity runs a cycle: there's a fairly intense stimulus for me at the time of the heart operation; then when the patient comes off bypass and the heart starts, it subsides a bit; and when I get the patient into intensive care and he's okay, it subsides even more.

That's an overview of the technical side of being a head surgeon. There's also the leadership side. After the operation I debrief the surgical team. It's a lot more informal than from a space-shuttle mission. I touch base with every individual involved in the operation and get feedback on how they think it went. Also I tell them how I think it went, and we discuss how things could be improved. This is all one-on-one, and I make sure I tell every person that they did a good job. The individuals involved are human, and they need to have a pat on the back.

I can't rely just on professionalism—that my people do a good job, know they did a good job, and are motivated by a job well done. They have a strong professional motive, but I can't let that suffice. I *tell* them that they did a good job. Such positive feedback is very important to all of us.

When there are mistakes, they are fairly obvious, and the people on my team are conscientious enough to know that they've made a mistake. In dealing with mistakes, there's a very critical balance. You need to make every effort to see that it's corrected. To do that, you have to have the most competent person in the room to take care of it. For example, say the profusionist makes an error. He clearly is the most competent in the room to correct that error—I can't break scrub. When he's made the error, I have to point it out in such a way that the correction maximizes his function. I can't belittle him or severely criticze him, especially in front of others. I have to keep him working at his most effective state.

If there is a mistake during the operation, I just very objectively say, "Here's a mistake; you correct it." I avoid making a value judgment about how the mistake was made or who made it. And I particularly try not to make any comments that would reflect on that person as an individual. Then after the crisis has been solved and the operation is over, we'll discuss it. A lot of times it's not until the next day, because that gives the person sufficient time to think about the problem that came up, how he solved it, and how he could potentially avoid it in the future. It's very important for people to be allowed to exhibit their ingenuity in correcting their own mistakes.

It would be extremely inappropriate, in my opinion, to go on a rampage and to express what a worthless person made the mistake. I've always been able to control that. Sometimes it is frustrating to hold it in, but I know I must. After the operation is over, I may be very critical of him and point out that he made mistakes which could be and should be avoided. I try not to belittle people as individuals, but I'll say, "That's a problem we—I take a great deal of care to use the term we—should be able to anticipate and avoid. Please do what you can to ensure that the problem doesn't happen." Also, I'll ask the person to give me specific followup, later on, as to what he's done to avoid the problem in the future.

I also make mistakes; therefore, I use a style that encourages the team members to give feedback to me. I encourage the feedback, accept the criticism, and try to correct my mistakes.

What distinguishes leaders from nonleaders is that for leaders, the mistakes—yours and others—provide a foundation for learning and improvement. How one deals with mistakes is very important. What types of thoughts and behaviors do you develop as a result of mistakes? You need to walk away from the mistake realizing that it was a mistake and that it points out areas that can be improved. Then you formulate a plan that prevents those mistakes from happening in the future. You also have to make sure that your initial reaction to the mistake is not dysfunctional to your own performance or to that of any team member.

During my training as a surgeon I got a lot of exposure to a lot of different people. I not only picked up surgical skills, I also tried to pick up the leadership techniques that appeared to work—those which allow the team to function at maximum efficiency. I've seen surgeons who become irate. All that does is tear at the foundations of the team.

This low-key style also goes along with my personality and background. I trained at a university where the style is very easygoing. They try to make the operating experience a very positive one for everyone who is involved, rather than an intense and stressful experience. I think this style is very important in making the team successful. Also I want my people, on their own, to draw conclusions that are consistent with mine. You could draw the conclusions and say, "This is the way it is." But it's very important to allow team members to come to the conclusion on their own.

Likewise, it's very important to do what you say you're going to do. People have to respect you not only as a competent surgeon but also as a person. And they have to know if you say you're going to do something, they can count on your willingness and ability to do that. Integrity is very important.

Motivating the team, as I said before, is a very important leadership function. I give them personal feedback. More importantly, I have the patients do so. When I see the patients after the operation, I find they are now healthy, happy people. So I encourge them to go by and visit (a) the people in the intensive care unit, (b) the people from the operating room, (c) the physicians, and (d) the profusionists so that the team members can see how well the patients are doing. Unfortunately, we don't usually spend a lot of time with patients who have done well. They have their operation, get well, go home, and we never see them again. We spend a lot more time dwelling on how to make the system better and how to correct our mistakes.

In the operating room, I try to make the team more comfortable. I try to reduce the tension. Telling an occasional joke is one way to do this. Another thing, I have music—soothing background music—piped in. People behave differently with music and even with different kinds of background music. You can really reduce the tension by having soothing music.

How I relate to the operation that needs to be done can also affect the level of stress. During the planning phase, if I come in and say, "This is going to be an easy operation," then everybody takes a deep breath and says, "Fine.

It's going to be easy. The risk will be minimal, and it's going to be a nice, pleasant day." Whereas, if I come in and say, "Gee, we really have a tough one today; I'm not sure we can do it," then the tension level is increased significantly.

For me, fatigue also has to be considered. I take steps to avoid lapses in concentration or to avoid fatigue. I set a pace with the operating schedule so that it doesn't wear me down too quickly. This is akin to long-distance running. If you want to perform well in long-distance running, you have to set a pace. You can't be sprinting and walking, sprinting and walking.

I have not had trouble with concentration for up to 48 hours. I have been in circumstances in which procedures had to be done, there were emergencies, and I've been able to perform up to that period of time. But after that I've found that I'll go to other surgeons and ask them to perform the procedures. After 48 hours I can feel that I don't really care what happens to a patient. Once I've crossed that line—say we have a critically ill patient, and we try something to make him better. It doesn't work. I find myself saying, "Well, that's okay," or "We've done all we can do." This all indicates a lower degree of intensity than my usual go-get-them or do-everything-you-can-to-make-them-better spirit. Then I know that I'm losing the concentration and the energy that's required to direct the effort. So I pull back and ask for some assistance.

I've been talking about heart surgery in general. With the heart transplant the actual technical aspects in the operating room are the same for the recipient. Yet there's more time involved—I'll be on the go for 18 to 24 hours—because there are a lot more logistics. I need to coordinate the harvesting of the donor organ so that it can be done at a time that allows implantation with a minimum time interval. Here we have an urgent procedure rather than an elective one. Once the recipient is cleared as suitable, he actually wears a beeper so that he can be called quickly if a donor comes up for him and the match is good. He can be called to the hospital and be receiving his new heart within 6 hours.

When a donor is available—a donor is declared neurologically dead and the involved relatives have said they do want the organs donated—tests are done on that party's cells to find their characteristics and to find who the best recipient would be. There's usually a large pool of potential recipients and you want the match to be the best it can be. The donor has been declared dead, but his kidneys, heart, liver, and other organs are functioning normally. He is still in the intensive care unit on a respirator. This can be five hundred miles away from the recipient. Once the decision is made as to who the heart recipient is to be, that person is called and brought into the hospital. He undergoes prompt testing to ensure that he doesn't have a contraindication to proceeding.

Then the recipient is taken to the operating room, put to sleep, and his operation is started. The donor heart is harvested by another team at the donor site. All the logistics are worked out beforehand such that the donor heart will arrive at the recipient operating room as soon as the recipient is ready to have his heart removed and to have the donor heart implanted. Usually the head surgeon does the coordinating so that the donor heart arrives just as we need it. So it's a very long day; I have to coordinate the logistics, oversee the preparation of the patient, open and bypass the heart, and then perform the transplant.

If the recipient is uncomplicated—i.e., if he hasn't had a previous operation—then the operation is pretty easy to do and doesn't take very long—about 4 to 6 hours. From the time I get a beeper call that a donor is available until I get into the operating room is about 12 hours. Then the operation takes about 5; so from start to finish the heart transplant operation can take 18 to 24 hours. I'm working that whole time, but I set up the system so that I'm under stress for a minimal portion of it.

You set up the system so there's more than one surgeon who can perform the transplant; there's more than one who can harvest the organ. The transplant coordinator—the primary person responsible for deciding when each facet is to be done—need not be a physician. It can be a nurse—after they've lived through a few of these and know what's going on, then they know what the pitfalls are and how to avoid some of the predictable delays.

In the early days of transplants, the head surgeon was involved with everything. But now we've trained a lot of people so that they can help with the surgery or do it themselves. Delegation is a very important ingredient in setting up a system. I want it to run well in the transplant operation, but also I want it to function independent of any one person.

Even with all the right planning and with good delegation, there are times of intense stress. Sometimes things don't go as I would like them to, or I find something that I didn't anticipate before the operation. The heart problem can be very complex, and we give a lot of forethought to how we should handle the various alternatives, depending upon what we find in the operation. If something comes up in the operation that we haven't previously considered, then we have to make some very important decisions rather promptly, without a lot of research or mulling over the alternatives. They're not hasty decisions, but they do have to be made quickly.

And there's frustration. On the operating team we have a lot of experience, and usually the nurses and physicians can deal with the problems effectively. Yet it's most frustrating to catch a problem that I thought would, and should, respond to the treatment we had planned. But the patient doesn't respond at all. Sometimes we can review the situation in retrospect and say, "We should have done this and anticipated this." But usually we go over things again, again, and again only to find *no* red flags to indicate what the problem was.

And there's death. To keep the team from getting down and frustrated with death, I impress upon them that in general our record has been very good. Our results here are as good as anywhere in the nation, and we should all take a lot of pride in that. We can't dwell on the tragedies. Most of the deaths are a consequence of our limited ability to treat problems rather than a mistake per se. It's depressing, but we have to keep plugging along because there are going to be a large number of patients coming along who we need to help.

For me, it takes about 36 to 48 hours to recover from a patient's not surviving. I'm constantly mulling over what could have been done to make the system work better. After 48 hours I lose more of the emotional aspects of that death and become more objective about it. I talk it over with the team members at the time of the death so that they have a chance to describe their feelings about it and to get their feelings out. At that time I try to suppress my feelings and be upbeat. Try to reassure them that everything that could be done was done. There was nothing else we could do to make the outcome better.

Then I talk to other people here about the death. Here, a lot of physicians experience the same problem. There's support here plus suggestions as to how we can improve.

Perhaps I'd like saying to the team and to myself, "We'll try a little harder on the next patient." But everyone on the team always does the very best; therefore, we don't have the luxury.

Operator, Body Builders' Gym

I have a lot of drive that has to be satisfied in one way or another.

A lot of times I find that people, when they're interacting with me, are caught off guard. At times they don't respect me, or they don't expect me to be as assertive or as aggressive as I am. Also, I'm petite so they underestimate how strong I am.

For example, my landlord at first would call me—he's real macho—and tell me to ask my husband to pay the rent early. That happened only once! And men will come in, give me a little squeeze, and pat me on the head. When they try to get by with stuff like that, I will just let them know I'm not taking it. When a construction worker who's in a class gives me a squeeze or a pat on the buns I just handle it myself. Usually one good cold look is all it takes. I have to be more firm with people than a man would be. For example, when I order stuff from suppliers, they don't try to get it here on time, so I have to go to them or tell them, "You have this or this here by a certain date or we won't take it."

At first, I think, I appear to be a pushover. I'm petite and small-framed so some people try to take advantage of that. It would be different, probably, if I were six feet tall. But for some men you can use being petite and attractive to your advantage. Sometimes if you're very nice to them they are very gentlemanly. A kind of tit for tat. And sometimes you find they'll take more from a person like me than they would from a person who is overbearing in stature.

In our operation here, we sell a service. People come in wanting to lose weight, to get into shape, to build strength; we have classes that help them do so. I recruit my staff, teach them, and then motivate them to provide what the customer wants.

In motivating my staff and keeping their quality up, it seems that intrinsic motivation is most important. Everyone wants to make enough money to live on, and they like bonuses, but I think most people here are doing a good job because they take pride in what they do. Also, they're competitive, so they want to be the best and work hard at it.

My staff just wants to be considered good people, so I play on this. I tell them they're good, and I suggest if they do this or that then they'll be better at what they're doing. "Maybe you could even do this, and that would make you much better." Being up in front of people also helps. They know they're being watched, and the customers provide them with a lot of strokes by saying things like, "Hey, that was really great."

When people are doing a bad job, then that's the bad part for me as a manager. Say a person can take a hard workout and she's in great shape but she just can't teach. At first, I didn't handle that very well, and it was embarrassing to both of us. Now if I find a person's not a good teacher, then I put her in a class that's not very important. If I see she's not improving, I just leave her there. Yet if she improves, I put her in an advanced class.

Sometimes people ask why they're stuck with one class all the time, and I just have to tell them it's because they're just not doing a good job.

That's hard, because I want everyone here to feel like a big friendly family and to have a feeling of pride in what they do. So it's hard when you've got this friendly feeling going, and you've got to go in and tell people something that's going to hurt them or make them mad. It's a lot like diving into a cold lake. I just hold my breath and do it. I say some positive things and then touch on the negative. The person usually responds well and you both feel better about yourselves once it's over.

That's been the toughest part for me as an administrator. I'd never had to give criticism. As a teacher, I did some of that, but it wasn't as important then because I wasn't planning to teach all my life, and the person's performance didn't determine my future. Here, it does.

In managing my staff, I try to keep a close relationship with each one even though that's not my natural style—I'm not a "close" person. I guess I could be around everyone and chitchat a lot, but I really prefer to keep it one-on-one.

In my interactions I found that there are so many different personalities around here. Some of these people I get along with really well, and I naturally get close to them. Their philosophies, personalities, and bodies are a lot like mine. Others I don't naturally get as close to, so I have to work hard to establish a close relationship with them. Then if that fails, I just keep it on a more professional level.

This operation has been really successful for me, and a part of the success I think is due to the fact that I've laid out our mission for the people here and for myself. We concentrate on exercise and getting people into shape. We're not offering baby-sitting for the mothers, and it's not a social club for housewives.

Secondly, we have a better product. I know I can squeeze more people into the classes to make more money, but then the classes are too crowded; that's not fair to the customers, and I lose my good reputation.

Our music is better—I choose music that is cool, appropriate for this type of place rather than the pop hit or the loud type. And my instructors, male and female, are attractive. I don't have the "centerfold" type, but they are attractive to the customers of both sexes.

Finally, I'm aggressive in this business. I want it to grow; I want to franchise it; and I want to publish some sort of publication in this area. I want to be stimulated, to grow, to be productive, to do a good job at something, and to be successful.

While I'm aggressive and willing to take risks for my personal success, I have to admit that I want to do well *for* females. I want to do well as a female to show others we can be successful and maybe to serve as a role model.

Over the years I've grown a lot and learned more. I've always thought a lot of myself, but it was mainly that I knew I could do well in school. There I knew if I was given a task I could do it. Now it's the real world, and I'm excited to find the same is true here.

I've got more drive now. When I first got married I wanted a certain kind of existence—I never regarded myself as a businesswoman. Instead, I wanted to live down on a farm in a run-down house, work part-time, and be self-sufficient. 'Course I grew out of that quickly. I was really bored. And I learned a great deal about myself. I'm not that kind of person. I need challenges; I need to perform. And every day I go up there, I find these challenges.

Or I, on some days, stay at home to reflect on where we are and to plan for the future, to be creative. This gives me time to think about myself and where I want to go. As I've been successful, I've become a lot more introspective in a classical way; I now think more about myself—as a person and as a female. I've found that I have a lot of drive that has to be satisfied in one way or another; most females do. We've simply been underrated, and if we put our minds (and bodies) to it, we can be successful in anything we're brave enough to try!

Antisubmarine Mission Commander

It's satisfying knowing you were the boss and everything went well.

I think of my crew as a team. Twelve people flew out for nine hours to find and/or track a Soviet sub, and maybe only one had a problem. He had a problem, and I, the mission commander, should have been able to ask the questions that would have gotten him back in the ballpark. Okay—*we* messed up; what should *we* have done? Perhaps you should have fed me your information so I could have come back there in the plane and we could all have made the call together.

I've taken all the tests that say what kind of leader you are—Are you an achiever, a democrat, an affiliator, a coach?—that sort of thing. And I always come up as a coach. Whenever we have a problem, I'll say, "Okay, here we go, team. We didn't do too well this time. We're going to have another chance tomorrow night, and here's how we're going to do it better." And usually we are better. We talk over each mission. Some missions go perfect. Some missions don't, and it was totally out of your hands. But if there was something we did wrong—something we could have done better—we usually talk about it. We do that as much as possible on a "no rank" basis. I let the junior guy say, "Well, you know, you messed up," or "If you'd done this, we'd done better." If they're scared to talk to you and say what they think, then you're missing something.

I think the most important thing a mission commander does is to let the people know why they're flying out. Now some of the crew are going to know what's up, especially those who got a tactical briefing. You've got a Yankee sub out there. He's there and you're going to track him. Other people who didn't go to the briefing may have some idea as to why you're going out, but they're not going to be sure. There are all sorts of things we fly on—training flights, bounce flights, tactical training flights, fly to pick up somebody and take them somewhere. You do all sorts of things. So I have to clarify what we're to do and why. Another point I keep in mind is that certain flights are more motivating to the crews than are others. Nobody minds flying on Wednesday from 8:00 A.M. 'til 12 midnight, no matter what the mission. But it's different if you're flying on Saturday night. You've got to take off at 8:00 P.M., and you're not going to land until 6:00 in the morning. Therefore, it's nice to motivate your crew. You can say. "This isn't just another training flight that we're going on. There is a Soviet sub out there. It is one that's of high interest." And within the limits of classification, you let them know why you're going out there.

I always have a plane-side briefing before takeoff. I get my whole crew together and say something like, "Hey, the reason we're flying tonight is this. . . . We suspect there won't be contact when we get out there. We'll have to put out a search pattern." Or maybe, "The guy on station in front of us has already made contact with the sub, and we'll be able to track him."

I think the crew is pretty much motivated by that. The people are there because they enjoy this type of thing—the *real* thing. It's not one of the training missions in which it didn't really matter if we tracked the guy or not. This is a submarine that the navy is interested in. Certain things happen in the United States according to where the Soviet submarines are; we mobilize in certain ways. And that pretty much motivates them.

If you're going on your fifth mission of the week, it gets a little harder every time to motivate them. They say, "Well shoot, we did this yesterday." Then I might use competition to motivate them. I could say, "Crew 4 went out, and they just got the guy real well. They got fourteen CPAs, and they got one as close as two hundred yards. Really did a good job. Let's see if we can't beat that."

The crew also needs to believe that *you* believe in what you're doing. If you say, "Well, I have no idea why we're going out there. They know where the guy is. They know he isn't doing anything. We're wasting time; we're wasting money," they'll have the same attitude. So sometimes if you don't believe there's a good reason, you have to get yourself up. But that's a fine line. They might know you're just giving them a bunch of crap. So what you have to do sometimes is go to the point of saying, "Hey, they think we need to go out here. From my opinion, at my level, it doesn't look like it's the most important mission in the whole world, but it's at least important enough that the higher-ups want to spend sixty thousand pounds of gasoline. So it means something to somebody, and really I don't have all the puzzle pieces. Somebody up the line has more pieces. So let's do a good job."

If you give your crew this honestly and say you don't know why we're going out, either, but we're being tapped, they'll pretty much respond to that. If you're honest with them and you let them know what you're doing, I found they do a pretty good job.

We fly about one hundred hours a month; that works out to about two or three patrols a week, normally about a nine-hour patrol. Being an antisub-type aircraft, most of our tasks are against submarines, mostly against Soviet submarines. First, we brief three hours prior to takeoff. The tactical crew—that is, the pilot, the tactical coordinator, the acoustic and nonacoustic operators—goes for this. We all go over and get a briefing. They'll tell us which submarine we're going out after today and where he's located. Sometimes we track a sub, and sometimes we go out cold trying to locate one. Then we learn what's happened on events previous to us and what our tactics are to be.

And we get acoustic briefing. Our main sensor is acoustic. Anything that makes noise does so at a certain frequency. Submarines, according to their class, make a noise according to a certain frequency. So operators will brief us as to what frequency this sub is at. It might be a "book" frequency. Consider a certain Soviet submarine such as a Delta—a ballistic-missile submarine. He may always put out the book Delta signature, but this particular Delta might also put out something different, according to some piece of special gear he has. Or they might get a brief saying, "We've never seen this guy before; you'll have to look for the book value until you find him and see what he does have."

The nontactical crew—ours consists of twelve people—three pilots, two flight engineers, two NFOs, three sensor operators, one ordinance man, and an in-flight tech—goes out to the plane, fuels it, puts the sonic buoys on board and loads any weapons. After we are briefed, we meet up with them, check out the plane and equipment, file a flight plan, and take off.

I've had plenty of flights where I stayed on station six hours and never saw anything. But sometimes you drop two or three buoys and before you get the whole pattern in, you got contact.

It's possible that the sub is there and we don't know it. There is shipping noise or maybe a noisy sea. If it's a diesel sub, he can run on batteries at slow speed or shut down and be very tough to find.

With a nuclear sub it's easier. A nuclear submarine has to keep his nuclear plant up. He's not going to shut his reactor down. He's got hotel power, which is ship's power, to keep up—his air conditioning. They've got to keep cool for all their computer equipment. Air has to circulate for the crew; blowers and fans. He has to keep water running over his reactor. Sure, he can slow down to a couple of knots, but he can't be absolutely quiet.

In addition to finding and tracking subs, we simulate killing them, putting them through an attack. When we do, I have to decide what is my best method of getting him in a position where I can make the kill. Then we simulate the attack.

I like the job. Maybe it's the power motive. I enjoy being in charge of a flight, knowing that myself and eleven other people are going to go out here. We ourselves are going to be in charge of an airplane. We're going to take off, do an antisub mission, we're going to land. This whole thing is going to be done by us, and I was in charge. I get a lot of satisfaction out of that, and I get a lot of satisfaction out of saying that for a certain period of time we knew where one of their assets was, and we could have, had we been called on, taken care of that circumstance—killed it. There's a lot of satisfaction in that. It's a little bit of knowing you were the boss and everything went well.

By the same token, the most frustration comes when things don't go well. Whether or not it's your fault, there are times you go out there and nothing goes right. A piece of gear is bad. You have trouble fueling. They lose your clearance. All of a sudden, everything starts snowballing and you get later and later. You're not going to make your takeoff time. Perhaps you're relieving somebody. He expects you to be out there. So all of a sudden a submarine that he's hot on will be cold because you weren't there on time.

Likewise, it's frustrating to get on station and have something go wrong with an engine or some piece of gear, so you have to turn back around. Your crew was motivated; they were all ready to go. You had them up for the flight and now you won't be able to do it.

The most frustrating thing—we've all had it happen—is to lose the sub. No matter what happens, you feel responsible. For example, a piece a gear can go bad. I had an OTPI fail on me. That's an on-top-position indicator—how we find our sonic buoys. It's pretty hard to track a sub without one. You might know that buoy 1 has contact, but if you can't find buoy 1 and the sub's moving, how are you going to be able to get another sonic buoy in the right place? I lost a sub because our OTPI failed and I kept getting further and further out of the picture. I dropped three more sonic buoys to try to get in the general area; they would come up real weak, and I lost him. That makes you feel bad even if it's beyond your control. You always say, "What could I have done?" All sorts of Monday-morning quarterbacking that you go through. I hate to go back and tell my superior, "Well, they turned the sub over to me hot, but I had to turn it over cold to the next guy." Whatever the reason, you're so embarrassed. And my operators feel the same way; they do the same Monday-morning quarterbacking on themselves.

In addition to the equipment problems I can have, sometimes the crew can get too motivated. For example, each crew has a drinking flag. Whenever you get together as a bunch of squadrons or crews, you carry your drinking flag, and usually the junior member of the crew or squadron is responsible for it, makes sure the flag is there and that it's not stolen. But we all try to steal the other squadron's flags. It's supposed to be stolen by stealth, not by five guys overpowering one guy. Once it went too far. We had a couple of crews that went into one of the British bases, and they had a certain type of flag that was presented only by the queen and only to certain select RAF squadrons. It was in a nice case, but the guys got in there and stole it. And we got a letter from the State Department to get it back as soon as possible. The CO was about to be relieved, and it was becoming an international incident in Great Britain because there were only a dozen or so the Queen had given, and we had stolen one of them.

I have a few problems with people being drunk. You have to decide what to do with them. You're ready to leave and so-and-so shows up drunk. Should he be put in the airplane to fly back with you? Can he do his job? You also have the judicial problem. I write him up, turn it over to the executive officer or CO, and he handles that. The punishment is up to the command.

Never have I had a problem, however, with drugs. The navy at one time had a tremendous problem with drugs, and that's when Admiral Hayward was in charge. He said, "We've got to stamp this out or it's going to stamp out the navy." So we went to a very strict urine-analysis screening. Now everyone is tested. It's done by last digit of the Social Security number. If the admiral's number is called, he's tested. Everyone is. We do about 10 percent a month. That has gotten the problem under control. Conversely, alcohol, being a legal drug, is increasing as a problem.

Some frustrations come from the top. You're scheduled to fly at 8:00 A.M. You get a call to come in at 6:00—"We've changed the brief time." So you say, "Okay," and set your alarm different. Then you get a call—"Things have changed; come in at 9:00." That doesn't really give me problems in managing the crew, because *we* just get peeved at the same people at the top.

But in the Carter administration I did have trouble keeping the crew motivated. We [the military] weren't very popular. And it didn't ever look like we were given the equipment we needed. Continually we were being told, "You can't fly on this mission because there's not enough money. Don't drop but more than twelve sonic buoys because we don't have the assets." I got frustrated. My crew got frustrated. We're frustrated with each other when we're told, "Fly on this guy. And we think doing a good job is necessary for the protection of the U.S. But we're trying to save money, so don't drop more than a dozen sonic buoys; do it cheaply." So here we are. It costs the navy about $1 million to train me. They buy this expensive plane, burn sixty thousand pounds of fuel on the mission, and now I'm being told to risk the mission in order to save $400.

That's frustrating. We—me and my crew—see the sub as an enemy. He's out there and he's trying to get the advantage on us. And the only reason we're not at war is he realizes that we have this capability and we realize that he has it. A mutual deterrent. Neither one of us is going to win. And if we ever say, "Hey, he's never going to launch those missiles—let's just forget about it and save our time, the gas, the buoys," he'll naturally do a better job than we will. We are out there so war hopefully never happens.

None of us have any hate of the Russian people. But we feel they're ready to do it to us. They've never heard my name. They have nothing against me. But their whole ideology has been that capitalism is bad; the United States is their enemy and will try to destroy them if it can. So if the call comes in from Moscow to launch the missiles or to hit the battle group with cruise missiles, they'll do it. It's our job to get them before they get us.

Director, Drug and Alcohol Hospital

It's a lot easier for them to take orders from a man.

I grew up with my father, who is a corporate executive, and I use him frequently as a role model. He has a lot of subordinates. They all love him, and they will do whatever they have to in order to get the work done. They just adore the man! So I really use him as the basis for my management style.

I'm sure I can't even come close to his management style. A lot of times I call him and ask him what he would do in such-and-such situation, or I just think, What would Dad do in this situation?, and that has pulled me through a lot of times.

I've found that a lot of bosses are intimidating, and I hate that. It just doesn't do any good for me, and I don't think it does much good for anyone. My current boss at times has a tendency to be intimidating, so frequently I have to work against that. I've always said that I never, ever would be an intimidating boss. I just didn't feel that it worked that way. But I am finding that you sometimes have to be intimidating to get things done.

When I first came here, I wanted the employees to respect me and to have a loyalty to me; therefore, I made an effort to talk to each employee about family matters—How are your husband and the kids?—so that they would know that I'm concerned about them. I think that really helps; but there are times when you just have to get downright tough with them. It was really hard for me to realize that I had to do that. Even though I wanted to be the good guy all the time, I found I had to be the bad guy on occasion to get the job done.

To be a good guy, I do one thing my dad has always done. It always impressed me that every year he sends a Christmas card to every employee, and in very card he writes a note in his own handwriting. Every year, starting on December first, he would start writing them. I saw how long it took, but it was always rewarding because he would get replies from his workers. I recall one from a janitor saying, "You are such a marvelous boss!" So I did that this year—I've got only about 35 employees—and for me it also was rewarding. It shows concern and tells employees that I'm thinking of them.

I'm the administrator of this hospital—a drug and alcohol rehabilitation hospital—so technically all the decisions here are mine. My boss will support my decisions, and there are a lot of times that I confer with him first and we make a joint decision. I really don't care if my subordinates know that I'm conferring with my boss, and I don't mind saying, "I'm not sure about this question," or "I don't know what we should do; therefore, I'll check and get back with you!"

I report to my boss—the regional vice president—and reporting to me I've got 7 people—a business manager, head of dietary, nursing head, my program director, head of maintenance, head of housekeeping, and a medical records head—and below them there are about 25–28 people.

We run a 21-day program for our patients. First we have to detox; so if we have a person come in who's been using drugs half their life, it takes a while for the drugs to get out of their system. After we get the drugs out, we put the patient through an intensive three-week program. From 8:00 A.M.

to 7:00 P.M. they are in group sessions, individual therapy sessions, personal
assessments, educational groups. And from 1:00 or 2:00 'til the end of the
day, we really encourage the families to get involved. It's a very intense time,
and the weekends are very family oriented; we really encourage the family
to be here a lot and to work with the patients.

Usually, by the end of the 21 days, patients have improved. (If we find
that a patient isn't doing as well as we think he or she should, then we ask
them to stay a while longer.) But they still have a long way to go. What we've
given them is a start, and we continue that by bringing the patients in for
a group therapy session once a week for the next year. We watch how the
patients are doing. For the first four or five months, most will come every
week. Then they'll pretty much start dropping out.

Our clientele, in terms of age, ranges from sixteen to eighty-four. Previously we weren't taking adolescents, but the problems with younger people
have increased so much that we felt obligated to start taking them. We tend
to have a lot more males than females—about 70 percent males and 30 percent females—but I think it's going to become a lot more even.

More women are entering the working population, and they're moving
up within this population. As they move into the more stressing positions,
women will, I believe, be more vulnerable to drug and alcohol abuse because
they use these drugs to cope with stress. Plus I think as women start to come
out of the closet, they'll also be more apt to use drugs and alcohol.

It might be surprising to you that most of our patients are blue-collar workers.
They aren't poor, and they aren't wealthy; they're just middle-class blue-collar
workers. And most of them are in their late twenties and early thirties. As
for their problems, almost all, say 90 percent, have alcohol as a primary drug,
but about 50 to 75 percent of our patients are multidrug users. That is, they
are on alcohol *plus* another drug—prescription or illegal.

Why did I get this job? I don't know. It's funny. I felt a woman wouldn't
get this job; plus, it was may first interview. So I had a good time and just
considered it as practice. Usually I don't interview well, but here I just relaxed and I guess I left this wonderful impression. Then I had this interview
over the phone and he said, "I want you to fly to Chicago tomorrow." I flew
in the next day, and—this sounds silly—I had this marvelous taxi driver who
had me very relaxed by the time he got me to my interview. He saw I was
nervous and started telling jokes and talking with me to put me at ease. He
helped me so much that again I interviewed really well and got the job.

When I first came in here, I immediately did two things wrong and one
right. The first *bad* mistake was that I didn't want to play the bad guy, so

when my boss said to put up with some people that I didn't like, I did it. I was *really* unhappy with some of the people here, but he said, "Just work with them!" I wish I had not worked with them because I eventually did have to fire five employees; my original assessment was a correct one. No matter how much I worked with them, they were problems. I should have stood up to my boss and said, "I disagree with you. You're not on the spot every day. I'm firing these people."

The second mistake I made was that I tended to put the blame on my boss a lot. If I needed to have something done and people didn't want to do it, then I'd say, "Mr. Jones told me to do it." That was really stupid. It took the blame off me. I wasn't the bad guy; corporate was. But I was losing a lot of face with the employees. They started to think that corporate was running their facility and not me. So when my new boss came in, I tried to correct that mistake. I told him that Mr. Jones is gone, I'm running the hospital here, and I'm making the decisions. His reply was, "You've got total control of the facility, and I'm just there if you need me. You make the decisions and I'll back you up."

Those were my mistakes. What I did right was to get my hands dirty. I literally got into every department, spent three to seven days in every department, saw what each person was doing, became able to do their job, and got to know the people there. For example, when I went into dietary, I went in there and made food for two days. I went down with the housekeeping and swept floors and made beds for two days and saw the chemicals they used. I really got a feel for the operation and what they were doing. I helped the nurses, worked in medical records, etc. And I had weekly meetings with the employees to ask what they liked and didn't like.

I got my hands dirty because I wanted to know what they were doing so that when I told them to do something, (a) I knew what I was asking for, and (b) I knew I could do it just as well as they could. Right now I'm running the show, and I consider my boss as a consultant, not as a boss. Still, I feel real comfortable calling him up and saying, "I really don't know how to deal with this situation."

When I came in I expected more paperwork, but most of my work has involved people. People are my biggest challenge—knowing how much you can demand of people, how much you need to document your interactions, etc., lots of personnel issues. I walked in here and the first week I had to fire two people. I had never fired people in my entire life, but I've gotten much better at firing; I'm good at it now [*laughs*]. But still it's real tough.

Thinking back, I find that I've really learned how to be direct with people. I didn't know how when I first came in here. It's tough to tell a person that they're really messing up without attacking them as a person—telling an employee that his work is bad without telling him that he is bad. Those are two different things, but it's very easy to get them intertwined. You've got to work on your techniques, because there's a tendency to say, "Tom, you're really messing up. Your work has been horrible lately." Instead, you've got to learn to say "Your work performance is really poor; consider what you've done and not done over the past year!"

What I *don't* do is tell the person some good things about their work and then also point out the bad. I don't sandwich the feedback. I break the bad news to people, especially if I'm going to fire them, right up front. I don't pussyfoot around. I just say, "Your work is poor," or "I'm going to terminate you." Then I explain it to them and don't let it take a long time. After that I'll touch on their good points. But first I get my clear, unambiguous message across. In a nutshell, it's one, the bad news; two, an explanation; and three, some good points.

With disciplining it's good to get the cards on the table quickly. My employees get nervous when they have to come see me; especially when I close the door, they get really paranoid. So I hit it right off—"This is my concern with you; let's talk about it." A lot of times people honestly don't know why their work is poor; so I start probing. In that probing I'll point out that they're good at this or this and ask why they can't apply the same approach to other areas. I try to pump them up.

When I first started disciplining people, I was real nervous, and that made it worse for both of us. Now I'm confident; I know what I'm going to do when I bring them in. In earlier times, I went home and cried after I fired a person. One fellow did something wrong and deserved to be fired on the spot. I did fire him later, but I was hesitant and felt like crying. That's simply not a problem anymore.

I'm a lot nastier now. That's been hard, but it's also been good in that employees realize that they've got to shape up or hit the bricks. They know it's my hospital now, and I call the shots. I recall recently when I screamed at someone, I said, "This is *my* hospital, and I'm angry at you." Then I really started yelling. I did it purposely, and everyone heard it. When I walked out, everyone was hiding like little kids in a corner, but it was really good because it let people know that I meant business and that everybody had better shape up. So when I yell at a person, I yell loud enough that everyone can hear it. I know what I'm doing, and they better listen to me because the reins are in my hands.

I'm assertive because it helps with my employees. It's necessary also because alcoholics and drug abusers are very manipulative. They admit that. They have manipulated people, and they try to manipulate us and the program here. And I wasn't used to dealing with that. Here we have to manipulate them to get them to do the things we want to do.

We use some of our graduates in the program here, and some are still very manipulative. They went through our old program, which was for 14 days. Now it's 21 to 25 days. So things we do are a lot different. When they see these changes, they resent it and try to change the program. For example, when they came through, we did not allow them to watch TV because we wanted them talking to each other. With the longer program we weren't as strict—we didn't want to deny patients TV for three weeks. So our grads started complaining loudly. Now they are the best referral service we have, so I don't want them unhappy. But I decided they weren't running my program. We are going to run what we think is a good program. If people are abusing the right to watch TV, that's one thing. But we're not going to deny them TV privileges for about 30 days because some graduates want us to.

As an administrator, I don't just punish. I've also got to know how to reward people. When someone does something good, I try to make a really big deal out of it, personally and in front of people. Also I'm sure to put a memo in their files. And we use merit increases here, not across-the-board increases. So I remind people of that and I reward good performance with large salary increases.

Since our salaried people, especially the department heads, tend to work well over forty hours a week, I feel comfortable in rewarding people with time off. If they're good workers and need to take off in the afternoon, then I give them an okay. From the corporate side, that's not permitted, but I don't tell them and the practice works out well for me.

In the month-to-month matters I do what I want. Corporate generally just holds me accountable for the budget. We have monthly meetings with the president of the company, myself, my boss, the head of finance, and my boss's immediate supervisor. There are five people in this room and they are throwing questions at you about your finances. I've got a budget that I'm supposed to meet, and if I don't meet it, then I get a lot of questions. So I'm in the middle here. I try to run my show and not take too many problems up to my boss. And I try to meet my budget so that corporate doesn't cause problems for the people running the hospital.

I don't think corporate is any easier or tougher on me because I'm a woman. And I think most of the employees like me. Some think I'm a bitch, uncaring, but that's okay. There's *no* problem in being a woman, but there has been some problem with age in that all the people I manage are older than I am. Even my assistant is a lot older than I. I wondered, How is she going to feel about taking orders from this young punk? Most people have adapted well.

I think you might say I got this job in spite of being a woman, not because I am one. It seems the company doesn't care if you're a man or woman, as long as you can do the job. A man can walk in and he, as well as his subordinates, have a lot easier time because it's a lot easier for people to take orders from a man. It's a lot easier to look at a woman and say, "Come on now . . . ," whatever. It's just a lot easier for most people to take orders from a man. But I've overcome that by being open and honest with my people. Once, early on, my boss and I decided not to be open on a situation, not to tell my employees about something. They found out about it anyway, and I lost a lot of respect. I learned a lot from that.

On the other hand, sometimes you can use being a woman to your benefit. You can show a little more caring because you are a woman. You can be a little more physical with people, and people like it. That's a little bit more accepted for a woman. You don't do it to an excess, but it's helpful.

Both the men and women seem to accept me. Sometimes the women, depending on their security, differ a little, but in general the women do accept me as well. It's the ones that feel a little more insecure that don't accept me; I'm a secure woman, and they're not.

Where I'll go from here I'm not sure. I'll probably move to a larger hospital—ninety to a hundred beds—as the top administrator. It depends somewhat too on where my husband's jobs take him. I could move to a much larger hospital as an assistant administrator. I'm only twenty-four, so I've got plenty of time to explore my options.

Armed Robber

Whatever trips their trigger, I want to find that out.

There's such an excitement in robbing people. When you got a gun in your hand, you're dealing with people, you're the ultimate. It's the ego-inflating power that you have. You go into a tavern and there's forty to fifty people there. You throw on a shotgun and you tell them, "Everybody in the air." You know what I mean. People pee on themselves. It's a gas.

It's a gas for me. It's a gas for my partners. They want escape. That's what motivates them. Escape from the 9-to-5 routine. They want to be able to get up at 9:00 to go; get up at 12:00. Don't have to come home. They want complete freedom.

'Course they know they need money to have this freedom. So robbery gives them the money. They got to pay those bills. You have to pay your rent, your food, your gas, your cleaning. Or if you got an old lady, that's another mouth to feed. So they're in this to get that freedom.

Some guys got to have the cars, the good clothes, the flash. That's what they want. So I find out what they want and say, "Hey man, join up with me and that's what you'll get." They steal with me because I always got something going.

After the score, it's sit down and divide up the cash. Split the cash right there. I'll take a little extra since it's my score. That's why people follow me. I got something going, and they walk away with their part of the score.

Now you got to make sure they don't turn on you. You don't use fear. If you make somebody afraid of you, then they're going to shoot you. Plain and simple. If you scare someone bad enough then he's saying, "I got to kill him."

Who wants this? Not me. What I want them to realize is this: if he rolls on me I'm going to kill him. That's all. I realize if I scare you then I got to start looking in my garbage can when I go up the steps so you don't jump out of there and blow me away.

I don't want people scared. I don't want them to think I'll go around hurting them, but I want them to know I'll kill them if they do anything that makes me have to. See what I mean?

That's the reason, too, you don't go around punishing and threatening people. Right or wrong you stay with what you got. If a guy screws up, you pay him off and ease him out. Don't ask him back on the next score. You don't want to make him so mad that he drops down on you. It's just, "There's nothing happening. I ain't got nothing." You got to put them off like that. If you tell them, "Hey man, you can't work with me," he's going to burn you. Keep him happy as long as possible. If I'm really scared of him, put him in the bushes.

Give you an example. I tell this guy to wait in the car, and I go check this joint out. Come back and he's not in the car. He's window-dressing in the store. He's not taking care of business. That's not important enough to kill him. He just don't get asked back. Once I said, "Man, watch when this cat comes out. I got to know what time he comes out between 10:00 and 11:00. So you sit here and watch." I come back and he's asleep. I'm out of it, but I stay cool.

Another example. I think this other guy's cool. I give him a Magnum and tell him he's to go behind the bar. "Here's the piece, but I don't want you scattering nobody. If you fire this gun, it's yours." He says, "Okay." We go into this tavern and here's this drunk, this lady drunk. I'd already sent one guy in and he's sitting at the end of the bar so he can watch out. So I go in with the shotgun and freeze the bartender right away. "This is a robbery." And this other guy has everybody covered from the back. So we got these people whipsawed. We done it so quiet that the people on the other side don't know we've stuck these people up.

This lady gets off her seat and starts cussing us. Like I mean she is drunk. So this dummy takes the Magnum and hits her on top of the head. When he does, he discharges the gun, shoots into the top of the bar. Wood chips fly into the air. Then the cordite, there's a big blue smoke cloud in the air. Everyone wants to run, to break.

We could have let that old lady say anything she wanted. I mean she wasn't going to physically attack any of us and if she did, we had all the arms. There was no need to hit her on the head, and there was definitely no need to discharge the weapon. Next time around I don't even tell him nothing! Now don't get me wrong. That's if a man does his job wrong. If he does *you* wrong that's a different matter. You can't let that stand.

In leading a score, picking people is the most important. I got to find people who when they're under pressure don't visibly show it. They don't get flushed in the face and they don't stammer, scream. You don't go into a robbery screaming. You go in real nice. "This is a stickup. We just want the money. We'll be real cool and let you be and be right out of here." So the owner says, "Okay. Just don't hurt my customers."

I've got a group of people that I choose from. I don't have five people that I've got to take. I pick a man with a good reputation or someone I've done something with. The loyalty—trust—is more of value than anything. When you're sure of the man's loyalty, then you don't look behind you to see if he's there.

See, when I say, "Hey, I want you to throw the gun on this dude; I want you to freeze him there," he's going to do it there. And if push comes to shove, he *will* shoot this guy. This is what it's all about. And he isn't going to make this guy panic. He doesn't have to talk to him. "Just keep your hands where they are, and you'll live." I don't want him to hit the guy in the head, because if you do he doesn't know what's happening. He's liable to start kicking, screaming, and the next thing you know, you're shooting.

Sometimes there's a dress rehearsal so that everybody knows what they're doing. They got confidence in themselves and in you.

Hey, I put the plan together with people but I prefer to do it myself. If I make a mistake, it's on me. If I get caught, it's on me. If I get told on, it's on me. If I get five guys with me and something goes wrong, then it could be two shot and three in jail because of me.

Or let's say I got this guy, John. He's in to me for $100. Now he knows come Tuesday it's double-up day; he owes me $200. So instead of paying me Tuesday, he drops a dime on me Monday. Tells the law some job I've pulled. Every dude what's working for you when you take down a place has an insurance policy. Now, he can go around and commit any crime he likes. If he gets caught, all he'll do is turn on you—cop to a minor plea and testify against you. He walks on his crime, because the cops want to get me.

So you don't lead unless you need more hands—to drive the car, hold another gun, scout out the place—or more brains—like to take down a safe. Sometimes after a hit a guy will get scared and start to talk, or he gets to bragging. Then you got to put him in the bushes, and that gets everything too complicated.

I like being a loner because it's easier to survive that way. Being a leader's stressful. You got to plan, worry about people. Take care of your people. You got to find enough scores to keep them in scratch [*rubs fingers together*]. One gets shot . . .

I've dropped people off at hospitals. Taken all their clothes off and left them naked on the street. I've given them that much. They got a bullet in them. Nothing I can do for them. I'm not a doctor. I take everything away from them. "Now you can tell them anything you want to. Tell them you's robbed." I take away all his clothes so they can't get no identity or association. I help them out that far.

You got to protect your people, and there's two sides to that. They're your people, so you got to take care of them. And they expect you to look after them. Like this fence told me he'd buy a load of liquor from me at $1.50 a bottle. So I told a few guys, "Let's go bust this place. We'll get $1.50 a bottle." So we get seven thousand bottles.

He says, "I'll give you $1.00 a bottle. I don't have $1.50."

I says, "Man, the deal was for $1.50 a bottle."

He says, "If you don't like it, drink it."

So I says, "We don't want it." And when he turns around I shot him. Didn't kill him; just shot him. Can't take that. I'm in between. This guy [a subordinate] hears $1.50 a bottle; now you're telling me $1.00 a bottle. We're talking seven thousand bottles. Where's the $3,500? He'll shoot me.

Look, your leader has got to know the subject you're dealing with. In my case, robberies. Since I did so many by myself, I learned all the details. Like to keep something between me and you. I don't care if it's a ballbearing. When I'm sticking you up, as long as that ballbearing is there, you're going to think before you come after me, Do I step around it, over it, or . . .? So I know to keep something between me and you. But I know better than to block the situation so I can't see what your hands are doing. So I know about my subject.

The people. The people I'm going to lead have to want to be involved in this subject. Now I've got to show them that I know what I'm talking about, and I got to show them that by my track record, what I'm talking about is right.

Now if you've got a good idea, I'm going for it. I'm not going to be pig-headed about it. I got rules about robbing, and if the troops got an idea that fits in these guidelines, then it goes. If it doesn't, we throw it out. In crime you don't have a research shop, no R and D. You can't do no experiments and trial and error. So you can't stretch out too far.

And I got to know what these people want. This guy wants this. He wants that. And this guy wants to get next to me because he wants the fattest slice of the pie. So I want him to push these other two. Drive them; get more out of them so he can get next to me. I use people by giving them what they want. Whatever trips their trigger, I want to find that out. Their hole card—what's their hole card? Show me what that is, man, and if I can produce that, then we're in like flint. If I can't produce it, then you can just pass me up.

So you get the system and the troops set up to do this robbery. Then I got these people who I know can do the job, and I got to keep them busy. It's a twenty-four-hour job. Because if I don't keep them busy, I'm going to lose them to somebody else.

You got to do all this. Still, you can run into problems. Like touching women in robberies. Because of the time, that's a real problem. I got enough trouble just dealing with the robbery. I can't worry about my *own* guys molesting women. Like this time we jammed a tavern and made everybody take their clothes off. Well, I had this guy—nineteen years old, good, and he's always putting his hands on women. But I got him straight on the job before this one. "You touch a woman and I leave you there."

So we've jammed this bar and we're ready to go and there's an accident outside. The cops are there and the getaway car's blocked. So we got to be cool; can't have the people running out of there. Can't have no screaming. So we have everybody take off *all* their clothes, and we roll them in a ball. I see what this guy's thinking, so I just ease the shotgun over at him. He gets the message. He's cool; don't touch no part of no broads.

I go outside and find this old brown Chevy that's at the end of the block. Come back in. "Whose brown Chevy is this? Give me the keys, man, and we'll be out of here."

All went cool.

7

Leading by Example

E FFECTIVE leadership is based on fundamental heuristics. Leaders have learned that without protecting and motivating those who work for them, they cannot be successful themselves. When it comes to motivation, a system of rewards and punishments has been proven to be helpful, but nothing motivates as well as the leader's example.

Leading by example is so obvious that it often passes us by. It's not emphasized in texts; it's so simple that it's often not taught in classrooms. But it works.

Consider the advantages of this approach. It allows the leader to communicate what is important. How leaders spend their time is the best indication of their priorities. Subordinates hear what a leader says, but they are truly impressed by—they understand and remember—what he or she does.

More important, setting the example motivates. When the leader expends time, energy, and sweat on the job, the message is clearly, "I'm interested in this job." There is no need for a lecture. Simultaneously the worker senses, "The boss thinks enough of my job to do it. I'm responsible for this job, therefore I'm valuable, and the boss knows it."

Not only does exemplary leadership communicate and motivate, it tactfully hones precision. If a picture is worth a thousand words, an example is well worth a million. Exhortations to a subordinate to work harder, pay attention to details, be more careful, and so on, are blunt and often ambiguous, whereas a leader's example (in overhauling a motor, saving a patient, or massaging a client) is tacit, instructive, and reassuring.

As the SEAL team leader's commentary reveals, setting the example motivates by demonstrating the correct behavior. He and his men play and kill with chilling abandon. As they do, the leader takes the initiative in everything, from machine-gunning motorcyclists to eating sharks. He participates in crazy exploits with his troops. Simultaneously, he retains their respect and his leadership position.

While the worlds of the city bus maintenance foreman and the federal mediators' director are far less exciting than the world of the SEALs, their leadership by example demonstrates a benefit at least as significant; examples are educational. Being close to the job allows these leaders to understand the capabilities of their workers and to recognize opportunities to train them. In the words of the bus maintenance foreman:

"Often I'll have people come up to me and say, 'Hey, look, I'd like to have the opportunity to, say, overhaul a Detroit 671 engine.' He wants the opportunity because that would give him new training. He wants to expand his capabilities. Sometimes I go along with that, and if I do assign somebody a job that is going to be a learning experience, I'll either assign another mechanic—a higher-level mechanic, or someone I know knows the job—to stay with him or I'll stay with him myself. If it isn't too complicated, I'll just run through the process with him."

The federal mediator is even more the teacher. He demonstrates first, and follows with a debriefing:

"We're always bringing in new guys—not mediators yet—and I try to show them the techniques I use and why I use them, leading or teaching by example. I do this type of debriefing right after we've finished a case. I don't care if it's been a ten- or twelve-hour negotiation. I sit there with the guy for one and a half, two hours. I say, 'Remember I did this, and I did this, and I did this. Here's why I did it that way.' And it means a lot. I've had guys two or three years later thank me for that. They thought that was one of the most important things that happened when they were going around. Not only did I tell them the problem, I said this is why I did that, and here is the results."

The mediator's comments indicate another payoff of leading by example—the subordinates prize the leader's efforts. Not only do they appreciate the lessons, they also value the effort devoted to them. Soon this appreciation translates into loyalty. Usually subordinates reciprocate, doing the best job they can for the leader. Occasionally the reciprocity is turned toward fellow workers as the subordinates model their behavior after the leader, helping colleagues and setting industrious examples for them.

The massage parlor operator and the paramedic helicopter director also teach by example. But the paramedic wants his example also to set the emotional tempo for his team. He wants to promote an action orientation; a positive attitude, a perhaps-wrong-but-never-in-doubt approach:

"On the other side of it, I always approach the task with a positive attitude—it will work out okay. I won't use and I can't be forced to use a negative attitude. I always think the job is there; we will rise to the occasion and get it done. That's very important, because people take their lead from me. I set the tempo.

"At the same time you can't ever, ever in front of that group let your guard down by being indecisive, because you're training them by example to be decisive.

"A constant example has to be set for these people, a very firm example. The worst thing you can do with these students is to be wishy-washy."

SEAL Team Leader

They're so excited that they're leading the guy they're supposed to be following.

Well, the SEALs are the navy's version of the Green Berets; we're trained to fight on sea, air, or land. And I guess you could say these fellows are just people waiting to be led. A SEAL leader just tells them what the mission is, goes with them on it, does his part. He leads by example. SEALs can do anything; all they need is to be pointed in a direction.

Becoming a SEAL is almost impossible. One hundred and twenty started in my class in San Diego, and twelve finished, survived. We all started out as good swimmers. So at first they started us playing water polo all day. Play, play, play; can't touch the side or bottom. Then after a few days they take us out to the ocean. Here's the ocean, boys. Just get acquainted. Swim out to that island and back, about two miles. You could wear flippers, but most didn't because you couldn't get into a good crawl with them. I hit my head on a rock coming out so I got stitches and couldn't go back in the water for a week. So I had to do the elephant walk while they're swimming, hold my ankles and walk. They told me that I set the Guinness world record for the elephant walk.

Plus there were the push-ups. Everything you did was wrong, so that was fifty push-ups. I must have done thousands each day. Every morning we'd stand formation all sharp in clean uniforms. They'd always find something wrong. Run to the ocean, do fifty push-ups, crawl in the sand, do push-ups in the surf, run in the water. We'd be filthy after twenty minutes. I can't believe how strong I was after that. I could climb to the top of a rope, using only my hands with scuba tanks that weighed eighty pounds on my back.

We'd run everywhere. Mostly in the sand in combat boots. They thought it built up your legs. And they taught us weapons, explosives, underwater demo, navigation, mapping, everything. Then we got teamed with a partner. I got to know what he was like, how he swam, how fast he swam, everything. Out there under forty feet of black cold water, he's all you got, so you better know each other.

Mine was fun. We'd always get in trouble of some kind but get off okay because we were good. Like we were swimming a simulated mission in the dark at about sixty feet. It's dark and you hear all these sounds—ocean sounds, motors, whales—it's real eerie. And the guys on the surface are circling in boats trying to find us; like we're the enemy. Trying to capture us. And these porpoises start bumping into us. They were curious or playing; first time it happens, it really scares you. So one bumps my partner and he screams. So he loses his mouthpiece and needs to use mine. I get tickled and start laughing and lose mine, and then we had to surface. We came up laughing like kids. They didn't have to see us. They could hear us. So we got captured.

Sometimes sharks would bump, and that's especially scary, but we're trained to go on with the mission. In war, if a shark eats somebody you just go on. When we were in Florida, one of the team was swimming with his girl. He had gone out and she was coming when he got hit by a shark. He yelled for her to go back. Shark bit him on the shoulder, bit him on the leg, and then ate out his stomach. We all went in and pulled him out. Then we caught that shark and ate it. Kind of a revenge.

Being a SEAL leader was easy. I think it was because everyone thought he was his own leader. We were all the same. We didn't wear ranks in the field or on the base or ships if we didn't want to. We didn't salute our officers. Oh sure, back on base or on a ship we'd do it to them, but we'd laugh as we did. But sometimes we wouldn't salute them there or salute other officers. That got us in trouble with the brass.

On a mission, I would go over what we were to do to make sure each guy knew what he was to do, make sure he had checked all his equipment. I'd go over the procedures, time, distance. Make sure the explosives were okay. I'd just ask a lot of questions. You had to get all that straight because at sixty feet below the ocean you can't start asking questions about what you forgot. After a mission I never told them they did a good job; we all knew we had, and we all laughed and bragged about it.

Whatever the mission was, everybody was ready to do it. Nobody wants to get up at 3:00 A.M. and drink gallons of coffee so you can urinate in your wet suit and stay warm. And nobody wants to go out from a submarine sixty feet underwater in ice-cold water. But we're the only ones who can do it, and we did it.

You and your partner are put out of the sub at sixty feet in dark water. You know there's an obstacle, boat, or tower five miles in this direction that you've got to blow up. So you have a compass on your wrist, and you read it with a flashlight as you swim. It's dark, you're sixty feet below water, and you got to tell how far you've gone by the number of kicks you've made. That's tough because you're swimming through kelp and dragging maybe two hundred and fifty pounds of explosives behind you. Then you get there, set the explosives and get far enough away so that you're not blown apart.

A pickup boat waits just beyond the horizon. So at *a* time you've got to be back at *a* place in the ocean. You all get there and it's—you've seen those World War II movies?—just like that. You get in line, and they make one pass, and you all catch this hoop with your arm and get pulled into the boat. Hurts like hell, and they come in fast. In war if they miss you on the first pass, that's it. On our missions we'd have to give them a case of beer if we missed. Maybe that's why they came in so fast.

Missions for us could be very tough. Everybody's up, ready to go. They're so excited that they're leading the guy they're supposed to be following. Once, on the coast in the Mideast, the State Department thought we might have to take some Americans out. And it might be under combat conditions. So contingency plans were made to bring them out. Our team went in off subs to recon. It was perfect, cloudy, dark, no moon, and we have all-black equipment. Not even the mask will reflect light. And this beach was really fortified, obstacles and antiaircraft guns pointed toward the ocean. There was a coral column that needed to be blown out so our ships could come in, but we could do that. So we mapped the beach and swam back out.

After that they got us together and went over the plans. The column was to be blown, the guns were to be taken out. And they needed some of us to volunteer to go in, blow some obstacles, and then infiltrate the town, locate our people and lead 'em to the right beach. It was a suicide mission. So they asked us, and there's silence for about five seconds, and then everybody volunteers. All of us, and we're cheering, yelling, jumping around, slapping everybody on the back, shaking hands, giving high-fives. I couldn't believe it.

Being a SEAL is everything. When you're wearing that patch, nobody fools with you—no sailors, no marines, nobody. You got respect. When I's on this boat one time I had free run of the ship, and I'd be free to go up to the captain and talk and drink coffee with him. And if somebody fools with a SEAL, that's it. One time two of our guys got cut up in a bar, and we came back from a training mission all blacked up and in gear. We went down to that bar like we were, carrying weapons. Told the owner to tell us who did it or we'd shoot up his place. We found the guys and evened the score.

And you're asking about leadership. The SEAL leader leads by example—takes the initiative, initiative in anything. One time we came into Norfolk, and we're in this van with all our gear and weapons, and we stopped at a Kentucky Fried Chicken place and loaded up on buckets of chicken. So we're trucking down the road eating chicken and puttin' the bones in a big tub we had. And these four motorcyclists came up behind us. They're waving with one finger. We're waving back. So two SEALs open the back door and throw the bones all over them.

They went on around us, and about fifteen miles later we came around this curve and there must have been fifty of them waiting on us. And they're all over us, trying to run us off the road and wreck us. Now we got this strap over by the sliding door. So I took the M60 and put in a belt of blanks and hooked up to the door. And then we opened the doors, and I'm swinging out on the side, cutting down on them with this machine gun. And they're everywhere.

That was crazy, and being crazy is fun and everybody knows SEALs are crazy, and they respect us. Like we were over near Greece and the French SEALs, or whatever they were, were having a celebration for us. And we're drinking and eating and then drinking Ouzo and getting half drunk. So then they have this ceremony for us. They all got in a circle and took their clothes off and one guy got in the middle and put toilet paper where the sun don't shine and someone lit it. And he danced around as long as he could and then ran to the ocean. He could only put it out in the ocean. So they all take turns at this.

After it's all over, we're plowed, and this helicopter is taking us back to the ship when the pilot points out some marines camped on the beach. To make it short, he says he'd certainly like to get back at them for a reason. Well, we go back to the ship, black up; this is late at night. We went back and captured all the marine sentries and tied them up. Don't know how we did it in our condition. Then we set charges and trip flares all around them and left us a way in and out. Then we went in and broke into the mess tent and got pots and pans. We all set off quarter-pound charges of TNT, and we started running around the camp beating on pots and pans. These marines are screaming, running everywhere, tripping over flares. And then we ran down the beach. We were laughing and rolling in the surf. The flares and yelling are still going on. Then we hear these helicopters coming from across the water, and they put their searchlights on us. I forgot to mention that we did all this naked. One lands, and this colonel or general hops out, and we're there naked, and he wants us to salute and explain. So when he hears the story, he just laughs and says only SEALs are crazy enough to do that.

There's some problems in leading SEALs. One time a bunch of guys almost got blown away, and one of them couldn't handle it after that. They were setting five hundred pounds of plastic explosives, and I ran down the beach checking the wires and found them crossed. Anything like that will set off the charge—ship vibrations, radios, anything—so I ran down there and got it fixed. Then we went way out on the ship before we blew it, and it blew boulders the size of portable TVs out on us. This guy just turns white and is shaking. So we had to talk it over and get him into some other job.

And there's stress. They put us on a battle-readiness status sometimes a day or so before a mission. We're there isolated, ready to go. Top readiness and we're tense. So we had boxing matches and fistfights just to relieve the stress.

And there's drugs and alcohol. Alcohol is there, like a part of us. We do our mission and then get drunk together. We sober up and do the next one. We drink to loosen up, to come down. But it doesn't hurt the mission. Drugs are a problem. I just tell a guy who's too much on drugs to get off or it will hurt him doing his job. If that doesn't work, we put group pressure on him; that works.

I understand. I've had trouble with drugs and alcohol. I started thinking about what we were doing, blowing up everything. Saw the effects of what we did—maimed people, blown up boats and buildings. People who are gone now.

Lebanon was especially a problem for me. The CIA or State Department— one would find which rebel groups are active in an area, and if they wanted to have them blamed for something, they'd have us go in and blow up something so that those rebels would be blamed.

Would you blow up ships or buildings?

Both.

Whose were they? Were any American?

Yes, some were.

Were any Americans in the targets that you blew?

I can't say. Maybe. Probably.

City Bus Maintenance Supervisor

The key for me is matching skills to problems.

I don't think there's anything here that I assign that I can't do myself. That's one thing that's kind of unique about our operation; both me and my boss have a maintenance background. Now you could have a supervisor who doesn't know the technical aspects. He can supervise, but *what* can he supervise? Because of our situation, we have the lowest maintenance costs for any large city in the state.

The key to being a good supervisor is knowing what you're supervising. I'm in charge of the maintenance of 64 buses, 5 ride-carry vans, and 10 trans-aid vans. And I can take any one of those vehicles apart and put it back together. I, without the help of anyone, can fix anything that breaks on any one of those vehicles. So I've got a real advantage when it comes to supervising. I don't have to try and impress my mechanics. They know I know my job and theirs too. When a unit is down, I quickly look over it, along with the report, to see what's wrong and then assign it to a mechanic who is capable of doing the job.

Generally I come in a little before my mechanics do and look over what we got to do that day. I'll talk with the working foreman who's been in charge of the night shift. When the mechanics some in, I'll tell them what jobs to pull, and if there are some questions on what's wrong, I'll go out and troubleshoot a job. I also got a parts man that handles purchasing and keeping parts on hand. That's, generally speaking, my day. I'm out in the bays most of the time and there are intervals when I come into my office and do some administrative work and maintain certain records that I have to maintain.

As you can see, it's a large operation here. This garage is about 75 yards long and 50 yards wide. These six bays cut through the center, and each bay can accommodate six to eight buses. There's a portion set aside for changing tires; some for realigning wheels and putting in bearings. One half of one bay we devote to washing buses; another half we use for changing oil. Then there's lubrication, inspections, steaming, fueling. We handle all of that.

Most of the operations take care of themselves. I've got someone changing oil. That's his job. He does it. Buses come in; he's here; he changes the oil. On occasion I'll come down to chat with him, but I don't have to assign him jobs or help him with problems.

With the other mechanics, it takes a little more work. We've got mechanics with varying trades, skills, and educations here. A couple of them have two years of college; some have been to trade schools; and others, we've got some that can barely read. So I've got a wide range of problems that come in every day. I've got to match the two—problems to skills. That's not easy sometimes. First I have to know what I'm doing; that is, I've quickly got to figure out basically how complicated the problem is. Then I've got to know the capabilities of the people I'm going to match the job to.

That's my big pressure every morning. It would be heaven to say, "I've got ten buses down. You ten guys go work on them." It isn't that simple. Mentally you run through the possibilities. Well, I can't put this mechanic on that job; it's over his head or he's going to mess it up. He's not going to do it right, and when it goes sour, the bus will be back in here again. Or I'll think, No, don't put him on that simple job, because he'd be wasted.

So you definitely have to pick the jobs and then treat people as individuals. What goes a long way in supervising is treating people as individuals, knowing their skill levels, and putting them on a job that they do their best on. You don't want a man over his head, because he doesn't do the job well and he's under stress because he's afraid he'll mess up. Also you don't want a man underutilizing his skills. He's bored; you're wasting good talent; and he loses some of his polish.

Often I'll have people come up to me and say, "Hey, look, I'd like to have the opportunity to, say, overhaul a Detroit 671 engine." He wants the opportunity because that would give him new training. He wants to expand his capabilities. Sometimes I go along with that, and if I do assign somebody a job that I know is going to be a learning experience, I'll either assign another mechanic—a higher-level mechanic, or someone I know knows the job—to stay with him or I'll stay with him myself. If it isn't too complicated, I'll just run through the process with him.

That's the major thing I love about my work—being able to be there with the mechanical problems. I've got a mechanical background, and I *love* troubleshooting—we've got a problem and we've got to figure it out. I love being faced with a problem.

Quite honestly, I think that at times it causes problems for my mechanics. I know my job. I'm considerate; I'm fair; and I'm a good mechanic. But when I'm in there doing the troubleshooting, the mechanic many times loses the opportunity to do it himself. You see, a lot of a mechanic's motivation and satisfaction comes from *finding* the problem. Unfortunately, sometimes I take that from him. Because of my experience and knowledge, I may quickly wander through the problem and spot what's wrong very quickly. I've got to learn to share the troubleshooting with the mechanics.

When I put a man on a job, I set up a work order. It lists who did the job, when he starts a repair job, and when he punches out. The mechanic also lists briefly what he did and any parts—oil or stuff—he used on that particular vehicle. Now this file is maintained so that if we have a problem with that repair job—for example, we line a set of breaks on a bus and a week later it comes back with a brake block loose on the shoe—we can get back this work order and see who did that repair job. What to do then depends on the severity of what the incident might be. If this is something of a minor nature, you say, "Well, look, you didn't tighten this up properly; you make sure you do that." Generally, even if it were something that costs a major amount of money—say, somebody built an engine, and it came back and went sour—we would ignore it the first time. If I have continuous problems with a mechanic, I put him on simpler jobs, or it could get to a point of using progressive discipline.

My major problem is that the only way for me to advance is to replace my boss, if he moves up, or to move to another city. There's a catch-22 to doing that. I'm a good supervisor because I know the machinery. When I advance—and I've had several offers—I'll be getting away from the machinery. Now, I've read *The Peter Principle*, and I don't think that I'll get promoted to where I'm over my head. But I'm pretty sure I'll get promoted away from what's fun.

Federal Mediators' Director

Right there at the negotiating table is where the action is. That's the war zone.

The good mediator is a bit psychiatrist/psychologist, a bit priest, a bit of a humorist, a bit of a conversationalist, and a bit of a person who definitely understands problems from one side and another. He has sincerity, confidentiality, and acceptability.

We are goal-oriented. My goal and every mediator's goal should be the resolution of the problem at hand. If it takes a little wheeling and dealing, you do it. You run over here and talk to this side, then you run over here to talk to this side a little bit. You say, "What if I can get this back from them? Would you go along with that?" And they say, "Yes." Then you go back over to this side and say, "I think I can get this done." And you get the sides together. It's cutting the wheat from the chaff and getting down to the heart. That's important to both parties. The facade is knocked away.

It's exciting, exhaustive, and stressful. We have a very high incidence of mediators with heart problems. It's very stressful. I've been off caffeine for ten years. I drink one caffeine, and I have to drink water all day. Within this profession we have all the signs of stress. The statistics relative to heart attacks and strokes are very, very high. You get into one of these negotiations at 9:00 in the morning, and things start jelling, say, at 7:00 that night. This little bit is coming together, and this little bit is coming together. You can't then say, "Well, I've missed my dinner. I'm going to walk out now." You don't do that. You stay with it. It could be 4:00 the next morning or 5:00 the next day before you get your next meal of any kind.

Now it doesn't happen all the time that way. And I'm not saying that it's rare either. I've had one heck of a lot of meetings that were very long—I mean 14–15 hours. I had one meeting recently that was 39 straight hours. It's exciting, but it's stressful.

Part of my job as their director (I have twenty mediators reporting to me) is to help my mediators deal with this stress. There's a lot of frustration, and the mediator can't go to the union or the management and talk his frustrations out. I'm a buffer. I'm the guy they talk to on this. When you're the third party, everyone talks to you but you've got no one to talk to. So they come to talk to me.

Maybe it won't be a formal way. Maybe it's over coffee. "Gee, this problem over here is bad. I really hate what's going on." He knows what he says will never go out of the room. It's between us. It's something that'll never be discussed with anyone else. The discussion usually leads to an alleviation of some of the mediator's frustrations. Maybe the mediator did okay in a bargaining session. Maybe he didn't miss a thing—he's just frustrated.

A big part of my job is leading by example. I know what my men are in charge of. I'm in the war zone with them. I help them mediate some cases. I don't get involved until my actual physical presence will make the difference. Sometimes the mediator gets into a mean labor dispute, then myself is called upon. The mediator might say he is having trouble and needs some help, or the parties could ask me to enter.

When I mediate, I always think ahead, use a strategy. One of the first things I do is to get the trust and confidence of both sides. So first I make it a point to talk to each side separately. I do this for both sides; I get the good feel for the management side; what's the truth, the whole truth, and nothing but the truth. I do the same thing for the union side; what's the truth, the whole truth, and nothing but the truth.

Then I look for ways that both sides can get a little of what they want. Say the management will give 50 cents an hour. Then I talk to the union and they say, "We get 60 cents an hour or we hit the bricks, period." So what in the world can I search out that will not cost the company 10 cents but will give the union the 10 cents an hour? What comes to mind is a holiday. Ah, an extra day of vacation. An extra day of vacation wouldn't cost the company 10 cents, but I can mathematically show the union that it is 10 cents an hour. Since all the workers don't take a vacation at the same time, what you lose when one employee is gone is made up by the other employees on the workforce at that particular point in time.

I might find the committees on both sides, management and labor, are voting down proposals. I'm just not getting through to the two chief guys. They're not really talking because they're playing on the stage of the other nine. I may say to them, "Let's go to a small table. Any objections from you?"

"No."

"From you?"

"No."

So I get the two head people in at the small table. Solve the problem without the stage lights on. Get down to the problem.

Or I could pull the chief negotiator away from colleagues and associates at the big table and say, "I'd like to talk to you for a minute if I could." So I sit down and just outright say, "You know, where you're headed is for trouble." I would *not* do that if I could see that the chief negotiator has a tightrope on him. What I mean by a tightrope is that the parties don't want no one talking to the chief negotiator except in front of them. That if you were to make the move, it would do nothing but deepen your problem with the whole committee.

Then I get the table started up. I start looking eyeball to eyeball. Then they start talking better, and others start falling in line. It's an amazing thing. All of a sudden the other people start being quiet and listening. The chief negotiators start to talk and add and subtract things.

It's hard to work with committees of 15 on each side. That's 30 in the room, and you take a pet peeve from every guy in every department, you got one heck of a lot of issues. So what I got to do in this game is get rid of the issues as fast as I can. Get down to the resolution of the conflict, which means money, hours, and working conditions, as fast as I can. That gets both sides back to making their widgets and making money.

And you got to remember you got just so many chances to use my techniques. Pick out my best techniques and start running with them. Don't think, If this one fails, I can use this one. That's a very dangerous approach. I'm limited. Think about it. It's 2:00 in the morning, and I used a few things up. Everyone's pretty frustrated, mad, and angry. So I say I think we should split up into committees and go in such-and-such a direction. And the guys are liable to say, "You go jump in the river. We did these other five things you said and now this. What for? They didn't work. Now this isn't going to work." Now I'm ending up defending what I did and becoming a part of the problem. I got a bag of tricks. So I run with my best, get my best lined up. Be sure that when my number one fails, that my number two is not what a reasonable man would deny me.

Prior to becoming a mediator, I attended law school at the university and had a degree in labor relations. Then I had about fifteen years of labor relations experience with the labor union, and prior to that I was a private consultant to management. So I had exposure on both sides. Mostly our mediators come from one side or the other.

I've been a mediator for ten years and director for five. As the director, I assign cases. As the cases come in, I look over the cases numbers and decide what impact they're going to have. Then I assign each one to a mediator and try to equalize the load. In other words, I try not to give twenty cases to one guy in a certain period of time and one to another, so that one guy is working day and night and the other is having a pretty easy go of it. At the end of a case, the mediator fills out a report, which I review. If he gets into a problem, we'll have consultations and discussions on what's going on. If he needs some help, he'll let me know, or if I decide on my own initiative that he needs some help, I give him some help.

Sometimes I suggest on a very hard case that there's some good reason that it's so hard. I'll ask the mediator, "Have you tried the technical assistance program with those people? Have you tried training sessions with the stewards and the management supervisory-level people so that they understand the contract and the grievance procedure better? Have you suggested to start with the higher-ups, the possibility they need some more communication? Then at the next negotiation a lot of the problems wouldn't come to the negotiating table. Maybe they would be washed away by an ongoing congenial relationship during the life of the contract." See, there's a lot that could be done during that period of time rather than wait for it all to come out at the bargaining table. There is a sore festering there all the time that caused the problem.

In addition to helping old mediators, I train new ones. I did as a mediator, and I do now. You really can't describe what goes on in a mediation. You've got to really get involved in the case at the beginning and watch the different moves. We're always bringing in new guys—not mediators yet—and I try to show them the techniques I use and why I use them, leading or teaching by example. I do this type of debriefing right after we've finished a case. I don't care if it's been a ten- or twelve-hour negotiation. I sit there with the guy for one and a half, two hours. I say, "Remember I did this, and I did this, and I did this. Here's why I did it that way." And it means a lot. I've had guys two or three years later thank me for that. They thought that was one of the most important things that happened when they were going around. Not only did I tell them the problem, I said this is why I did that, and here is the results. They could see the whole picture that way.

Sure I've got a supervisor, but my relationship with him is okay. He lets me run my show. It has to be that way. My people and I are caught in the middle between the union and the company. If I got caught between them and my boss, then it would be unbearable.

I just have to be on top of anything he might ask questions on. I keep him advised of any significant-impact cases. For example, there's a company out here; it's a really big company. And if I thought they were going to strike, I'd keep him advised. I'd alert him to that fact so we could alert the national office, so they could decide what moves we wanted to make down the road—whether we wanted to accelerate it or put a panel on it. Maybe he wants to get involved in it, or maybe the best we can do is get it to Washington and handle it that way.

So the stresses and frustrations come from the bottom up more than from the top down. Right now the new negotiators are most frustrating. When you're with a guy who's been at the bargaining table for a long time and has been through all kinds of negotiations, that's okay. It's the new negotiator who's inexperienced that's the most frustrating. And the frustration comes in when you're trying to lead them the right way, trying to guide them, and they just won't listen. They think they been there fifty years and they've only been there a day. That's what hurts.

It doesn't hurt my pride or that of my mediators. It's because a calamity is going to occur and we can't do anything about it. People are going to suffer. And a lot of times I know if I had an experienced man in his shoes, I'd avoid this. Maybe he'd walk away from his committee and I could meet him in the restroom or the hall and say, "Jim, you know I know what you want, and I hear what you're saying, but it seems to me that rather than pushing for a three-year agreement you'd be better off with a one-year agreement for what the company's trying to give you. They'll make that compromise; why don't you take it and call it a day." The old negotiator will go along with me, but a new one trying to prove a point, trying to make himself look like a top-notch negotiator in the world, says, "Oh no, I'm going to accomplish what I want. It's got to be done my way!" And I know with my experience that the negotiations are going to go down the toilet and the contract and all that just isn't going to happen. But I can only suggest, recommend, give my best advice and judgment. I can't force anybody to give an offer, take an offer, recommend an offer.

But as I said, if I didn't like it, I wouldn't be in this. Right there at the negotiating table is where the action is. Right there when that contract is about to expire. That's the war zone. If there's a strike, a lot of people are going to lose their incomes, and their families are going to suffer. And on the corporation's side, it might mean the difference between them staying in this community with their manufacturing or not staying. Or expanding or not expanding. So it's a war zone. And I get in there in the trenches with them. And it's tense. Someone's in there with their feet set in concrete, and they're not going to do this or that, not at all. So I get what you call marathon negotiations going. I get them here at 9:00 in the morning and we keep on going until we get something done. That means it could be 2 days, 48 hours. I tell them, "Look, it's not my problem. It's your problem. If there's going to be suffering then you're going to be doing the suffering."

So I turn up the burner, create an atmosphere of tension. This is important. A strike means a lot of people lose. So I push, suggest, be the priest, the psychologist, the torturer. And the deadline starts coming so I freeze the clock and keep going. Then it's over. Sometimes I lose—there's no agreement— but I still come back to work the next day.

Massage Parlor Operator

I set the example and she follows.

The Parlour, located on the outskirts of town, can be easily distinguished from the adjoining buildings by its coat of electric-pink paint. Inside, every customer is greeted by the manager, who is dressed in tight, very short shorts and a long-sleeved top that exposes both her midriff and an appropriate portion of her ample bosom. She welcomes customers cheerfully and leads them to a dimly lit front room, where they can choose between sitting on a stuffy sofa or a plastic chair. She eases herself up onto the front of her desk, which faces both the sofa and the chair, and places one high-heeled foot on a nearby stool in a Mrs. Robinson gesture. Then she explains her business.

A massage from a girl in a negligee is $20. A massage from a girl topless is $25. Specials are . . . well, the way this and other things work is that girls work for tips. Once they're behind those locked doors, they're on their own. Kinda like private entrepreneurs. They get so much for each massage they give. Plus there are tips. Gentlemen want the massage done a little specially, and the girls do it that way and get tips. They have specials they can do. The gentlemen ask for quotes on the specials, and the girls give their prices. (I don't give them a price sheet on the specials. Each girl has her prices, except I set the prices for the massages; the price on massages includes the shower.) My girls are on their own in there. Some charge more than others. Some won't do specials that others will. We just collect all of the basic massage charge and get a percentage of the tip.

Mainly what I do is answer the phone, greet customers, hire and train girls, settle problems that come up, and evaluate the personnel. Then there's the usual stuff—getting someone to come in and fix things, keeping records, banking, paying the bills. My hours are long—10 A.M. to 2 A.M.—but I'm my own boss and I like running the show. Actually, the owner is the boss. I started at the bottom of the totem pole just like everybody else, and then I started learning the business and how to manage it properly. So the owner realized I knew what I was doing and put me in a manager's position. He's now over at the other place. Lets me run the show over here.

On the heavy nights I have five girls working, and for the slower times it's only about two. A customer comes in and picks who he wants to give him a massage. Most gentlemen have a favorite, but if she is busy they have to wait or take who's available. Before they go in for a massage, they pay me, and I send them down that there hall. We got seven rooms down there, three on one side and four on the other.

One of them is the dressing and makeup room for the masseuses. It isn't used by any customers. We also got the Executive Suite. It's got a heated king-size water bed, a table, easy chair, and a small shower. The other five just have a bed and some chairs in them but they all got their own showers. And they all got locks on the doors.

I send a gentleman down the hall to the right room. A girl meets him in the room, and then he comes back out this way after his massage. I ask him if he had a good time. I ask him to come back. And if he's a regular, I ask him if he wants an appointment. But I do that only for a regular.

I'm like any manager. I do a little bit of everything. I greet customers and try to make them feel at ease. I also spend a lot of time on the phone, explaining what we do, giving gentlemen directions, and quoting some prices. In general I try to get gentlemen here and make sure they're satisfied when they're here. But if I get them here in one piece, then the girls can handle the satisfaction side of it. I can give massages too. But it's my own choice. I'm selective. See, if I get too caught up in massaging, then that doesn't leave me free to handle other duties. I have to have another girl to greet gentlemen, answer the phone, etc. Usually if we're packed, I never go back, even for my favorite customers. But there are some exceptions.

I hire and train the girls. They fill out an application form, and then I talk to them personally about their past experience. Then I make my decision. I train them, too. First I give them a written sheet of paper that is a kind of a sales speech. It tells them how to answer questions that gentlemen ask. It lists how much each massage costs and what each massage includes. Then they have to memorize it; I ask them the questions, and they have to be able to give it back to me like I was a customer.

The first few times the lady is chosen [by a customer], I take her and the gentleman into the room and show her how to do it. So he actually gets two girls for the price of one.

I show her how to give a good massage and how to speak to the man. That's kind of my quality control. I set the example and she follows. As I said, it's a good deal for the gentleman—he gets two girls for the price of one—but if he's getting something special then he gets it only from one girl. But gentlemen don't usually ask for specials when there are two girls in the room.

So I go in the room with the ladies to teach them. And sometimes I go in to kind of introduce a new gentleman to a girl; it's kind of a public relations role. And I go in when there's customer complaints. I get in and try to smooth over the situation as best I can whether or not it's the girls' fault or a customer is just being rowdy. Sometimes a customer thinks he's bought more than he gets. Sometimes the girl makes mistakes. I just try to keep everything quiet and smooth things over.

If a girl makes a lot of mistakes, then I fire her. And I have evaluations— each month I tell the owner who has done the most and who has done the least—who gets asked for the least. Those who do it the least eventually get fired. Me and the girls have some problems. This is a hard business, but I let them know right off who's in charge. I tell them when to be here. They gotta memorize my list and do the massages the way I say.

It's not a bad job. I handle my part; the girls give good rubdowns; and the customers leave satisfied. And we got good public relations here. We run a respectable business. We don't allow people to hang around and get rowdy. Sure, the girls provide extras for tips behind locked doors, and they can make arrangements to meet gentlemen later. But the police haven't ever arrested one of our girls or shut us down. No, we've got someone who makes sure that doesn't ever happen.

Paramedic Helicopter Director

Lead them to the decision you want, but make them feel it was their idea. If you get to the bottom line, dictate to them.

When the call came in that our helicopter had crashed, I felt my insides tighten up because I knew we had a pilot, flight nurse, and patient in there.

One of our paramedics in emergency was on the phone to a doctor in another hospital when the doctor said in the middle of a sentence, "Oh my God, your helicopter just crashed." That's all he said, and then the line went out. I quickly put into effect our accident plan; that is, a plan through which certain people are notified as to what they are to do immediately and the priorities of each action. So we implemented this plan, and it took us about twenty minutes to find out that it wasn't a crash, just a precautionary landing.

For twenty minutes, though, things were really tough. There were a lot of quick decisions to be made. There were a lot of immediate things that had to happen. People had to move, and I had to do a lot of quick directing of what people here and there were to do. And I was here, directing over a phone, being essentially blind or ignorant as to what was happening miles away.

When you've got to make decisions fast like that, with limited information, that's when you earn your pay. But that type of situation really suits my leadership style. I approach everything from a very open perspective. I try to use a very analytical approach. I watch the situation and see how it develops. I depend a lot on the information that is supplied to me and never, ever, ever overreact. I try to avoid that at any cost, deemphasizing the pressures and trying to keep everything in perspective.

On the other side of it, I always approach the task with a positive attitude—it will work out okay. I won't use and I can't be forced to use a negative attitude. I always think the job is there; we *will* rise to the occasion and get it done. That's very important, because people take their lead from me. I set the tempo.

I try to work with people in a very creative sense, one that allows them a tremendous amount of flexibility and self-management. I have certain rules that they don't break, but other than those, my subordinates manage themselves. They are very creative people and I want them to use that creativity to the fullest. In general, I just oversee them, and when they start going in a bad direction or if I see the program taking a direction I don't want to see, then I step in. But until that time, I let them do what they want to do. There are times—this is one thing that can be frustrating about this approach—that I see them making mistakes and I want to step in and correct them. But I don't because I want them to learn from mistakes. (Understand that there're some decisions in which you let people learn by mistakes and some you can't. Some mistakes equal death or suffering to the patient or pilot or flight nurse. These you monitor closely in order to correct or avoid mistakes.)

When I make decisions, I do so quickly. What I have learned from my field experience, from my crisis experience in the field, from dealing with people who are deathly ill or very critically ill, has been beneficial to my leadership because it taught me to make *immediate* decisions. You can't look back; the only way you can look back is to learn. It requires you to decide right then and there what to do. And if you don't, then the outcome of that patient, the outcome of that situation is going to be marginal. You're going to take away from the potential outcome. So that's been excellent experience for me and made me the leader I am. It's given me the ability to make those decisions that have to be made.

The other side of it is that I use a book that I call my bible. It's Dale Carnegie's *How to Win Friends and Influence People.* When I deal with people, I use all the points in that book, just because that's the way people like to be treated. That helps for dealing with people in crises and for leading people in crises. If you can be cool and remain cool when people blow things all out of proportion, it helps a lot.

It especially helps with flight nurses, because their personalities are so aggressive that they frequently lose their temper. That provides me with the opportunity to say "Well, look at it a little differently. Let's step back and look at it again." And that's within the role. Being A-type personalities, these nurses have a tendency to lose their tempers because they're perfectionists, for the most part. They're very, very aggressive, and when things don't go the way they want them to, they get very upset.

In my position, I'm always on call, and I have to be available. The other night, for example, I was up teaching a paramedic class, and I got the call to come to the emergency room right away. In this case it was with the alleged helicopter crash. Or, another time, we had a 'copter heading back and it needed fuel, but they wouldn't accept our credit card. (A little hindsight told us there was some problem in the coordination of the flow of the money. Visa had to change their standards a little to offset the bureaucracy here. And we were paying the bill; it just wasn't being received on time.) The pilot was trapped there, so our service was out of action and I had to be accessible to tell him what to do. He called the dispatcher here, who called me, and then I, working with the people at Visa, got it resolved in five minutes. But these are the types of things you've got to be accessible for. I supervise five people directly—my secretarial staff, the paramedic staff, and the chief flight nurse, who directly supervises the individual flight nurses. We lease the helicopter, two pilots and a mechanic from a helicopter company. I interact with these three personnel, although I have no direct supervision over them. So the way that works is that the chief pilot and I interact on a routine basis about problems or changes in format—programmatic changes. I also work very closely with their regional director, who the pilot actually works for.

It's a good relationship, because the pilots and I can sit down and they'll say, "This is a problem." Then I have to take that problem, consider it from the hospital perspective and decide which way we're going to go with that. My interaction with the pilots is kind of a strange thing, appearance-wise, because if you drew the organizational structure there would be no official line between me and the helicopter pilot, even though that's the most important link. It would be a dotted line, simply because we pay their company for a service and the direct responsibility goes back to their company. In an organizational structure sense, that seems strange, but it's real common in this country. I think only one hospital owns its own helicopter.

I have three major functions here—running the helicopters, PR, and teaching paramedics. Keeping the helicopter operations running smoothly takes most of my time. The helicopter provides unique experience because it goes anywhere, anytime, and *rapidly* moves the sick and injured to the emergency room. It's a full-time medical helicopter that transfers patients from accident scenes, between hospitals, etc. We also have the mutual-aid component, where we support the fire department and a number of other agencies throughout this area for the floods and major fires that occur. We have a primary ship there with a spare also provided by the helicopter company. When we go down for maintenace, then we put the spare into service, or if we have two flights at once, then we can press it into service.

While my responsibility is to oversee the helicopter-rescue program, it in general runs itself, and I don't have to deal with the flight-to-flight operations very often. A call comes into emergency. The pilot and flight nurse fly to pick up the patient; they transport him to the pad; and then the hospital emergency staff takes over. I do all the paperwork to make sure everything is in order so they can make those flights without any hitches. The only time I get involved with specific flights is when there's a problem. If they go where they're supposed to go, then I never get involved. I just step back, monitor, and watch where they go. If there are problems with the aircraft, one with the pilot, with the local agency, problems resulting from transport or staffing—operational problems—I take care of them.

It might surprise you, but PR also is a very important facet of my job. We're very big on image because this program has a very high visibility and that's either good or bad depending on the image we have. We're very, very sensitive to that, and we're also very sensitive to the way we interact with the local agencies. If they feel for some reason that there's been a bad interaction, they notify me and I try to pick up and run with it, not let it sit around.

Let me give you an example that'll help explain. A doctor in a nearby town might be offended by our operation or by one of our people. The feedback from that most typically comes back from the pilot or the flight nurse who was on duty that day. So I would talk to both of them individually and try to get as much information as possible and get their impression about the incident. Then, depending on the nature of the incident, I would make a contact back with the physician in the town, or a medical person would. We're really sensitive about medical courtesy. If it were hospital-related, I definitely would make that contact. I'd be on the phone and after picking up information here, I would then come to a decision and take an action based on that. I try to avoid punting or passing the buck, because I despise that and so do most people that I know. Sometimes I have to, but usually I make the decision right then and there.

Good PR requires also that I go out and make presentations about the helicopter service. It, quite frankly, is selling the service. I don't say that to those people, but I describe the service, let them ask questions about it, and at the same time, in a low-key I convince them that it's a good service. I've spoken to Rotary clubs, the Kiwanis, etc., where you really find the pillars of the community. We go out and try to work with them because this type of service requires good public support. A *very* important part of the helicopter service is for it to be accepted by the community.

We saw, very early, some horror stories in other communities, where the service wasn't accepted for some reason. It could be the press. One program had a fatal crash two weeks into the program. (That kind of thing happens in in this industry, and it's accepted that it does; it's not acceptable, but it does happen.) So we wanted to get out very early and start developing a positive relationship, not only with the public but also with the providers—the physicians, agencies, and hospitals—whom we serve.

When I work with the paramedics, there's a creative side and a responsibility side. On the creative side, I get to plan, implement, and develop new programs. Then I have to plow those programs through to the implementation stage. On the responsibility—teaching—side, I'm basically taking students and training them to be aggressive so that they can be successful. You've got to be aggressive when time is short and lives are in your hands. And you train them to be good decision makers. At the same time you can't ever, ever let your guard down in front of that group by being indecisive, because you're training them by example to be decisive.

A constant example has to be set for those people, a very firm example. The worst thing you can do with these students is to be wishy-washy. That statement might lead you to believe that directing paramedics is a dictatorial position. It is. But there's another side in that you can do what Harry Truman used to say, that the best way to handle people is to lead them to the decision you want but make them feel it was their idea. Now, that's what I do in handling the paramedics. That's better than dictating to them what to do. But the bottom line—if you get to the bottom line with them—is you dictate to them and show them examples of what you want done.

Trying to wear three hats—helicopter director, PR man, and paramedic teacher—at the same time can get you very frustrated. You work with a bureaucracy and a lot of bureaucrats. The lack of authority is a problem, too. I know what my authority is and I know where I can or cannot go, but that's constantly changing.

On the positive side, this job has been exceptionally educating to me. And I get to work with everyone from the hospital director to the housekeeper. Everyone has a little different attitude, a different approach, and I learn a lot from each of them. I probably learn the most from the housekeeper.

Most of all, I *love* the pressure here. I thrive on it. That's when I do my best work. I'm not a person who lays things out terribly well in a plan. I don't organize myself as well as other people do because I don't function well if I organize that way. I'm a last-minute-type person. When I speak at meetings or go to a national convention, I don't write the speech until two hours before I give it. I'm a last-minute person and always get the results I want. So I like pressure and I don't function well unless I'm under pressure. That's great here, because there's always the pressure of being behind; I'm always overextended. I like the pressure of always having to make a decision and live with the results. And I like being under the pressure of making important decisions. If I make a wrong decision, then someone could needlessly suffer or die, and if it's the right one, I can reduce suffering and help save some lives.

8

Primum Non Nocere

As noted earlier, leaders are caught in helter-skelter, high-pressure worlds in which they use simple, basic, down-to-earth leadership. It consists of two essential elements—protecting and motivating the troops. On these two pillars, leaders build their individual styles. Perhaps they use a coaching, laissez-faire, participative, democratic, 9-9, system 4, considerate, or autocratic style. Whatever the style, it rests upon a base of protected and motivated troops.

Some leaders abide by a dictum from the Hippocratic oath, *primum non nocere*, which means "First do no harm." Or in modern lingo, "If it isn't broken, don't fix it." Many leaders find that little or no leading is called for, because "leader substitutes" are in place. In that case, it is best to stay out of the way. As the brick foreman has found:

> *"In fact, I don't have to do any managing if there ain't anything new going on. I just walk around looking for mistakes. That's all I got to do. This place runs itself."*

This foreman allows the highly technological structure and the incentive system to substitute for his leadership, thus freeing him to fight fires and look after his men. Up and down the Mississippi, the riverboat pilot relies on the experience of his crew:

> *"Like I say, I don't spend much time telling the crew what to do. Only orders I really give is like when we're making up tow and I see something that will help them do it faster or better—like laying wire a different way—then I tell them. Or at times I go out there and show them how to do something they're not used to.*
> *"You see, a lot of your mates have been out there longer than I have. That's all they want to do. They don't want to become a pilot or captain; they just want to*

stay a mate. . . . They've been out there twenty to thirty years and know more than I do, so I don't have to tell them a thing."

For the Amish sawmill operator, the work ethic eliminates the need for "managin'." Through his comments we sense his pride in the Amish—in their frugality, hard work, charity, reputation, weddings, even their stainless-steel cookware. Within this setting, the operator need only "get them broke in." To exercise strong leadership over his "hands" would be an insult not only to them but also to his own Amish tradition:

"When I'm managin' my hands, there's not a lot I got to do. You get them broke in, show them what to do. Then I get on the logs—or my brother-in-law does— rollin' them in, measuring and sawing them. I push them through, keep them moving. The hands know when the boards come out they got to be stacked and edged. Not a lot of managin' to do. You kind of set the pace and they know what to do. Sometimes you got to make sure they're not gettin' too tired. No need to worry about motivatin' them; we work hard, take pride in it. Never had to tell one of us to work harder. 'Course, I never laid on a man who I didn't know was a hard worker."

In the comments of the Washington-Moscow hotline translator, we again encounter the concept of professionalism. Along with peer pressure and the maturity and self-discipline of the subordinates, it serves as a leader surrogate. In addition, the system downplays the leader's importance. The translators are trained, even overtrained: their knowledge of the rules, procedures, and regulations is exceptional. Also, their mission—the prevention of nuclear war— keeps them from napping.

Finally, the tribal administrator's reflections serve as a bridge between this section and the next, on pragmatism. The old chiefs, he notes, did very little leading, because norms, traditions, and gossip guided Indian activities. Today, the tribal administrator is expected not to lead *unless* there is a problem. Then he muddles through with whatever works—action, examples, participation, planning, and always, patience.

Brick Foreman

Time comes when a supervisor's got to look after his men.

He is sixty-three and a half, one and a half years beyond retirement age. He stands about five feet six inches tall; weighs 190 pounds; is stout with no neck. His head just sits on his shoulders. He wears a hard hat and in every season sports dark blue pants along with a blue long-sleeve shirt.

My philosophy is treat workers right and they'll treat you right. In fact, I don't have to do any managing if there ain't anything new going on. I just walk around looking for mistakes. That's all I got to do. This place runs itself. Used to be we had a foreman who would watch the hackers. They'd be working and he'd just stand there day after day watching them. They didn't like it. Soon they'd start yelling at him to get out of there. Go sit in the office. One came up to him in the yard and said he didn't like the foreman. Starts cussing him. Like, the foreman should have grinned and walked away. But no, he starts shouting and cussing back. And there was some shoving. All this because the foreman kept too close of an eye on these hackers.

I run the brick manufacturing line. Ground clay comes down a shoot into that mixer, where it is mixed with water in a hermetically sealed unit. Then it shoots out in a long solid brick, about seven inches across and three inches in height. This here endless brick comes out of the mixer real fast and gets sand washed into its surface. Then it is cut by wires, and the bricks is laid on a conveyor belt that shoots them down to the hackers. They's twelve of them standing at da belt, and they pick up the bricks and lay them on six-by-six-foot railroad flatbed cars so that they can be rolled into the kilns.

That belt moves fast, but ma boys move faster. They're lean, and they really can grab and load a pile of bricks.

You can hear them talking, shouting to each other—"Give me brick," "More on," "Move it, mother," "Let's go, you mother," "Let's go"—and if you listen, you note they're chanting and coordinating their moves.

You see, all twelve of the hackers are in line on one side of the belt. The first hacker takes all the bricks he wants and in the order he wants—like he takes 4 and leaves 20. He stacks them on the cart and then takes some more. The second hacker takes what he wants from what's left. Like he takes 2, leaves 6, takes 2, leaves 6, and so on. It's up to him. The third hacker takes what he wants, etc., and then the twelfth hacker gets what's left. And them bricks come fast, so he sometimes gets a lot.

Every one of them boys is on a piece rate. The more they stack, the more they make—some earn twenty-nine hours of time on an eight-hour shift. And every day I shift the positions so that every boy gets a shot at the first brick.

These hackers are the only ones that will give me any trouble. Sometimes they like to lay out. Once they're here there's no trouble; if one don't work, then the others get his bricks. They got an incentive system: harder they work, more they make. So I just leave them alone, 'cept I make sure they got plenty of music. See that white boy up there in the T-shirt, he likes different music than that white boy down there. Give them what they want, I say. All hack workers need music.

Had one hacker, stout like me. Worked hard but just couldn't hack it. Fired him. Have to be thin and quick like these boys. Age is no problem; got to be thin and have a style, or a rhythm. See that black boy there, he's fifty-one and still one of my best.

I got twenty-eight men working under me, and back when we were working three-and-a-half- to four-hour days, we didn't have no problems. People wanted to work. Needed the work. Now we're up to working seven days and need more men, I'm afraid we'll get into some problems. But I can handle them. I handled all those marijuana problems, so I'll handle the next one that comes up.

I don't have much education, never finished high school, but my common knowledge, my hands, ability to get along with people, changing with the times helps me. I get a man here early—6:00 A.M.—each day to get the machines up; then I come in about twenty minutes 'til seven and check on him and the machines. Then we run this place flat out, and I walk around to chat with the people and point out mistakes.

I like people, and I don't have to work, but I think I'll keep on doing it as long as I'm useful. I'll quit when I ain't helpful. I need to go out to make sure the line is full, to measure the brick, to mark the carts so that people down the line know how to fire them.

That's about it. Sure, I got a boss, the plant manager, but he doesn't do a thing. We supervisors carry him. I guess they had this fellow that didn't have anything to do, so they made him a plant manager [*laughs*].

This place just runs itself. The clay comes in, a presser presses out brick. Another machine cuts them and lays them on a conveyor belt. And everybody works hard. The more bricks loaded and coming out, the more they make. You'd think them boys would like to see the maker or conveyor belt break down. No way! Something breaks down, everybody's over there to fix it. Everybody's on the incentive system—piece rate—and the money's good. They're union. They make good wages for this part of the country, and they like to work hard.

Don't have any people problems here. Like I said, we carry my boss, so he don't bother us. Sometimes a boy will get to layin' out. Say he comes in here at the front of the line and works like a dog all day. Say he earns twenty-five hours. Well, he knows he don't have to come to work for two days, and he's still ahead of the game. So he might lay out, do a little drinkin' or fishin'; tell his wife he's gone to work. That don't cause no problems; we got them boys there, who's pickin' up scrap. They're dying to be hackers, so we just put them on the line. Maybe the other hackers just decide to handle it themselves; they want a little extra money to put some meat in the pot. That's okay by me.

Sometimes I'll say to a boy what's laying out, "Okay now, listen, boy. You're messin' up, and if you lay out anymore, I'm gonna fire you." That *always* works. I don't usually say much, so when I do they listen. Usually everybody's here; the machines are running. Everybody's part of the line, and if they want to make good money, they work hard.

Sometimes we do get a problem from a 'ministrator up the line. Like with a new rule that if you're out a day that you got to bring a doctor's excuse. And if you don't, then you get a warning. Well, lots a times a man is sick enough to stay out and don't need a doctor. Say he gets the flu. Go to the doctor, and you can't get out for under $30.

I'd be embarrassed to give a man a warning in his file for not having a doctor's slip. And it'd embarrass him. Here he's been with the company for thirty odd years with no warnings, and I put one on him. So I don't do that; time comes when a supervisor's got to look out after his men.

Riverboat Pilot

On the Mississippi, heading south is pure pressure.

A lot of people, they got the wrong impression of a pilot or a captain on a riverboat. They always want to think of Mark Twain. It ain't nothing like that. Basically my job on the boat is getting it up and down the river. While I'm on watch, I'm in charge of the guys who tie and fix the boats, but as for being the main man on the boat, that's the captain's job.

Different size boats got a different size crew, but the big line boats I work on have about ten to fourteen men on them. When I'm on watch and doing the tow work, I'm over the mate, the second mate, and two deckhands.

I work the back watch—that's from noon to six in the evening and then midnight to six in the morning. The captain's watch is just the opposite. Now your line boats average from 140 foot to 200 foot long, and they're anywhere from 40 to 55 foot wide. Your tow, which is pushed in front of the boat, is usually 25 boats, 5 long and 5 wide. You don't ever go over 5 long going down; you always go wider. If you have 30 barges, that would be 5 long and 6 wide, because you don't want to go over 1,000 feet long. A barge averages, say, 200 foot long, so you've got a 1,000 foot of tow out there, plus the boat is 200 foot. And each barge is about 35 foot wide, so with 6 of them that's 210 foot wide. So heading south you've about 1,200 foot long and 200 foot wide—that's a mighty big piece of real estate to be moving on the river.

Pressure is the name of the game when you're heading south. Of course, a lot of it depends on the boat, the tow, the performance of the boat, the river stage. Lot of these bridges in particular can get mighty bad; like the Vicksburg bridge is a real bad bridge. It's just a real bad set—it's in a bend for one thing; then right there at the bridge is a hard set. On the Vicksburg side there's the piers and you got to hit the channel just right to make it, and if you don't, you hit the bridge. There's been a lot of barges hit the Vicksburg bridge, the Greenville bridge, and the Cairo bridge. There's a lot of barges sunk there. Lot sunk on the Cape bridge too, the water's just running so much faster there and you just got to do it right. You can't stop and try again. Once you start making a bridge, after you get past a certain point, there's just no stopping. You got to go.

A good pilot will see when he's getting into trouble and do what he's got to do to get hisself out of trouble. But a lot of people can't tell when they're getting into trouble, and those are the people that have all the accidents. It's too late to correct it when they do see that they're getting into trouble.

Pressure is just the name of the game when you're southbound. Northbound is easier compared to your southbound. You're going slower and you can stop in a few hundred feet because you're going up river and you got the current pushing you back. You just pull up the throttle and you stop in a little bit.

The other way you got all your weight. I think a 30-barge tow is 45,000 tons, not counting all the steel in the barge itself. It takes *miles* to stop, and some places you can't even stop. It depends too on where you're trying to stop at. Last week the Mason Landing was a real bad place to try to stop. Lots of people been having accidents down there. You can't stop at the place at all. It's just a bad bend. Corps of Engineers come in there and put some dikes across there, trying to cut all the bar out and help us to get down through there. But it ain't done no good so far. There's still just no stopping at that place.

Once you board the boat, you stay on for two round trips from St. Louis to New Orleans. That's an average of 30 days. Sometimes it's 28 and sometimes 36, but over a year it'll average 30 days. This last trip we took 25 loads of grain down to New Orleans from St. Louis. We delivered them and brought 25 empties back up. We didn't stop to relax at New Orleans. No, we cruised the New Orleans area until we had 25 empties, and then we headed on back to

St. Louis. Going down we had 25 loads probably averaging fifty thousand bushels a barge. That's quite a bit of grain. If we're lucky, we don't come back with empties; we load them with phosphate, fertilizer, or something like that at New Orleans and bring them back up. That's where the money's at, really. Your loads northbound pay more money than the loads southbound, but most companies don't have much going northbound.

'Course, going south is a lot faster. You average 10–12 miles an hour going down. Coming up you're doing pretty good to average 6, even though you're empty. See, you're going with the current, and the southbound traffic has the right of way. The northbound traffic has got to wait for the southbound to come down a small bend where there's no meeting. You got to wait for a southbound boat, and since there might be 3 or 4 of them in a row, you can get hung up 4 or 5 hours at a time.

You got a whole bunch of radios—sidebands where you talk to your company, VHS where you talk to other boats. So that you don't meet nobody in a bad place, you monitor your radio all the time so you know where everybody is at. You always check if there's anybody coming when you come up to a place where you can't meet another boat.

That's the major portion of my job. I don't spend much time ordering the mate and deckhands around or following what the captain says. I got to communicate with these other pilots. When you're coming upriver, you got to check at the tight holes and then wait. When you're heading downriver, you make sure they know you're coming.

When you're northbound, you ask the southbound pilot if he's far enough away so you can squeeze through a tough hole before he gets there. If you think you can make it, you tell him. Of course, there're a lot of guys who'll make you wait even though you could make it through, but you pretty much have to do what they say. They can help you out, slow down a little bit, pull back and run slow to help you get up through a hole. Usually if you been sitting there for a while, they'll give you a chance.

When I'm southbound, I usually try and help the other fellow out. If a pilot calls me, tells me what he's got in tow, the time he's making, and says he thinks he can make it, then I pull back to help him get far out of the hole. I don't want to go in the hole with him in there, especially at some of the bad places, like bridges. You don't want to meet nobody at a bridge. If you get caught southbound in a tight, fast hole, that's it. You can't stop, so there better not be anything else in there.

There's a lot of money involved, for one thing. Each of those empty barges costs $300,000; you've got thirty of them, and that's not counting the wheat or whatever, that can cost up around $100,000 a barge. You're looking at 10 to 12 million dollars of barges and cargo, so you want to pay attention to what you're doing with it. You don't want nobody coming up in there with you and taking a chance of sinking something or getting you in trouble.

It really sets you back when you have an accident. I never sunk no barges, but I've had accidents. I've hit the bank before and got too deep down in a bend trying to steer places. Just can't steer it; just wouldn't push out. And I've run aground when water got too low before. But I ain't never sunk no barges yet; I'm not saying that I never will, because I've been close to a lot of bridges, but so far I've not hit any.

When I'm piloting, I'm the only one in the wheelhouse. You don't got nobody there steering for you. You've got your levers there. There's no wheels like in the old steam boats; just a couple of levers for your steering and a couple for your back rudders. Then there's your throttles, and you've got the radios and the depth finders. They started using those depth finders about ten years ago. Now most all have it. It doesn't help much southbound, but northbound you can check your places out, like you run up close to a buoy line in a bend and you can tell the next boat coming down that I got fifteen foot of water on my red buoy line.

In the wheelhouse, you're in command. If you want to call the cook and tell her you want your steak rare on Saturday night, then you can. Of if you want to call Pittsburgh, your sideband is right there. Your lights, radars right there next to you, everything is in reach where you can just get it. And you can phone home.

My job is to keep that boat running, because them boats are expensive. They're expensive to buy and they're expensive to operate, especially with the high cost of diesel fuel. When I first started on the river, it cost six cents a gallon; that was when the river business was good. We got to keep this boat moving to make money; it costs about $800 an hour to operate it. So my job is to keep it moving.

I keep it moving, but like I say, I don't spend much time telling the crew what to do. Only orders I really give is like when we're making up tow and I see something that will help them do it faster or better—like laying wire a different way—then I tell them. Or at times I go out there and show them how to do something they're not used to.

You see, a lot of your mates have been out there longer than I have. That's all they want to do; they don't want to become a pilot or captain; they just want to stay a mate. Mate's a good job out there, pays good money. They've been out there twenty to thirty years and know more than I do, so I don't have to tell them a thing. Sometimes you get on a boat where a fellow is green, a mate or someone don't know a whole lot; then you have to show them or help them.

When we're making tow, I tell the mate how I want the barges arranged and tell him where we're going to pick up a barge at. Then I call down on a walkie-talkie to tell him to get set up to pick up or drop a certain barge. I tell him what to do and he does it. As far as other chores on the boat, the captain handles getting all that done.

Me and the captain, it depends on the captain you're working for. Got some guys who're really hard to work with. They want it done their way, and their way is the only one that's right. But most of the time you make decisions together. Say we're going to pick up 25 barges at St. Louis and drop 10 before we get to New Orleans, then we'll usually talk about how we're going to do it and stuff like that between us. We both agree on it, and that's the way we do it.

You got to be able to work with the hands and the captain, but being a good pilot depends a *whole* lot more on communicating well with the other pilots. You got to cooperate with them moving up and down the river. What is more, I depend on them. Like if I was off for 30 days, and when I left there was 20 foot of water on the Memphis stage, say it's now about 5 foot, I need to know that because there'd be bad places. I've got to get information from them.

We get to talking, helping each other out, and you get to know other pilots real well out there. You couldn't pick them out of a crowd, but you just talk to them for years out there, and they tell you where the shallow waters are, better stay off a certain buoy, better stay away from a certain place, if there's any hard sets working and all that. You talk a lot to the other boats and help each other out.

I like this job and wouldn't give it up for nothing. I like the money. When you're working regular, the 30 days off is great. And when you're working for a good company you got insurance, disability, and dental.

And being out there is a challenge 'cause there's not many of us. It may not be an elite profession, but it's not the easiest job in the world. When I was working for this other company, we had two airline pilots ride with us and they said I had a harder job than they did, what with pushing what looks like a city block around in the river, using only four levers and a throttle to guide it. 'Course I know it was harder back in the old days when they didn't have no radar, but I know they didn't have the tows we got nowadays—the size, the weight, or nothing else.

I like driving these big boats: 30-barge boats with 6,000 to 7,000 horsepower range or a real good 5,600 horsepower, 25-barge boat. Of course, 30 barges isn't big. Lot of your 10,500's are out there with 40 loads, and that's a lot. You wouldn't think that 10 more added on to that 30 would be that much, but it's big, really big. And it's expensive, and you're under a lot of pressure not to make no mistakes. That's part of the challenge.

What can be most troublesome is to have to rearrange all your barges. You're heading south and you tell the crew to make it up like you want it to be; *then* all of a sudden somebody up the line changes orders on your barges in the middle of your tow. You got to drop some before you thought, and of course it's never a barge on the side that you can just peel off. No, it's always there in the middle somewhere. So you got to dig it all out and put your tow all back together, rearrange them, and it messes up your whole thing. So you got to tell your crew to dig out the barges that you got to drop and then to put the tow all back together. That's a pile of work, and the crew's cussing and swearing and sweating.

Then you start off again with the tow arranged like you think it should be, and then they change the orders on you again. You're never told why. I suppose they sell this grain to some person, then he sells it to someone else while we're on the river, so now we got to drop in a different place. You tell the crew what to do. They don't like it; you know it's got to be done. You don't know why there's a change. They start to think you don't know what you're talking about. It's a real hangover.

Amish Sawmill Operator

Sometimes a fellow like me kind of gets the blues of it.

I got me a good reputation down in the town. So when they'd say, "Where's the Amish? I need to get me some good lumber," the people down there'd say, "Go north up this road, and it's the first sawmill you get to."

About twelve years back, I got married; didn't have no farm, and in fact I's laying in the hospital. Had my leg broke and my buddy I'd been running around with come down to visit me and said, "Joe's gonna sell his sawmill." I said, "Oh my God, I got to buy that sawmill," and I bought it. I never gave no thought 'til I bought it.

He had this guy Lamech working for him from Ohio. He was a square boy. He was a big guy. Not the fastest, but every move he made counted. And he'd really got Joe on his feet in that mill. So I know'd I had Lamech to run it for me for another half year. (That was in August, and he was servin' two years here and had six months to go.)

I's on crutches where I had my leg broke. I's on them from July to December, s'posed to be, but I pitched the crutches around about October. I guess I suffered for it. But anyway in February, Lamech broke his leg. That set him off; he didn't serve no more time, and I's just depending on him. He could run the mill. He's used to it, and I'd worked there but never run the mill hardly. I never had the response on me to take care of the saw. I'd took care of the customers, bought the logs and such as that, but as far as running the mill, I didn't do that.

We had some tough pickin' when we started out. Had nothing, you might say. Had to borrow money to buy the mill. Didn't have a log in the yard. The yard was clean, and had to sell some lumber to pay for another load of logs. Times were rough. But I don't know, with the help of friends and neighbors, and experience, we got on okay. We got a little more money, bought a few more logs, stockpiling them. Then I got too many logs and they rotted on me. Got poor management there, I guess.

Little while after I bought the mill, my father-in-law had a stroke and he was paralyzed. He couldn't do nothing, and he had a renter who was going to quit 'im, and Dad-in-law, he couldn't hardly stand that. He couldn't sleep at night because it was working on his mind. He didn't know what he was going to do with the farm. I went over there one morning. Me and my wife talked it over and I made him an offer, said if he wanted to consider selling the farm, we'd consider buying the farm. We could move home, and we could start dairyin'.

I come back home and my wife said, "What are you going to do if he accepts your offer?" Said, "I ain't worried." That night I stopped in, and Grandma come to us and said, "If you didn't mean what you said this morning, you shouldn't said it, because he fell for it." Oh, I's in trouble; had me a sawmill *and* a farm to run. Work as I had to.

So I got down to work; I got the sawmill paid for; got the house we built paid for; in fact, I loaned quite a bit of money out. But what happened then was I bought a load of timber. I thought I better keep these logs—they're the cheapest logs I'll get. You know, I bought the timber lump sum; therefore, I made money on the timber. Had a lot of logs in the yard for practically nothing. So I stockpiled them; should have shipped them and had some money in my pocket, which I would 'ave if I'd knowed I'd bought the farm. (Fact I paid these loggers to cut and haul the logs for me—paid them $10,000. 'Course I'd turned a lot of logs to pay for it.)

And when we did saw, the loggers brought the logs in here and put them in front. And then the logs in back I couldn't get to because I's using horses—we don't use no tractors. I'd run out of one length of logs, so I bought some more, and that's where I goofed it. When I bought the farm I should have sold more logs.

I like running the mill. You're dealing with the public all the time, and you find all kinds of people when you're dealing with the public. You find them good and you find them bad, but I never found them so bad I couldn't handle them, I guess. I take care of them. People come from about a 50- to 75-mile range to trade with me. In fact, I've got a lot of customers from way off, and there's sawmills between here and there but they come to me. Lot of them come up here and know what they want. They just place the orders. Quite a few give me mail orders—write me through the mail and tell me what they want. I aim to satisfy my customers the best we can. Aim to give them pretty good lumber, but onst in a while a log is bad and we run short on time. Sometimes I take some boards I'd rather not, but I aim to satisfy my customers. I guess that's one reason they keep coming back from so far off.

When you're working with the public, you've got to keep up on your numbers. I's making some boxes for this one company—one of those big companies. I never give it a thought that you'd have to be right on their heels or they wouldn't pay. I'd send an invoice in whenever they got a load of boxes. I guess I's busy; that was in the spring and they quit buying'. Then they come back in the fall, and the guy picking the boxes up said, "Did you get paid for all those we picked up last time?" I said, "Yes, well, I don't know. I guess I did."

He said, "You better check. You know sometimes them big companies, you got to watch them. Sometimes they misplace a ticket or something. You might not get your money. You should have, and if you're keeping records you ought to check."

I just never give it a thought. I figured I'd got my money. I guess I had enough customers, enough money rolling, had enough going that I never give it a thought. So I checked and found that the ticket wasn't paid—two hundred and some dollars. I'd turned it in to this fellow, and he got right on it and got me the money. Then they got some more lumber from me—4-by-4's—and they had the check all ready for me, except they'd left off the tax. So I told them they'd have to pay the sales tax. So the fellow hauling the lumber said, "Give him another invoice," and I did. He said, "We'll either bring it out—the check for the tax—or send it by mail." So all right. Then in the mail comes another check, $319.25; they paid me twice for the same lumber [*laughs*]. Looked good, a $319 tip. And the time before that, they pretty near would have chipped me out of that if I hadn't caught on to it.

Lot of my customers give me a lot of bull, but as long as they do it in fun, I joke with them. Sometimes they just razz me all the time. I have my fun with them. But there's a few guys—like I said before, when you're dealing with the public, you find them all—that you can't just handle good enough. They'd gripe if you'd hang them with a new rope. Them's the type of customers I don't appreciate too much, but I've got customers that make up for that. But I can't complain overall.

And on bad checks, I've had a few. I's had a few fellows come in, get lumber, take off and never paid. I can't collect. But overall, I can live with that.

'Course, my loggers give me a lot of baloney too. They come in here and I measure their logs with my scaling stick to see what I pay them. They call it my cheatin' stick. But I aim to be honest. Always when I'm scaling they gripe; so I just kid with them, tell them, "Don't come back." One hasn't, but he was a scromp, griped wherever he took his logs. He don't get along nowhere. He brought me one load of logs and never come back. Actually he's doing me a favor staying away. I aim to pay what's fair, scale the logs according to my stick, and if he can't get along with that, he better straighten up and stay away. At first he made me feel bad the way he cussed and all that, but then I found he does that every sawmill.

People tell me I'd do better if I had a phone down here. Now, we don't have a phone of our own, but we got this milk station down the way. The creamery put a phone in there, and I've told a lot of guys, the loggers too, about it. All of them kind of rave and carry on that they can't get ahold of me on the phone. Well, I give them that number and there's always someone there. So if they want to call—which they have—somebody's there. Fact is, I've gone there and called them, my customers. Having that phone really gives them a lift, and me too, far as that goes. Using that phone's a good break.

Dealing with the customers and loggers is a snap compared to running this mill. You got bad logs; pay $10 to $12 each for them, and you can't cut nothing out of them. You got to get about 10,000 feet in here before you start sawin'. And once you got them in, it's hard work—hard, hot work. Like today, it's real hot, and if you got any breeze, you can feel it. Now if the breeze is coming from the wrong direction, then it brings the heat from the motor over you, and it's hot, mighty hot. Like last week it was 100 degrees in the shade up at the house, and the wind was coming in from the west over the motor, and I mean it was hot.

Now all this millin' can be automated. You could snake the logs in with a tractor and then use hydraulic lifts and then move the logs with conveyor belts. Lot of cranks could be put in. All my competitors do it that way, not by hand, but that gives them a lot more expense. They put out a lot more lumber than me, but they got to pay for all that automation. They got 10–12 guys working for them, maybe 15, and all them got to be paid.

Me, I just run it myself with my brother-in-law and a hired hand or two. Usually it's just one, Elic. At first when you're breaking them in, you got to tell your hands what to do. Now I just tell Elic what we're sawin', like you get an order or you tell him this guy wants a hundred 1″-by-6″-by-14′.

Elic knows what we're sawing when we start out and just does what he knows to do. Lots of times he takes care of stacking the lumber and I take care of the logs. I get the logs in, run the saw, and he kinda takes care of his end—edging and stacking. He knows what I'm doin', so if someone comes, he takes care of the customer and collects the money. But when it comes to buyin' logs, he won't do that. Scalin' the logs and buyin' them, I can't get him to do none of that. So far, he hasn't done that.

Elic don't run the mill much either. I understand. When I first started, it was scary. I's timid and afraid I'd get the saw hung; afraid I'd tear up something. That's the same with Elic. He just don't trust himself. And I'm trying to develop his trust by having him do more and more. The more you do it, the more you trust youself, and the more different things you do, the more interesting the job is. If he sets down on that end and just edges and stacks all day, the job's not going to be very satisfyin'; it's just boring.

Still, you got to be on your lookout; it ain't going to be too satisfying to lose an arm. It's a dangerous piece of equipment to run. A guy told me yesterday about a shaft breaking off right there and the saw blade took off running all over everywhere. I've heard of fellows who fell in the saw. And I've been caught close enough to that saw so's my hair stood on end. It's dangerous, mighty dangerous. But I've said, if it's supposed to happen it'll happen. If you're supposed to get hurt, you can get hurt going down the road in your buggy. You've got to have your trust in something else.

When I'm managin' my hands, there's not a lot I got to do. You get them broke in, show them what to do. Then I get on the logs—or my brother-in-law does—rollin' them in, measuring and sawing them. I push them through, keep them moving. The hands know when the boards come out they got to be stacked and edged. Not a lot of managin' to do. You kind of set the pace and they know what to do. Sometimes you got to make sure they're not gettin' too tired. No need to worry about motivatin' them; we Amish work hard, take pride in it. Never had to tell one of us to work harder. 'Course, I never laid on a man who I didn't know was a hard worker.

I like runnin' it. Sometimes a fellow like me kind of gets the blues of it. I guess everybody else does too, maybe. Get tired of it. I get to thinking sometimes, Shoot, it'd be a more quiet and peaceful life to be out on the plow, out on the farm, you know. Not working with public, just by yourself, with the horses, work with the family. But more or less, I enjoy running the mill. 'Course, there are days when things go wrong; you have them days on the farm, too, I guess.

I've modernized this place pretty much. We don't believe in using tractors, but motors like this is okay. They don't move themselves. Twelve years ago I bought that motor new, and it's had one valve job done on it. I tell you, the motor's been good. It's in good shape. It runs good; I change oil and use good oil. I think it pays to take good care of your equipment.

The first years, this thing—motor, saw, and tracks—wasn't on level concrete, so when you'd get a big log on your carriage, the track sagged one way and then another. And about every day you had to shim it up; your saw's got to be perfectly level, and your track has got to be perfectly level. If you don't, when your log is run through here, it rubs on your saw and makes it run hot. Then you get odd-shaped lumber. And you got to have the saw rehammered to get the tension back in it. I've had my saws hammered quite a bit in the first years, but after I learned from experience and put in a concrete floor, I haven't had to have any hammered.

I don't use tractors, phones, or any of that because I'm Amish. We—the clan of about three hundred families—are from Pennsylvania and we moved out here to the Midwest some time back. Some way we's "hook-n-eye Dutch." (We're not Mennonites—Mennonites have automobiles and tractors but dress the same as we do.) "Hook-n-eye" because we don't wear buttons on our clothes, just hook 'n eyes. Aim to wear black and our womenfolk wear a bonnet. They got a white cap under the bonnet, and they hardly ever take that cap off. They don't wear no makeup, don't cut their hair, they can't wear jewelry. 'Course sometimes they got some—a pin or something—and put it on the inside [*laughs*], where we can't see it. We got watches but no rings.

At home our women use stainless steel cookware—best you can buy—and don't use no aluminum or porcelain or granite or nothing like that. We got a sink, but that's as far as we go. We don't have no cabinets. Got hardwood floors that really shine, finished right to a tee; no rugs. Curtains are just a blue piece of straight material. There's no electricity; got gas lights, and it's just as good as 'lectric lights. Don't know if you've even seen gas lights or not, but they're real white.

We marry on Tuesday and Thursday, mostly Thursday, but that's the only days we marry. We're not supposed to have any money until we're twenty-one; when we got paid, our money goes to our daddy. That's the reason I didn't have money to buy the sawmill. So we're gettin' older 'fore we get married. And we marry in the clan, but it's distance. Lot of us go away and get married; a girl married a fellow in New York a while back.

When we have a weddin' a lot of people come. The wedding and a reception is at the house. There's a lot of food. Boys wait on the tables. And after the reception there's a sing-spiration, where all the men sing.

After we marry, we get our own place or stay on our daddy's farm. If we stay on hissen, we'll build a separate house. You'll notice there'll be two or three houses at the same place. We'll stay and work the same place, but we always say, "There's no house big enough for two families."

Girls stay and work for their parents until they're twenty-one. They work out a lot—help other women clean house; they pull weeds out of bean fields, chop corn, and other stuff—you know. They'll all finally get married, then go with the husband, have ten to fifteen kids; that helps when it comes to dairyin', 'cause all milkin's by hand. Some of our families just live on about ten acres, but they work out right smart.

We like big families; most of us aim to have ten to twelve children. We send them to our own schools. Here we got five schools, and 'ave one of our girls who graduated from the school to teach it. It's got eight grades.

Lot of people think we don't pay taxes, but we do—but not Social Security—we don't give it and we don't take it. And we have our own school and pay our own teacher. School's for eight months and there's a week off in the fall called huskin' period so the kids can help gather corn. Then the last day there's a picnic; everybody that's got kids at school and all others too that wants to take food and have a big dinner.

We also got our own churches and preacher. And when anybody's got to go to the doctor and hospital and has a sizable doctor bill—most of them are—we all make up the money and pay the bill. The clan makes up the bill.

We practice what we believe. We milk on Sunday, but that's all the work. We don't go to the field; we don't help nobody; and we don't transact no business. If we got a sign out on the road—"Eggs for Sale"—the sign will say "No Sunday Sales." Or when Saturday night comes, we take the sign down or throw an old feed sack over it 'til Monday.

When we work, we work hard. Anyone'll say we got a good reputation as workers; our youngins' are 'bout the only people that people can get to help to work on the farm. We do good work. Fellow down the road here shoes

horses. He don't shoe many for us anymore; just for English [non-Amish]—
he shoes for all these saddle clubs. Now you got to have an appointment
to get a horse shod down there; he shoes that many horses. Now he don't
even farm anymore; he just shoes horses.

We farm with horses. Some have motor units. When one of us buys a
tractor, he takes out the motor and puts it on the runnin' gear of a tractor
and pulls it around with a team.

We raise what we eat, and some sell strawberries. One neighbor gathered
near on 350 quarts of strawberries yesterday. That's a lot of bendin', wasn't it?

When we're not busy, we don't watch TV. We go out and pull weeds and
stuff like that. In the wintertime our boys like to ice-skate. We hunt, and
the girls read a lot and quilt and make rugs to sell; we don't have rugs. 'Course
I just as well should say this: some of our boys they have transistor radios
hid out at the barn. They're not supposed to, but they have some 'cause they
like country music. 'Course I don't have that at my mill.

Like I said, people come up here looking for the first sawmill—mine. Well
this other sawmill got started down the road, so when people's coming north
on this road looking for the first sawmill—mine—they caught him first [*laughs*]
because now he's the first one. 'Course I didn't care, because I always had
more than I could do. 'Course down in the town when they heard this new
mill's runnin', why, they'd tell people to go to the second sawmill to get your
best lumber.

Washington-Moscow Hotline Translator

How can a system give one person so much responsibility?

The hotline between Washington and Moscow is not what you think it
is. It isn't a telephone hookup with a translator somewhere on the line. Rather
it's a radio-teletype net. Originally it came through high-frequency radios and
land-line telephones. But they had so much trouble in the system during sunspot
activity that the high-frequency net was not reliable. Also the cable in the
marine telephone system sometimes failed or was cut. For example, there was
once a fire in New York that wiped out the cable so that we had nothing
but high frequency.

Well, the link is so vital that you cannot afford to have all of your communications broken. Therefore, they began using a satellite network using
the U.S. Intel Satellite and the Soviet Molnia—this is the Russian word for

lightning. Our signal goes through our satellite, and their signals go through theirs. We receive Molnia signals, and they receive Intel signals. The signal itself is encrypted, using cipher devices at both ends, and it's decrypted at the receiving end. The Russians always transmit in Russian, and we transmit in English. That is, our signal goes through a cipher device in English. It goes out through the transmitter to the satellite and then down to a receiver in the Soviet Union. Then it's through their decipher device, and it's printed out in English on their end. They have translators at their end who translate the English into Russian, just like I take the Russian and translate it into English and pass it to the White House. The actual mechanisms for relaying the message to the president are classified.

Most of the time when the line is "hot," it's with high-level messages. It's not used for State Department traffic, communications, or routine ambassador correspondence. It's strictly a line of communication between the two heads of government.

From the time the president makes a statement until it's in Moscow is really short. There's no way I can tell how long it takes the president's message to come to me, but once it is here we have it in Moscow in about one or two minutes. There are certain mechanical delays, like typing out the message, but other than that the communication is instantaneous.

How did a navy man get into this? The navy is seagoing, but if you don't want to stay at sea your whole career, you develop a subspecialty, which is a job category which is predominantly ashore. With this, you can perform useful service when you rotate from sea.

There are various things you can go into—training, education, etc.—that relate directly to the at-sea experience. Others are service-oriented, such as the hotline, which are in support of other strategic missions. The hotline very definitely is this, because the purpose of the hotline is to prevent nuclear war.

Years ago I decided that the world political situation was such that the U.S. was going to be dealing in one way or another with the Chinese and the Soviets. It was a question of whether I wanted to go into the Soviet or the Chinese side of the defense mission. I'm not entirely sure why I elected the Soviet side, but I did. The language training followed, with the original plan that I would go into military intelligence analysis when I was ashore.

My major loves have always been the ships and sea, but the well-rounded military officer cannot stay at sea. You have to come ashore, learn your staff duty, and gain some more expertise, because a ship is a small world. Once you learn all there is to know about a ship, then you have to come ashore to grow. Then you go back to sea with a larger ship and more responsibility.

So I saw this training as a key to enhance my service career ashore. This would give me more responsibility than some special-services job in which I would be counting golf balls or tennis balls. I wanted to be in a responsible position with challenges and what have you.

I took the basic Russian course on the East Coast. I took an intelligence tour for one year. I went back for several tours at sea; then I competed for the hotline position successfully and took intermediate and advanced training in Russian. I was certified for the hotline and took this position. In my command here there's just me—the translator—and my equipment communications technician, usually on E-8 or E-9. We're both of such high rank not because of the sophistication of the equipment or the difficulty of the job. We're here because we have the maturity and the discipline to stay with it. We are never caught napping. It would be difficult to keep an eighteen- or nineteen-year-old interested over long periods of time; his mind would wander. We older people have the self-discipline.

Here we translate and keep up with the mechanics of the system—the network of communication, how to keep up with and locate the president in any given situation, where is he in the world, and what equipment we use to get this traffic to him. We always track the president, and depending upon where he is, we use different techniques and equipment to get to him. If he's airborne, you're talking radio. The cryptic devices are different. We have one set for airborne, one for in the White House, and one for when he's in the States. This communications package goes with him, and we have to keep up with where he is and how to get in touch with him.

Plus we test the equipment very often as he travels around. We send dummy messages to the president's team and they send them to us to make sure that the equipment is active and that it will work. Simultaneously we make tests with the Soviet terminal. During each sixty-minute period, we transmit test messages to them. In turn, they transmit messages to us. Once in sixty minutes is a minimum; however, I can do it more often. If I have equipment that I'm a bit concerned about—it's shaky or I think it is—then I might want to test that equipment more often to isolate the problem.

Our messages to the Soviets are carefully selected to avoid anything to do with politics or diplomacy, armaments, treaties, or anything like that. We use a lot of Mark Twain and selected passages from magazines like *Reader's Digest*. *Reader's Digest* is chosen because the articles tend to depict the happier side of being an American.

If the Russians are having problems receiving, they will send us messages telling us so. But if they're getting plain copy, then it's up to them to translate it.

According to the memorandum of agreement between the two nations, each nation is responsible for the interpretation of the other nation's correspondence in the other nation's language. They interpret what we mean and we interpret what they mean. There have been several cases that were comical and a little embarrassing from a professional point. Despite the fact we are fluent in the Russian language, we do see messages that are not entirely clear. To understand them you would have to have the historical background; you would have to have lived during that era; or Granddad would have to have told you these things—the things the well-educated Russian citizen would know. An adult American who started to study Russian in his twenties, however, will not understand these terms. We're fluent, so we don't get thrown by words that embarrass tourists. For instance, we know that "hot dog" in Russian means a bitch in heat or that "jello" is translated about twenty-eight different ways. But some words and messages can give problems. For example, we had a test message that referred to a device which in Russian was "starie byuick." It was overtaking other vehicles out in Siberia. We had a great deal of difficulty in translating these words—an adjective-noun combination. So we passed our problem to our native instructor, who handled the retraining, and he couldn't translate it. He had ideas. He guessed it could be a form of troika, a vehicle pulled by three horses, because it was overtaking these other vehicles drawn by one horse. Ultimately we were forced to go back to the Soviet terminal and ask them if they could tell us what this adjective-noun combination meant. There was quite a delay, several days. Apparently, they had just sent the text and not bothered to comprehend it fully. Finally they came back and stated that they were not entirely sure, but the term had something to do with a General Motors vehicle that was passed to the Soviet Union during Lend Lease. The adjective "starie" means old, and "byuick" is the Buick. This was a type of round-robin way of bringing English back home by way of the Russian. And it gave us all quite a lot of fun.

There are a lot of questions that come up from the Russians—for example, they might want to know what Mark Twain means—and we are very careful to answer them. I can't say that there is warmth over the line. We do not chitchat. But there is a great deal of professionalism on both sides. When either side has difficulties, the other is quick to respond or assist in any way that they can.

We also get to know who is on the line, because during the call-up the sending person will have a certain rhythm—his "fist"—with which he strikes the keys. We recognize them, and they no doubt recognize us. In dealing with those people, I get the very clear opinion that they are as well trained as we are.

Both sides know we have our "fists," but it isn't necessary to worry about it because this is *not* an intelligence mission. We are *totally* separated from the intelligence side because our purpose is not to gather information; rather, it is to avoid nuclear war.

There are no names exchanged, no "How's the weather in Moscow?" There is no chitchat. All communication is professional—discussing equipment problems, translations, and things of that sort. This is no place for chitchat. We never let the sophistication, the discipline of the operation fall down in any way. If you become lax between "hot" messages, then you might also be lax when the line is "hot."

We are so professional because of the level of responsibility here. We all have a basic respect for professionalism, and we pull it up when the job demands it. Our people are so professional because they are heavily screened, and they're all long-term career people who have proven their professionalism. Then there's the nature of the mission. When you're working directly with the president, you're not going to be making mistakes. Plus you don't allow people in here who will make them.

We are the direct link between the president and the leader of the Soviet Union. If we don't do our job well, then the link is broken. We all know that, and we behave accordingly. So what we have here are mature people who are professionals and who know that the job they're doing is very important. On my shift, it's just me and my technician. That—commanding only one subordinate—has been quite a change for me. At sea, with my rank, I commanded a very large number. But it only takes two of us to do this job.

Leadership in this situation is unique for me. The system is established in such a firm way that there is very little need for leadership decisions. The people who have the responsibility know what they're doing and do it. There are some administrative duties that go along with this. But by and large the management and leadership responsibilities were made when the organization was established. We have to know what the rules and regulations are, train the new people that come on board, do our job well, and make sure the tech does his well.

I'm probably the only leader who'll say this to you, but I've never had a single leadership problem with my subordinates here. Of course, that's unique for me, too. In all my other assignments, I've had problems. But there are none here. There are no problems with people not knowing how to do their jobs, not wanting to do their jobs, or being lazy. There are some administrative decisions, like someone is ill or has to be replaced and the first priority for replacing him has difficulties taking his place. These are just problems of administration, coordination, and getting the job done. These are mechanics, and you'll have them everywhere.

You have to realize that these people are very, very carefully screened, and they went through an intensive training program. The attrition rate even after selection was very high. I can't recall a single individual, officer or enlisted, who was assigned to the line and was later replaced. The screening and training is that effective.

The morale is high here. We—the ten translators and eight technicians— get together socially. And there's strong peer pressure. We file all of our translations and then go back and critically review each others' versions.

In general, I like it here. For the first six months the thrill of being here kept me real sharp; now my knowledge and expertise are the driving forces. By the time the thrill is dulled, you know fully what your responsibilities are, and the thrill is replaced by professionalism.

I like the responsibility because my decisions are vital, and if I don't do my job when I'm called upon, then we will have a disaster. When I say "we" I'm not referring to just the people in the United States and the Soviet Union but to the people in the entire world. It's rare that an individual is placed in this kind of position. Yes, I'm proud of it, and yes, I take it very seriously. We all do. Where else do you find that your decisions mean so much to so many millions of people? We hold this responsibility in awe. How can one person such as I (we all know that we're basically human) have this responsibility? How can a system give one person so much responsibility? Yet it does.

And there's just one translator here, but my training is and has been so intense that I can handle it. If you think of the nature of the correspondence that's exchanged, you'll find we're talking about two languages that are simple—subject and predicate. We're not talking about a literary work where you're bringing in flowery adjectives. We're talking about an event, the description of an event, and an opinion of that event from one side to the other: "We are concerned about your actions in . . ." That's pretty straightforward Russian or English. We are overtrained, if you will, because the correspondence that is passed is quite simple compared to the translation duties we perform between the real messages. So there is no concern about a mistranslation or that I can't handle the job.

I constantly think about what it will be like when the real thing comes. I will do the same thing; I won't panic or make mistakes. I will do exactly the same thing, although the stress factor will be out of sight. I've been trained, and I won't panic. My mission is the prevention of nuclear war. That's big stuff, and I'll accomplish it.

I was in various leadership positions on the seas before I came here, and that has helped me as a leader here. We operate in the Pentagon, and we're constantly dealing with senior military officers and senior White House people. The ability to deal with these senior people, to understand their needs and fill their needs, is important. I learned that in my other assignments. Certainly it helps. I am constantly dealing with senior decision makers who do not have enough information to make decisions, and they depend upon me and my team to give them the information they need. In coming up through the ranks on board ships I learned how to do this.

A lot of people think of good leaders as people who can handle the men under them. In many cases it's the capability to deal with people above you that's important. Sure you've got to manage your subordinates well, but at the same time you've got to deal with your superiors. You and your men are part of a team. I learned that early on ships, and it's been useful ever since.

Tribal Administrator

> There's a norm or feeling that I as an administrator am just another Indian. I'm advisory, like the old chief two thousand years ago.

When Kit Carson came through this valley, he tried to buy food from these Indians. They refused payment, saying, "Bread is to eat, so eat." They have been here for over two thousand years; they were not shipped in here from somewhere else. And they have never been in any kind of state of war with the United States. Traditionally their homeland was all up and down this valley and into Mexico, but now they have been constrained quite a bit; they currently have about 387,000 acres here and twelve thousand members of the tribe. These people have always had a reputation as being hardworking. They were farmers—agricultural—not gatherers. They dug canals, irrigated, or used plain ole river-flood irrigation. Relied on that for thousands of years.

As for their leadership, it's always been rather loosely structured, and I think that's the way it is in most Indian organizations. You don't seem to see organization going up; it's more along flat lines. What leaders they have had over the past came to the forefront because of a special situation—a bad crop year, some outside danger. The traditional enemy of these people was the Apache, who used to raid them; the Apaches were a nomadic tribe and lived at the higher elevations. A leader would arise or be appointed to deal with the situation.

And they had no laws. The only written information they had at all was the calendar stick, which would tell what happened in past years—big drought this year; lot of people died of such and such this year; twelve witches killed this year. They just followed norms and unwritten traditions. They were agriculturalists, and since this was such a harsh environment, they didn't have much of a choice but to get along with one another. This whole river valley is full of ruins, and one of the theories is that they only banned together and built these structures in times of stress. Where did these people go? They didn't go anyplace. Once the stress had passed, they dispersed again. They went back to their farming. They used gossip as a kind of a leveler. Someone got too high, then he was taken down by gossip.

This tribe was pretty well taken out of the agricultural business by the non-Indians. The river out here used to be a freeflowing river, and they raised all their crops from it. It's dry now because all the water has been diverted upstream. The records indicate that when they had water, they were highly successful farmers, in competition with the non-Indians.

Their thinking about leadership arose from that agricultural background. Everybody got together and worked to do the farming. Everybody had to do his part. There weren't some people telling others what to do. When there was a problem, everybody got involved in solving it. There was an attempt to solve all the problems and to make everybody happy. Also there was an enjoyment in being involved in the decision making. When they had a leader, a chief, he didn't have all that much authority. He was just another Indian, who, because of circumstances that were prominent at that time, became the leader. And this position wasn't sought, because these people didn't value authority.

Today there's still a norm or feeling that I as an administrator am just another Indian. I'm advisory, like the old chief two thousand years ago. And I have to take that into account. Exercise of authority by anyone on an Indian reservation normally has to be kind of loose. It can't be any kind of authoritarian, straight line. Rather there has to be a wide dissemination of information. Give you an example. About a year ago we were in a negotiation with a group who wanted to build a football stadium—an NFL football stadium—on our land. That took a great deal of politicking—taking it to economic development, taking it to the people involved, trying to outline the benefits, trying to find out what the fears were, going to the council, and their going to the people.

Here I have to go through a lot of people to get anything done, and a lot of times it's just by force of personality and good preparation that it gets done. I've got all angles covered.

I'm working with a group of people that expects me to be one of them unless there's a problem. If there is a problem, they want someone to assume responsibility. For instance, I went to a committee yesterday about a problem. A large bill had been received. My only purpose in going to the committee was to find out whether or not they wanted to pay the bill. Well, that went round and round for almost two hours. Everybody talking about everything. Finally I said, "All I want to know from you is whether or not you want the bill paid." And with that, there was an immediate motion to that effect, and it was seconded just like that. That was really all I wanted to do in there. And finally just by coming out and saying it, it was decided.

Many times outsiders will come in here with a proposal and they ask me how I feel it will go. I just have to say it's different every time. It can be a cut-and-dried proposal which goes to the council or a group of the people, and it ends up being tabled. Or it goes round and round, chasing itself around. I don't get too frustrated with that, because the tribe hired me to do a job and I have to realize that there are certain parameters I have to work under, and that's just one of them.

In sum, you could say my leadership style is action-oriented. When people come to me with a problem, I handle it, or I get someone to do it. With a general problem I'm very, very sure to get group participation. Sometimes the ball gets tossed into my court on specific things and I have to resolve them. The tribe hired me because of my [financial] background. This requires me at times to give them information or tell them something that will go against the grain or against their tradition. Yet that's what I'm paid for.

Now, when I screw up, they're like any other group; they are quick to tell me. But by and large they're very subtle, or they go through other Indians. I've been called into the governor's [head of the reservation] office many times and he'll say, "I don't think you should do this." For example, we needed a manager on one of our farms. We had a tribal member who had worked there for years, and I thought he was adequate as a manager. So I put him in as a manager and I got this feedback on that almost right away. I was called on the carpet with "How could you do this? This guy has told us a hundred times he doesn't like the business, that he isn't concerned with the business. You shouldn't have done this." At that time I thought I was looking after a tribal goal, putting tribal members into positions of responsibility, putting them into management. But I soon found out that perhaps he'd been there too long and he just wasn't perceived as a leader. I had just misread this situation.

Occasionally I run into problems like that, but on the whole I like the job a great deal. I like the extreme variety. I think one example I can use was back two years ago. There was a lady—little old lady—who came in. For some reason she couldn't get a pair of glasses. I wrote her up a note so she could get so much—$60. She got her check, went away, and bought her glasses. An hour later, I wrote a check for $1 million to the tribal farm. I got to thinking about that when I went home that night and said, "I can't believe it."

It's surprising how many projects you get involved in. Some you don't want. But what I like is the mix, trying to kind of weave my way through there and getting the job done. Most people are not going to tell you you did a good job, but still I enjoy knowing that it got done in spite of all the odds. I've been involved in quite a number of projects—the football stadium, the synthetic rubber project—and it's quite a kick to see that they went through. Someone comes along with an idea; you look at it, talk about it, and decide whether or not to do it.

There's also a lot of variety in the people I deal with. For some, it's one-on-one. Then it's a small group, with the council. And I deal with the government. Usually it's one-on-one; people come to me with money problems and I handle it directly. For example, I have a $200 electric bill and take care of it on the spot. I've *always* been able to help on personal problems. Right now we're striving for a good mix of funding so that we're not totally dependent on governmental development. We get grants and contracts from the government. We have the tribal farms; some light commercial ventures; and good relationships with private firms.

But meeting these goals is downright tough. A major problem is a pervasive attitude in the tribe that the non-Indian is strictly an economic animal, and if he does anything, it is for gain. There used to be a gentleman here, a tribal member, who got a bachelor's degree and then a master's degree. He came back, went to work for the tribe; but he was perceived as being, you know, up here someplace. He was no longer just a tribal member; he was a business-educated tribal member who had his own interest. And he was seen as no longer working for the common good. He resented that and described it as the "crab" theory—anytime this one crab tries to climb out of the bucket, the other crabs down there pull him back in.

A related problem is that the Indians have no role models. We have a tribal farm over here of 12,000 acres, and it was on the verge of bankruptcy under Indian management. So they got a non-Indian and he's been over there for twelve to fourteen years. And we nip at him from time to time for doing too much of this and not enough of that, but when it comes down to the nitty-gritty, he is going to stay there as the manager. He realizes it's a big operation and makes decisions. But the Indians would never see him as a role model. This attitude makes it difficult when I'm trying to run businesses for the tribe. The tribe wants Indians in managerial positions, but I have trouble finding anybody who has an interest in business or managing. If it's not agriculture, they're not interested in it. They can't bridge the gap and understand that there's not a dime's worth of difference between agriculture and running the store. It's still a process—economics—of making a living.

The only role model these people have is the Bureau of Indian Affairs, the government. If you want to go into something and succeed, and you want to stay in your reservation, you've got to work for the government. It's like the non-Indians first took their land, then their water, and now they've taken their role models, their heroes.

9

Pragmatism

W HAT kind of leadership is most effective? For some leaders the answer is simple: they prefer and succeed with a laissez-faire approach. But in most jobs stronger leadership is required, and leaders find they must experiment with a number of styles before they find one that works. Most leaders have not been to executive programs to learn about Theory Z, Path-Goal Theory, one-minute managing, or such. They just try an approach that seems to fit. As the heart transplant surgeon explained:

"During my training as a surgeon I got a lot of exposure to a lot of different people. I not only picked up surgical skills, I also tried to pick up the leadership techniques that appeared to work—those which allow the team to function at maximum efficiency."

After adopting a particular style, leaders observe the results of that style, and if the results are not up to par, they modify their approach. Through a sometimes lengthy trial-and-error process, most of the leaders I interviewed found that they had homed in on a style that was effective for them.

For the stockyard foreman, the style that works is rather indirect:

"I remember the boss I had back when I was first cowboying here. He was a hard ass; just like a trail boss. If you wasn't pulling your share, he'd come down on you fast and hard. If he found out you and a man was having trouble, he'd make him your partner for the next six weeks. That boss was real direct in handling problems. Guess I'm a little different. If I've got a man who's not working up to snuff, I go to the men in his group and say, 'Hey, that guy's laying down on you.' Then I just walk off. Or I just get the men on the feeder lot together and tell them, 'That man's laying down on you.'"

The head housekeeper finds that modifying her style to fit each subordinate is most productive. Her short commentary provides a fine example of contingency leadership. While she is uneducated and leads housekeepers in mundane, thankless tasks, this leader is savvy, street-smart. She leads by example, and as she does, she decides what will motivate each housekeeper. She "finds the mood and then reacts."

The commercial deep-sea captain offers another excellent leadership example. He protects his crew and motivates them—through cultivating a sense of humor, providing for some group decision making, and letting the crew handle the slackers. Upon this tandem base rests his style. He tells each crew member what his job is and when to do it, making sure, as he does so, to open up a two-way communication channel. If he has problems with a worker, he then puts into effect his three-step procedure: "one, questions; two, kick in the pants; three, fire."

The prison sergeant picked up his style in a school of (literally) hard knocks:

"When I'm supervising, I give my guards a lot of advice on how to handle inmates. If they try thinking, Well I'm tough and I'm somebody, the inmates will rebel against that. You can get 90 percent to do what you want them to without raising your voice. All you got to do is ask them. And the guards are the same way; all you got to do is ask them.

"The days of ordering people to do something is over with. You can ask people to do something, and nine times out of ten they'll do it even if they don't want to. It's just knowing how to talk to people. I admit I had to make that adjustment, 'cause I come down here with the contention that if the inmates done something wrong, then I'm number one and they pay the price. I said, 'You do this, this, and that.' "

Again, pragmatism is the guiding force. When he entered his job, the sergeant was a dictator. That did not work, so he altered his approach. His experience was analogous to that of the military academy sergeant we met earlier:

"You might say I'm an authoritarian, and in an army unit I got away with that. And that type of leadership will work as long as you use it wisely. Here, sometimes it'll work and sometimes it won't. You have to really look down deep inside yourself and decide how you are going to motivate these young kids."

For the mosque leader, God decides what works. The leader consults Muslim teachings and his flock; then he acts, praying that God will place obstacles in his way whenever he has made a mistake.

Stockyard Foreman

I figure this job is mostly just being stupid.

I've got seventeen bosses. And forty-two hands report to me. I talk with I'd hate to guess how many shippers a day, and I'm on call twenty-four hours a day, seven days a week. With all that, I've got to do a lot of thinking ahead. In a business like this, there's always something. Be nice if it could run every day without any problems, but it seems like they're coming up. A lot of times it's knowing when something is going to happen. You get a weird feeling sometimes, kind of senile about this. You know it's going to happen before it happens. So you're ready for things before they happen. You just kinda figure out things a day ahead of time. Like today I'm already trying to figure out what I'm going to be doing tomorrow when I get the sales over with and cleaning up done.

When I come in of a morning, the first thing I do is look at the receipts for cattle. How many cattle, how many hogs, how many sheep are here. Then I know how I'm going to get the people lined up on the scales. Then 9:00 is when the market opens. We have the auction out here on Tuesday and Wednesday. We sell what we call odd cattle—one, three, four, something like that. And there'll be a lot of killer cattle, killer bulls, and such as that. On Thursday, it's what we call our stocker, feeder sales. At the first of the sale there's got to be five head or more. And then at the end of the sale we clean up. If we've got one that's got popeye or is crippled, then we sell them at the end of the sale so that these people don't have to hold them over.

In the sales, we got eleven commissioners who do the sortin' of the cattle. They've been at it a long time and know what quality the cattle are, and the price they should be bringing for that day. They all go out there and sort these cattle up. They get the cattle ready for us. We furnish them with a place to bring them from the trucks, and we have men at the gates to count them in. And we order the feed on them, water them, sort them up a little, weigh them, and pen them.

Now we got a situation that we didn't used to have when I first came here. Today, everything that comes in goes out again because there's no packing houses here anymore. Most of them are out in twenty-four hours. Used to be that Swift was right across the river. There up on the top level was their pens, and there was a bridge that went across the river. We delivered the cattle to their pens, then their men took them across the river. Armour used to be up there. Meyer was right there. Armour drove their cattle across the river on the highway. They had their own bridge. Drove them across, not in trucks, they's on horseback and herded them across. After a while, the fence and all that got bad at their end, so they started trucking them over. The first week I started working here, I was cowboying. The first day I was cowboying was on Monday, and we had 25,000 market cattle plus 5,000 rail cattle.

I get along with the commissioners okay. I've been around for twenty-eight years and know my job. And they know theirs. Once in a while you're going to get a sour apple. I don't care what business you're in, there's going to be a sour apple in the organization. I just ignore them as much as possible. I try to treat everybody the same, even the guy who's kind of a pain. I don't treat him no different than the man who's 100 percent. I mean, they all get the same breaks, the same kind of treatment. I saw a lot of things happen, and I treat everybody the same, as near as I can.

We got it all set up so there's a president and a vice president. The main man I'm interested in is the president. As long as I keep him satisfied, he's not down here. He's kinda like me. He's a hardheaded Dutchman, and when you put two hardheads together, you're likely to come up with nothing. He's been here fifty years, and he's okay to deal with.

I came here to work for six months in 1955, and my six months just . . . I've had some chances to leave but could never get up the nerve. Every time I'd get to thinking about it, I'd change my mind. So I'll just ride it as long as there is anything to ride.

'Course I don't have the education that a lot of people's got. I've learned a lot as time's gone by, lot of trial and error. And I watch a lot of people and figure out a day ahead of time how I'm going to handle the crew. My hectic part really don't end. Even Saturdays and Sunday, if something blows up, I've got to see that it's straightened out. It's always going along with your fingers crossed. I can be wide awake and still something can sneak up on you. It's not like most occupations; every day is different.

I remember the boss I had back then when I was first cowboying here. He was a hard ass; just like a trail boss. If you wasn't pulling your share, he'd come down on you fast and hard. If he found out you and a man was having trouble, he'd make him your partner for the next six weeks. That boss was real direct in handling problems. Guess I'm a little different. If I've got a man who's not working up to snuff, I go to the men in his group and say, "Hey, that guy's laying down on you." Then I just walk off. Or I just get the men on the feeder lot together and tell them, "That man's laying down on you."

When you're working with people, there's somebody who's always upset. You're not going to please everybody all the time. You've got to tolerate them. If you get mad, then the next thing you know you're part of the problem. The best thing is to go sit on a fence for about forty-five minutes, get away from them, then come back and things are kind of worked around. Sometimes you can step right into the middle of it and all you do is just make matters worse. At times I do jump in. I don't know how to explain this, but there's a time to and a time not to.

I don't usually have any trouble with these men. Sure, some lay down on me sometimes. But they know I can do anything I tell them to do, so I don't have much trouble. Most of the boys respect me. I'm fair. I've got one man right now who's not too good a hand. His wife's got cancer, and it's just working on him. If I got mad at him, I'd just make matters worse.

I consider my men's personal problems but I don't let them eat on me. I got forty some people, and if I get to thinking about all their problems, then it would really eat on me.

There's some people problems here, but I figure whenever you get more than two people together you're going to have some wires crossed. Sooner or later, you know, they're going to get crossed. Most of the boys work their own problems out, sometimes back in the yards. If they don't, and it's hurting their work, then I just separate them like children—send one to one part of the yard and the other one to another part.

A lot of my job has to do with shippers. With them I treat everybody, near as I can, the same. The big shipper, I don't give him any advantages over the man who ships five head. Every day a lot of the shippers and truckers come in; I wouldn't want to say how many. Lot of them I know. I try to speak to all of the strangers that are in the sale barn. You know, it don't cost you anything to say "Good morning." Or I speak to a man and say it's a nice day or ask him how he's doing.

If I's picking another job, I'd never pick one like this. I'd be the man doing the work. It's easier. He has the feeling of doing it right, and he leaves it here at the end of the day.

When I got out of the service, I tried farming for a year and then came here cowboying. Wanted to go to vet school, but I hadn't had any chemistry in high school so I just couldn't hack that. I've stayed here, and I figure this job is mostly just being stupid. There's a lot of satisfaction, though, satisfaction in working with the livestock. You can smell them, talk to them, pet them, watch them. They do what you say; they don't cause trouble; they don't talk back. As long as I'm working with livestock, I can tolerate the people that come with them.

Head Housekeeper

I find their moods and then react.

She is petite—about five feet even—and she weighs ninety-five pounds. What is most impressive is her posture—straight as an arrow, whether she walks, stands, or sits. Her eyes are black as onyx and they complement her hair; they shine as she quietly but pointedly discusses her position as head housekeeper in a large western hotel.

I worked for fifteen years as a maid in another hotel before being promoted to assistant housekeeper. After five years in that position I was hired here as the head housekeeper, and I have been here for three years. Here I am in charge of six maids who clean three floors—120 rooms.

The key to managing is learning each girl's mood and then being flexible in telling them what to do. Each of my girls is an individual. When I first meet them, I say hello and show them what to do. I start by taking a girl to an average room and telling her exactly what I want done. If she doesn't understand, I speak to her in Spanish. If that doesn't work, I draw a picture. I don't know Vietnamese or Chinese, but I'm learning Vietnamese. If that doesn't work, I just sit her down and do the first thing myself and then have her do it—my way. They can change the way they make beds or whatever, but the end product, when I come to check, has to be my way.

My day starts when I check the ready rooms, those that are supposed to be ready for guests. My girls are on the floors, doing the "early bird" rooms first, then rooms without "Do Not Disturb" signs on them. I check each room behind them. I move around a lot, up and down the three floors I am in charge of. If there are little mistakes, I correct them myself, and if they are bigger, I go to the girl and tell her she made a mistake, in a nice way. I let her keep her pride; I try to humor her. That's important. For instance, if she put in the wrong color towels I'll say, "Did you run out of gold towels?" Then I'll say, "Because you got brown ones in 1712." I try to be nice; most of my girls are hard workers and pleasant to work with.

I don't do all the training. I show them once and then team them with another girl. My manager says to train them for five days and then give them just seven rooms—the regular girls have nineteen to twenty-one rooms each—for a week or so. But sometimes it takes longer, so we take longer. But we don't tell him. It always takes longer if the new girl can't speak English well. I try to put her with a girl who speaks both English and Spanish, but we've only got two of them and I can't ask them to train every new girl. It isn't fair.

Handling the girls as they work isn't always easy. When I start them, I say, "Watch what I do." I concentrate on the work. If they talk, open up a conversation, then I talk back, and we can get real friendly. Talk about family and all that. But I never break the ice; if they don't start being friendly and talking, then we never do. It's good to talk to them, and most of us talk and help each other out. But I watch what I say. I don't want to get burned. Say something personal to a girl, and you can get burned.

Talking is good because it helps me keep down the gossip. Bad gossip can get everybody way down here. And talking with the girls also helps me to learn their moods. Everyone has a mood, and I learn them. Some girls are crabby, some happy, some sad. Some talk about families. Some take pride in their work. Some try to get by on just a little. Some just want the money. Some want to please me. Some are afraid they'll make mistakes. I find the moods and then react.

For example, when I find a girl who wants to please me, I tell her, "I think you have done a good job!" If a girl is interested in her family and people, then I will take more time off to talk to her. Those who want money, I tell them what to do and make sure they do it. For those that take pride in their work, I act a little like a mother for them and tell them the job is really good.

I do this because I'm caught in the middle with these girls. My boss won't let me get a raise for them when they act [work] good. Their raises can only come once a year, so a bad worker gets paid as much as a good. We're in a big business here. So the big bosses say a maid that works for one year gets this amount; after two years, if she hasn't made a lot of mistakes, she gets this amount; next year she gets that amount. See, I got six girls and I have to pay them this way. It hurts me. I care. I'm surprised I don't get more complaints.

I can get them fired, though. With the first mistakes I talk to them, and usually we fix it up. We talk and if I want to, I can take them to the manager. But I do that only if I find them off their floor, or if they talk back to me. Of if I tell them what to do and they don't. Or if they lie. If they don't take pride in their work and don't do the job well, then we go to the manager. And if they get real uncooperative, then I write them up. If I take a girl to a manager three times, then he fires her.

What really frustrates me is that I can punish my girls but I can't reward them. My boss says to make sure the rooms are clean, and when my girls work to clean them, I can't do any more than tell them they did a fine job.

So they see me as a person who only punishes. And that hurts because I care for them. But that's the way it is. I punish when I have to, and I am as nice to the girls as I can be. Maybe I can't give them money for a good job, but I can talk with them. Or I can be nice. Or I can praise them. Or I can treat them like a daughter. And most of all, I can show respect to them.

Respect is very important. My boss has respect for me. He turns all problems over to me. He doesn't go around me to one of my girls. I handle it or we go talk it over with the girl. Because I take pride in my work, my boss trusts me. I do [take pride in my work]. I don't expect to get promoted to manager or to make a lot more money. I just do my job well, and my girls and manager have respect for me. To me that makes this a good job.

Commercial Deep-Sea Captain

If somebody don't work out well on the team, I got a three-step procedure: one, questions; two, kick in the pants; three, fire.

In the john of an inlet cafe, someone has etched the following words:

> *It's not my place to run the ship*
> *The horn I cannot blow,*
> *It's not my place to say how far*
> *The ship's allowed to go.*
> *It's not my place to chart the course*
> *Nor even toll the bell*
> *But let the damn thing start to sink*
> *And see who catches hell!!*

These brief lines of poetry kindled my interest in the managerial style of a modern-day sea captain. In my quest for someone who could tell me how he runs his ship, I came across the captain of the Mary Gray, a 20-year-old wooden seagoing vessel that drinks fifteen hundred gallons of diesel oil per filling.

We'll run off the South Carolina coast for seven days at a time, and there the crew—three men—and me run twenty-four hours a day, around the clock. Come daylight the crew lays two miles of cable along the bottom, with three-foot wire leaders and one-inch hooks on the cable every twenty feet. Every two hours, half the hooks are changed. At night, each crew member pulls a four-hour watch, fishing with wire-frame baskets for black bass. So each of the crew works sixteen hours and has eight hours at night to sleep.

The work is routine. But it's not boring, because you never know what is going to be on the next hook. It can be a ten-pound bass or a five-hundred-pound shark. And you drag up lots of interesting shells, and lots of interesting stuff floats by—for example, on the last run we came back with some coconuts.

I'm sixty years old, and fishing has been in my blood for fifty-five of them. It's like gambling gets into a gambler's blood. You always are waiting for the big catch. When you hit it, you hit it big. Like last week, I made $5,000 after expenses. Then you're out there again and the cards don't come up so good.

Managing the crew—about three to five—isn't too hard. They get a percent of the catch, so they work hard to get a good catch and they don't stand for slacking off from other crew members. The crew has *got* to be easy to work with or we can't get anything done. More important, they have got to work together as a team. They're on deck with the wrench pulling in a cable real fast. The deck's wet; the boat's rocking; and they're each handling five fish per minute, as a minimum. These can be some big fish. They're rebaitin', throwin' out line, and loadin' the fish into the hole. It all has to go fast and orderly, or it doesn't go at all. And they got to get along. They're the only people they'll see for seven to ten days, and they're there sweating and smelling together. They've got to work together as a team.

If one fellow doesn't pull his weight or gives trouble, then I fire him when we get in after the trip. But that doesn't happen often; I've had some crews be together for five to six years.

Sometimes we'll pick up a fellow who's hanging around the docks; always seems to be someone doing that. He might be hungry, with noplace to go; usually they have a drinking problem. So we carry him a while; take him out, train him, give him a place to live, a little spending money. And he'll dry out in the ocean. Strongest thing he'll get is a Pepsi. If he works out, we keep him on or put him to working the docks. You see, we understand that out, at sea, when a fellow needs help, we're all he's got. If he runs into trouble, he can't flag down a motorist. That's what you woodsers [a person not from the coast] can do, but at sea we have to look after each other.

Running men on a boat isn't like in the movies. If you start being a pick or kicking asses all over the boat, then you won't have a crew. No, got to learn to joke with the crew; slavery went out a long time back. But the captain usually does make all the decisions. I pick where to fish and how long to fish a spot. And when the crew works, I'm at the wheel. I'm the captain and I'm in charge, but I'm friendly. Out there there's only the wind, waves, and a bird or two. If you're not friendly, it can get real lonesome.

Some decisions I share with the crew. Say a trip is scheduled for seven days and the fishing is good. I'll ask the crew if they want to go or stay, and here I've got only one vote, same as the others. Other decisions I don't share. If there's a question about the weather, I've got the barometer and weather information, so I make the decision. Also, I decide where to fish around the Gulf Stream. The Stream is funny; you can be on this side and the weather is bad, but you can cross over and the weather's good on the other side. Sometimes when the wind's holding from the south, you can fish the Gulf Stream, but stay in it too long and you'll find yourself in New York somewhere.

When I manage people on the boat or here on the docks, I first tell them what their job is—what to do and when to do it. But I make sure that they are able to talk to me. You have to work out problems your men have and work out problems between men. I learned that back in World War II when I was the head of the engine room in a submarine rescue vessel. People would bring me problems and I'd work them out or take them up the line. I was good at that.

See, most people are afraid to speak to someone above them, to a captain or to an executive. This shouldn't be the case. They should be able to talk to their managers. You need these people, the ones below you; therefore, they should be able to talk to you. It's got to be a team; teamwork. But one person has to make the final decision.

If somebody don't work out well on the team, I got a three-step procedure: one, questions; two, kick in the pants; three, fire. But like I said, I first tell people what they're to do and when they're to do it. If they don't do it, I say, "You're falling down. Why?" Some people are just simple and can't remember very many steps. Say you tell them to do something that has fourteen steps and they can remember only seven. Well, they aren't going to do the job well, and lots of times they're afraid to come to me and say they've forgotten. So you have to work them through it a few times.

Sometimes people aren't doing it right and they don't know why. Sometimes you get another fellow to help. Some people simply aren't bright enough to do the jobs we've got to have done on the boat. They don't work out. They *can't* get good enough; so they don't work out. I let them go. They'll have to stay on shore and dig clams or something like that.

If a fellow can work—he's smart enough—and just doesn't, then I just prefer to fire him. I'll ask him why he's falling down. Then if he doesn't pull his weight in the crew, I kick his ass—but not often. I'm a quiet person, as you can see; I don't yell. Just usually put up with the bad apple for that run and let him go. Don't like to get upset with people. The sea's a good life; it's in my blood. Every run can be a big winner; every hook has something different on it; every day's got something different to deal with. You might lose half your line on a wreck; a storm can drive you in; you find a coconut or see a new shell or fish.

My crew and I like it—seldom have any problems. When we do, I handle them.

Sergeant, Medium-Security Prison

You can't take your frustrations out on those around you.

This is a medium-security prison. Prisoners have to earn their way here. They come in as maximum-security cases. After ninety days they work themselves down to medium security, and after another ninety days, they can work on down to minimum, provided they don't got no violations. And it depends a lot on your crimes. A lot of prisoners never get to the minimum unit, because you've got to have less than ten years. And there's risk factors to take into consideration; you don't want a real violent person in here.

I'm assigned one side of the dormitories during the day, so that's about 350 prisoners. During the day you got a lot of activities going on. Inmates are sick and got to go to the hospital; others are going on interviews.

State law requires that a guard goes with each of them to the outside; it's one-on-one, one officer for each inmate. So if you got four or five inmates, you've got to have four or five officers. That's the problem we're running into. We run out of guards; don't have enough help to go around. Lot of days we have only four or five on shift, because some call in sick, so that's a lot of inmates, about seventy, per guard. That's where the sergeants come in. We are supposed to be supervising, but at the same time we got to get in there and see that the work gets done.

So you find you don't have enough time to supervise, and you're supervisin' guards who are spread too thin. That's not too good, because these guards don't have that much training when they come in. They're supposed to learn on the job. You work a new guard a week on different shifts. Then you send him over to the training school. He gets a week's training there; then you bring him back and put an experienced officer over him. You see how he acts, and if something needs to be corrected as far as the attitudes, watch him close and work with him. Some of them come in here—I guess I'm guilty of that—with a hard-core attitude. (I actually thought I was cut out for maximum security; thought that was what I was gettin' into. Now I've come out here, and I had to make an adjustment.) When that happens we got to have some attitude adjustments.

As the sergeant, I help work with them—attitude adjustments—but more and more of my time's being spent doing the guards' jobs. I'm assigned a zone, and I don't have enough guards to see that the work's done; so I do it myself. And at the same time, I work out service reports on my guards along with my inmates that are assigned to me.

When I'm supervising, I give my guards a lot of advice on how to handle inmates. If they try thinking, Well I'm tough and I'm somebody, the inmates will rebel against that. You can get 90 percent to do what you want them to without raising your voice. All you got to do is ask them. And the guards are the same way; all you got to do is ask them.

The days of ordering people to do something is over with. You can ask people to do something, and nine times out of ten they'll do it even if they don't want to. It's just knowing how to talk to people. I admit I had to make that adjustment, 'cause I come down here with the contention that if the inmates done something wrong, then I'm number one and they pay the price. I said, "You do this, this, and that."

But we sergeants and guards can't go too far the other way. I instruct my guards not to be playing around with the inmates or anything like that. That's not a good policy. Treat them like humans, but at the same time you can't get too familiar with them, because if you get too friendly with a guy and something comes down where you have to arrest him, then he's going to say "Hey, you owe me a favor." You never know when that man is going to be involved in something and you're going to have to go in there and get him.

Of course, my guards mess up, and I have to talk to them; you know, we talk man to man. We're not hollering at each other and carryin' on. That's no way to talk. Sit down and talk man to man. I got my rules and I give advice to the guards, but if something comes up—they mess up or a difficult situation comes up—I also sit down and talk man to man. When we're talking, if they get to bringing up personal problems, I say, "Leave your personal problems at home. If you need time off, then go to the shift commander and take care of your personal problems, but don't bring them here. It's not my job to hear out your personal problems."

Maybe my supervision style will change; I don't know. I haven't really adjusted to being a supervisor yet; I like to do a lot of the things I did as a guard, like shakedowns, searches, and stuff like that. I've just not got the hang of doing the supervising. I like the doing part of it. I kind of still see the job from the guards' point of view.

Major problems I got with my guards is missin' work. They use up all of their sick leave 'cause of the stress. I understand that they're under a lot of stress. We're having to take people who don't belong out here really, but they don't have no place to go. So that's more stress on the inmates. The inmates get scared; some big dude makes a frail guy his bed monkey; someone puts a knife on a guy's throat. Anyone can get scared, and when they do, they try to escape. And that just puts more stress on the officers, because if the inmates can't get along, then you know what time it is.

And it's real tense at mealtime. Everybody reports to the dining hall at mealtime to help supervise because it's the most dangerous place in the institution. Inmates just keep coming in there to eat, and you might have three hundred people in there at one time. All that's got to happen is that someone throws something at somebody, and then a fight's ready to break out. That's a dangerous place; it's where most of your fights and stabbin's start.

When we get a fight or something, that's a hassle. You got to lock everybody down. Then the investigator comes in to talk to everybody—the guards, the inmates, who got stabbed—and all that takes a lot of your time.

My guards, they're on the go, just like I am, all day. Don't have much time to sit around. If you're caught up on your chores, then you're busy with shakedowns and disarming people. You constantly got to do that. People get well armed in here because they think they've got to have a knife to protect themselves against the other inmates who have knives. Then there's a fight, and everybody's got a knife except the guard. They make them out in the machine shop. Too many people out there and not enough supervision. A knife is easy to make; get a piece of steel and grind her down; use tape for a handle.

That danger all puts stress on the inmates, just like on the officers. The stress, it gets harder, and they just got to get out of here to get away from it. We've had inmates with only thirty days to go out here—they were short— and they'd escape. Just couldn't take the stress.

So one way of looking at it is that a good portion of my job is keeping the stress down. When it's down, we don't have so many fights; my men don't call in sick so much; not so many escapes. But keeping it down is awful hard, almost impossible, because this is a dangerous place for everybody. People just don't realize how bad the trouble is.

A while back, I was feeding the inmates who were in a lockdown when an inmate stormed out of his cell and jumped me. I got worked over pretty good, and they had to call for a big backup crew to get him off me and back in the cell, because he was storming mad.

The day after that happened I came back out of the hospital, and I kind of wanted to take it out on the prisoners, be real tough. But at the same time, I went down to where the prisoner was at, and he said right away he wanted to apologize, 'cause he said he was just mad. I understood him, to a certain extent; I get that way too, once in a while—hostile, lose my temper. He wanted to apologize about it, so I said, "All right, next time don't let it happen. Be a little cooler." I've learned you can't take out your frustrations on those around you.

You got to remember that this is a medium-security prison. The minimum unit runs smooth. People never mess up there because they're going home, whereas the guys in here think, What the heck! So you and your guards just deal with them as best you can. You keep moving, but you never set a pattern. You never keep a schedule; got to keep the inmates off guard. If you don't, then every day they'll get to watching you and knowing it's about time for you to be a'coming. You don't want that, because when they figure you out then they'll try for a break.

It'd be easier if we wasn't constantly having to bring in new guards. Lot of them come in here for a job, but few of them stay. They quit before they get the hang of it. After all, everybody who comes in here is looking for a job, and if they can find a better one, then they're gone. It's because of the people we've got in here. People aren't supposed to be here unless they got ten years or less of a sentence. But we do have some lifetimers, and we have some inmates who are too dangerous to be here but they don't really have anywhere else to put them. So we're stuck with 'em when they should be in maximum security or in a mental hospital.

Mosque Leader

As a leader, I am a shepherd led by the people.

If you are going to be a leader, you have to visualize yourself as a shepherd of sheep or goats. It is a very hot day in the desert, and you know that there is shade somewhere that you are supposed to take these animals to. If you try to push very hard, the sheep and goats—some of them—will just stand where they are, lose all of their energy, and starve. So you have to be very wise when you lead them.

And some will be very active, very uprising, and so and so. So you must have the wisdom to make use of this vigorous energy and at the same time give fuel to those who are lagging behind. It is very important. So don't push too hard but give enough guidance to get them all moving.

For instance, if I have someone I want to do something, I don't command or decree. I come in with some approach just like a proposal. "What do you think if we do so and so?" Just put it in the form of a question. I don't put it in a formal order. You have to use the most polite way so that people can cope with you. If people see that you are pushing and ugly, they will be that way also. But if you are polite, then they will be also.

In our faith, you do not strive to be a leader. That is, people who come into office have to be nominated by other people. Say a person is considered to be a leader; then he is nominated. Once Prophet Mohammed had a follower say, "Why don't you appoint me governor for a certain state?" And he told him: "We do not give such a thing—governor—to anybody who would run for it or like it for himself or ask for it."

And I think that is a good case. Because if you are running for it, then you might be having personal goals, but if others nominated you, it is because of your qualifications and not for your personal greed.

But sometimes a Muslim, living in a place or a society, knows for himself that he is *the* qualified one, better than all the others—For instance, if he wants to be the administer of finance and is from an accounts school and the others are farmers. In such a case, if the job is highly specified and it needs those qualifications, he can come and say, "These are my qualifications. If you think I am fit for this job, then I will do it." But still he leaves it to the people to decide if he can do it.

As a Muslim leader, I am guided by religion as to what to do and what not to do. For instance, a Muslim prays five times a day and will always first try to see what is lawful and what is unlawful according to what God has said. We do not do things to gain rewards here in this life. We do what God has said, and then Allah will reward us in the afterlife.

It is like the people who built this mosque. At one time we did not have the mosque, and the teachings of Islam say, "Wherever you are, come together as a group," because we know as individuals we can do nothing, but as a group we accomplish many things. And the mosque was the culmination of this group. So we worked hard to raise funds for the mosque, and funds came in from friends and relatives from all over the world. They gave because Allah said, "Whoever builds me a mosque on earth, I will build him a palace in paradise."

The people who gave for the mosque will be rewarded in paradise. Likewise, I will be rewarded for giving of my efforts to be a good leader. I realize that the position of leader is one of trust, and if I have shortcomings, and if I don't do it right, then I am responsible. You see, leadership is an act of worship. All of life is an act of worship. We see in Christianity that the worship is spiritual; but in the Muslim faith, all of life is an act of worship of God.

So we have as an example of this, doing sex to your wife is a worship. When Prophet Mohammed told his people that doing sex is an act of worship, they said, "How come, prophet, that I am having sex, and I am going to be rewarded?" And he said, "Yes, because if you don't do it right with your wife, then you will do it with another woman, which is wrong, and you will be punished for it. So if you do it with your wife, you are going to be rewarded for it."

So the Muslim sees all his life as worship. If he performs it perfectly—in leadership, physics, chemistry, sex—he will be rewarded. All of this is connected with the needs of the society, with the needs of the Islamic nation, and with the service of God. You will be rewarded for this, and you will be punished for acts that are classified as illegal.

There is Allah's palace, and he will put the people either in it or not when all people will come before him for judgment. He will judge them not only by their prayers and coming to the mosque, but also by what they did—how they behaved politically, how they treated their wives, and how they led their people.

So some people will become leaders to worship God, and then they will be rewarded for this. And in Islam, if people come and they say, "You are the one who can do the job," you have no right to decline. That is their consensus, and you have to do it. And another thing, they, your subordinates, will help you. They will not put you in office and then criticize or abandon you. Rather they will come to you at times and say that you have done good in this and bad in this.

And this is what I think is the difference in leadership in Islam and in the western democracies. In the western democracies, you come, you run, and then people back away and try to record your wrongdoings—"You have done bad here, and you have done bad here, and so and so." But in Islam, we have what we call "advice" from *Koran*. If you did something wrong, people will come and advise you, from the beginning, so as to correct you. So you have group guidance.

And the other principle is the one of consultation. The *Koran* says to the leaders that these are the characteristics you must have to be considered perfect Muslims:

Those who hearken
To their Lord, and establish
Regular prayer; who conduct
Their affairs by mutual consultation.

Anything you do as a leader has to be approved by the process of consultation. You must consult the group and discuss the matter with them in order to get the feelings of the group. Then they will give you guidance or broad lines, and you will lead within these broad lines. But this policy that you follow, and your leadership within that policy, should not contradict a fundamental belief or Islamic rule. If it does, it must be changed.

For guidance as a leader, I pray to God, and I do it this way: for example, if I plan to take such-and-such step as a leader, I say to God, "I am going to do this"—for instance, appoint someone to the head of a committee. "If that is not right, if it is not what you want, then please put obstacles in my way so that this is not done." First, I go with the decision that I feel is right in my heart, because God's guidance comes there, and then I ask God to put obstacles along the way if he thinks my actions are not going to be correct.

On a more day-to-day basis, my leadership style is one of depending on helpers. I believe in the principle of division of labor. If you divide up a task so as to minimize the load on one person, this works well *provided* that you have very strong and tight supervision. Otherwise it will not work, or if you don't have cooperation, it will not work.

So I divide up the work and have people do their parts, and then I check on them. If they are not doing well, I do not go directly to that person, but I go to his committee leader or to someone in his group. And when things are not going well, I do come in and correct them because I, not they, am responsible for getting the job done. And it must be done correctly.

When some problems come up, I first just ignore or avoid them, and people will forget about them. I know if I bring the problem before the group there will be at least two groups, one for it and one against it. So I take care of it myself or ignore it. Forget about it. Sometimes we have problems and people come to me and say So-and-So must be replaced, or you must solve this problem. Here I just talk to them, cool it down, give it two weeks or a month. People usually will forget about that problem and then maybe I will handle it later or we will discuss it along with another problem.

I try to give my guidance, for that is my place in society. And sometimes—this is very important to remember—sometimes you take a different viewpoint from the group. But if the group agreed upon a certain course of action, and even if you are the leader, you must neglect what you think and what you believe and do what they say, because we believe that many people will not agree on a false position. So I keep what I think to myself and do what the group thinks is right. We feel that if you are not going to hold to the group position, then you are going to do harm to the group; therefore, the personal interest of all individuals, even the leader, must be reduced below the group interest.

For example, consider one issue that has arisen for us—the role of women and how they are treated. You go to some countries and there the women do not work. They do not go out, and so and so and so. That is for the sake of the society; they agreed upon that. And you come for instance and go to another society and find women are going around without covering their faces and are making boyfriends.

So we come here, in the United States, and our group meets, and some from one culture say, "Women should be treated like this." And others say, "No, like this." Our cultures mix here and there is difficulty, but the group decides, and that is the way women are to be treated. I let the group decide. But still this gives problems for me, for each segment of my group still has their beliefs. But we come together, and we negotiate toward a position that most of us can agree upon.

When I find a person who is not behaving correctly, I do not push hard. If I can, I educate by example. Sometimes we do have brothers and sisters that cause trouble. So we follow the prophet Mohammed's teaching: "Take them as they are and try gradually to educate them."

Start by changing what is inside the mind. For example, consider a woman who does not dress correctly. First we change what is in the mind. We do not want her to dress a certain way because her husband or the society told her to do so. Rather, we wish for her to do so because she knows in her mind that she dresses this way for the society and for the group. So by the examples and by the education, we change people, but if they don't change, we don't throw them out; we tolerate them.

Sometimes, coming to this country, people slip away from our faith. Here I must, as leader, play an important part. What I try to do is socialize the person. I go and say, "Brother or sister, we have prayers in the mosque, please come." They may not. I then have people go talk to them. We meet and talk about the person, the problems, and how to solve them. Then we go back and ask the person about their general ideas about certain things. And we ask them if we can't get together again, once or twice a week, if not in the mosque then perhaps in a home. We give them a society to which they to demonstrate her belief that power lies with the people instead of he leaders. She admits that her approach doesn't always work:

hink there's a myth of egalitarianism that often crops up in groups who are menting with traditional forms of leadership, and it's this: if you throw a or so people together and say, 'We're all equal,' then good decision making adership will result. It doesn't. We make a lot of mistakes sometimes."

bar manager uses a street-smart style. All of his decisions—selecting , choosing a seat for himself near the john, buying liquor, building a er, and his leading itself—are guided by his wits. While his employees e bar, he puts out the fires. Whether his style is called democratic leader-delegation, or something else, it works:

me people can drink all night and be okay; others you got to watch. One and they're crawling. Usually I leave that up to Kay or Norma. I stay out way. If someone is giving them too much grief, I step in and tell the fellow to cool it or leave. That's my management philosophy. Let the employees e place. They think it's their territory. That's fine with me."

quality circle leader agrees with this participative approach. He finds quality s own "equalism" style works well, and he has transferred it from quality to his primary group:

cause I get so participative with the circle (I see benefits from participation—C people are so free to let their ideas flow) I say, 'Why can't it work over my group?' I've changed and developed a different vocabulary, a different express myself, and now I conduct myself interpersonally in a way that bet-s the resources of my subordinates."

limestone quarry foreman has less appreciation for participative manage-He confides in people to let them know that they are important to nd to build their confidence. Yet he offers a caution; "They can start k you can't do without them." Then they have to be taken down a or two.

lly, the marijuana dealer's style evades classification. To some extent black-hat approach:

hat they say is that the first impression is a lasting one. So I put on my npression to my people, and it's not usually a nice one. But I put it down

can come, to socialize with. Outside our society they have their friends, their good times, their fun, and they are not going to sacrifice this just to come and pray in the mosque or to be with us. So we begin and gradually, gradually, gradually socialize them. This is a sacred responsibility. We are the people who have got the right message, and if we let people slip away, we have not done the right thing.

When I find there is a conflict in the group, I act in a similar way. I am not very assertive. Consider the conflict over the role of women. I did not take the role of a chairman; rather, I just gave my opinion and discussed it as any one of the group. If the group comes to my side, that is fine, and if they reject that, it is also fine; I have to abandon what I have said and go with the consensus. I am not a mediator. I try to say my opinion, but go with the group.

But if the decision has practical consequences that are undesirable—maybe they would cause conflict in the group—then I would implement them in such a way that this problem does not occur. The issue might be agreed upon, but the way it is to be implemented is my decision. For example, if there is to be a change, I will implement it gradually. Or if I know one part of the group opposes a proposal, I would not implement it for them.

People always go along with what I say, because in our society—Islamic society—we have great respect for the person who is leading, because the qualifications on which he is chosen should give him that respect. So what you say is discussed almost automatically, because the *Koran* says:

> *O ye who believe!*
> *Obey God, and obey the Apostle,*
> *And those charged*
> *With authority among you.*

10

Whatacra

I N talking with leaders, I was most surprise
strated in their leadership style. Seldom w
describe it; it was the first topic they mentio
of concern; as a pimp confessed to me, "My
others, it is a source of pride.

Most of the leaders I interviewed chose style
to their circumstances; many of them have actu
of our knowledge. They approach the challe
curious, and inventive perspectives.

Based on their experience, some have chosen
tor of a mental health ward is one such leade
that in his profession there must be structu
autocratic approach, and it has worked well

"When we're making these treatment decisions,
conflict, and get upset; but they get over it. I don'
I handle it pretty decisively. A lot of this disagree
because the prior unit director tended to be pretty n
of a benevolent dictator, like I am.

"I don't think you can decide on treatments or
a democratic style. Someone has to make the fin
leader. This isn't a democracy here; you don't v

In stark contrast to the mental health directo
democratic approach. She adopts this tack becau
especially women—a different, democratic m

hopes
with

"I
experi
dozen
and l

Th
plants
count
run th
ship,

"So
drink
of the
or gal
run t

Th
that h
circles

"Be
my Q
here i
way t
ter ta

Th
ment
him a
to thi
notch
Fin
it is a

"W
first i

thorough. It's a tough image. Good language, to the point, professional. Scare them. Then I tell them what to do and how to do it."

His style is mainly results-oriented, pragmatic, and "loose":

"I just want the job done, and because of the nature of people in the drug culture, they can relate to it. Here it's a basic knowledge of who is, who isn't, what's right, and what's wrong. There's not all that formality. Here I'm free to use the leadership style that works. I don't have to use rules that my boss gives me. I don't have to be tactful. We just relate and communicate as individuals. We just relate together as men in the best way to appropriately get something done, if it's selling drugs, loading trucks, building buildings, or anything else. That's the way I operate, and my men respect me for it."

Unit Director, Mental Health Ward

I'm not a democratic leader. This isn't a democracy here; you don't vote on therapy.

We psychiatrists are trained to recognize our emotions and hopefully trained not to allow them to get in the way of our professional functions. What we do is deal with emotional problems. So we deal not only with the patient's emotional problems, we also must deal with our own.

In spite of that training, my staff and I do get emotional about patients. I do get angry with the patients. A therapist would be lying if he said a patient doesn't turn him on sexually from time to time. I do find some situations so disgusting that I wonder how people can survive through it. And I have times when I really feel sorry for a patient because they've had such a sad, tragic life. Anybody in this business who tells you otherwise is lying.

I would say generally that this unit gets the *most* difficult psychiatric patients. We get a lot of committed patients; that is, they have a civil court commitment because they are a danger either to themselves or to others. We have criminal cases here for evaluation. We try to determine why they did what they did and how they can be helped. And then we get the voluntary patient. So it's no picnic here. And that's what I like about it.

There are three aspects to my work as a director. First, there's patient care. Second, I'm responsible for teaching in the unit. I have two psychiatric residents, three to five medical students, and a full-time clinical psychologist. And third, there's the research end of it.

As the supervisor for patient care, I have twenty to twenty-five people report-ing to me: one psychologist, two social workers, two residents, four medical students, plus the administrative staff—about twelve—and three secretaries. The job entails a lot of interaction with the staff therapists. I meet with them at least three times a week. I meet with individual staff or groups of staff and social workers every other week. I meet with the psychologist two or three times a week. And I meet with the staff that are involved with par-ticular patients whenever problems arise in treatment. Presently, I have no primary responsibility for patients; rather, I assign that to the staff psychologists, social workers, residents, and medical students.

I delegate responsibilities because I cannot physically or professionally han-dle the tasks of my people. There are too many people for me to treat as a therapist, and I'm not trained to perform all the tasks. There are cer-tain things the psychologists do—testing and evaluations—that I can't do. Social workers are trained in skills that I'm not trained in. The residents and medical students, because they are so close to medical school, have better diagnostic skills from a physical point of view; so I have to depend on their judgment and abilities. Of course, I've never been a nurse, so I don't have nursing skills. I would be at a loss if I had to go out in a unit and nurse for eight hours.

Once I delegate, I generally let them run their own show. They do their job and I do mine. In general, mine entails making four types of decisions. I decide who gets admitted. I decide when people get discharged. I'm the final decision maker on the diagnoses. Most of the time people in the unit come to a diagnosis that I agree with. That's 95 percent of the time. The other 5 percent, no one knows anyway. And I direct a patient's treatment.

In patient care, I'm both a manager and a doctor. On the manager side of the coin, I decide who is admitted to the unit. I take just about all referrals—from a court or professionals (private psychiatrist, social worker, nurse in the community), because they don't have the knowledge or resources to treat a person. In addition I decide when patients are to leave, and I oversee the group decision-making process on treatment.

When we're making these treatment decisions, my people do disagree, come into conflict, and get upset; but they get over it. I don't view it as "healthy conflict," and I handle it pretty decisively. A lot of this disagreement and conflict arises, I think, because the prior unit director tended to be pretty much a laissez-faire leader instead of a benevolent dictator, like I am.

I don't think you can decide on treatments or be a leader in this profession with a democratic style. Someone has to make the final decision. I'm not a democratic leader. This isn't a democracy here; you don't vote on therapy or medication.

While I'm not a democratic leader, I'm not an autocratic one either. Rather, I use "shaping" in my management style. When a person does something right, I reward him; when he moves in the right direction again, I again use a reward, again, again, again. It takes time, but with my staff I have time to shape; I'm going to be living with them forever.

Our disputes have leveled off also because there's an agreement now that we use only four or five modes of treatment. Most psychiatrists admit nowadays that most of the theoretical formulations—the psychiatric formulations from which we derived our psychoanalyses—were nothing more than belief systems and have no empirical validation. So we tend to deal with those techniques that are supported by empirical evidence, like the behavioral, the cognitive behavioral, and the medical management—drugs and that sort of thing.

I like managing the small unit here, running the show, and being in on the action, because I can do my management face-to-face. In contrast, at a higher level the management has to be done on paper, and I don't do nearly as well on that. In fact in my job prior to this, for a period of four and a half years I was chief of staff of a 125-physician hospital—525 beds—and I actually quit that position because I got so sick and tired of the paperwork and the loss of the personal contact. I like the personal side of management; the impersonal, paper type of bureaucratic duties aren't for me. Here I'm tied up mostly with face-to-face matters, so I've managed to ignore the paperwork, or keep it to a minimum [*laughs*].

As a manager I also have to decide who is to be transferred. We have our share of violent folks, but for the most part they are treatable. For the criminally insane who are not treatable, we have backup systems. When I say the criminally insane, that's a judgmental call. A better description would be unpredictably violent. If patients do get too unpredictable or too violent, then we have backup units to which they can be transferred.

However, I find that to be one frustrating aspect of this job, because those types of transfers tend to be made very bureaucratically. Therefore I try to use the "good ol' boy" system. I have staff in my unit who have worked at other facilities, and I have them call someone they know, and they manipulate the system so we can get fast transfers. There's no reason to go through the bureaucracy; it would take weeks.

There are lots of times the patients want to pull and end run around their therapist and see me. My response is to tell them they have to work through their therapist to get an appointment with me. Then the therapist has to go through my secretary, who keeps my appointments, to get an appointment. And my secretary does a good job protecting me. But usually if a patient wants to see me, he or she can in a day or so.

They can come in with all sorts of questions, or perhaps a complaint about something. If they want another therapist, that's just not negotiable. When I make patient assignments, I generally try to take into consideration the people who are the primary therapists, their personalities as well as those of the patients. Then I make the assignments. It's not a democratic process, and I don't want the patient's inputs into it.

When it comes to the work relationships among the medical students, the residents, and the staff, I let them work that out, because they negotiate that out very fairly. I don't ask them to fill out a lot of forms for my review. There are spot checks from other people in the system, and if they spot flaws, then they bring them to me. Generally, residents and medical students are overly responsible, so I don't have to worry much about them. And with my personal contact with my staff here, I have a general idea of what their strengths and weaknesses are.

Being the leader here also helps make my life as a doctor more enjoyable. I don't have to follow the patients on an outpatient basis when they get out of the hospital. And here I get the cream. I'm a decision maker when it comes to their treatments, but I don't have to go through with all the scud. I know what patients generally have to go through in psychotherapy, and I've gone through it so much that it is actually boring. Now I have others do that, and I get right to the treatments of some very interesting patients. There's a constant array of these interesting persons coming through.

When working with the patient, you do experience some pressures; they don't like the treatment, the requirements, or the results. And the relatives come in and have their ideas. Usually I have the primary therapist handle that; if he requests that I help with the outsiders, then I'll step in.

I don't really like that part of the job. Some of the relatives and patients get mad at me, but I stand my ground and they get over it. Often I'm just telling people things they don't like. I'm blunt. I don't have the time to shape their behavior. They're here for a short period of time, and I try to get the message across as to what's going on and what we recommend. Very often it's upsetting to the patient, but I'm being asked for my professional opinion and service, so I give it. When a physician tells a patient he has cancer, the patient gets mad at the physician. Same with me. I tell a patient that they have schizophrenia or a manic-depressive illness, and I say "These are the types of behavior that are going to give you trouble, and this is the way you can change them." Then they get angry. That's not a lot of fun for me, but it's part of the job.

There's an ironic twist to my research, my role as a therapist, and my job as a unit director. In the research, I'm looking at the interactions among my patients' life stresses, the emotions they arouse, and the effective and ineffective coping mechanisms that they use. As a therapist, I'm trying to help patients cope with stresses. And in my job, I'm constantly being frustrated. I'm under stress and I'm trying to cope with it.

As I noted before, we get pressure from the patients and their relatives. Why aren't you doing something more? Why can't you make the patient well? Shouldn't you be trying this? Why can't my relative get into your institution? One time we had to bring someone in because the lieutenant governor wanted him in. Not only do I get pressures directly from these outsiders, I also get pressure from the assistant superintendent, who also gets pressure from the superintendent, who gets pressure from the director of mental health, who gets pressure from the department of mental health. That goes with the job.

My teaching gives me some relief from all this. As I said, I have four medical students. They do a lot of the scut work and the physicals and they sit in on the interviews. Also, when we have any trouble with the therapy, we'll discuss it with them. Then we'll all go see the patient and conduct some therapy with the assistance of the medical students.

In psychiatry a picture is worth a thousand words, but a moving picture is worth ten thousands words. They sit in and watch, and then we discuss what we've done. They question me, so I have to legitimize what I'm doing. In private practice I rarely had to do that.

But medical students aren't a free resource. When we get the juniors, the residents and I have to really be up on them. We have to watch them, double-check them, and then when we find out they're good—that we can depend on them—they get more autonomy; we then allow them to become primary therapists. Some of the good ones even end up having two patients that they have primary responsibility for.

With regards to my future, I'm not sure how I would respond to a promotion. At first in my career I wanted to get ahead and accomplish a lot of things. Now I like helping others—patients, medical students, and staff—just as much as personal accomplishments. My personal priorities right now are: my family is number one—that switched about five years ago; second is my research; recreation is probably third; and fourth, I guess, (you're going to think this is funny) is providing an enjoyable work environment for the people who work here. I really consider it important for the people here whom I supervise and interact with to enjoy what they're doing. I don't think there's anything better in life than enjoying it, and I want to provide that for my people.

Peace Camp Leader

The first victims of nuclear weapons are already dead.

The peace camp sits a few miles from Boeing's cruise missile plant in Seattle. In the summer the weather is kind, and the camp somewhat festive. In the winter, the climate is bleak, the mood in the camp is more sober. Whatever the weather, the leaders are always determined.

We don't allow men in our organization. That decision was made for a number of different reasons, and every woman I have talked to has had a different opinion as to why it's good that we're a "women only" group. Women's leadership has not been acknowledged, though it has been strong in this country, and that's one way to demonstrate without a doubt that women can do something together. Also, we are experimenting with decision making and the leadership processes. And women work together well because we tend to be more cooperative. We haven't been taught to be as competitive as men have in this culture.

We feel that women have a history of working for peace and for better lives, but that so often we have not been allowed to develop strong leadership skills in mixed groups of men and women. There is this natural tendency for women to drop back in a group of men and for men to come forward and to do the more important work. Here, this doesn't happen.

We do allow men here. They've formed a strong support group. They do child care, they bake bread, and they do fund-raisers. All the time during the day men are welcome to camp, but they must leave at night. The men who are in our support group understand that women have been kept down for so long that it is important that we are given an opportunity to demonstrate leadership. And they talk to men who don't understand and explain man-to-man that some reparations are in order.

We want to give women the power to believe in themselves. Women in general lack self-confidence because we have been taught from early on that we do not have the skills to pull things off. But we do, and we've got to teach women to believe in themselves.

We have always made decisions by consensus, and that means that our meetings usually run from four to five hours every week. Whenever a major decision is being reached, we each have an opportunity to contribute what we think or what we feel. If there are major disagreements, we each have to move to a position where we are in enough agreement that we can say "Okay, let's go with it."

Sometimes reaching decisions by consensus works—it brings in more people and yields a better decision—and sometimes it fails. I think there's a myth of egalitarianism that often crops up in groups who are experimenting with traditional forms of leadership, and it's this: if you throw a dozen or so people together and say, "We're all equal," then good decision making and leadership will result. It doesn't. We make a lot of mistakes sometimes. And when that happens, we leaders have a rough go of it; we're scapegoated. This happens because women have been kept down so much that we have this tendency to project our resentment on our own leaders. We see women treating us the way we've been treated by the world, sometimes unfairly. Sometimes we react like that, instead of understanding that we need to have leaders.

The way I view leadership now is kind of an amalgamation of working with the traditional systems and these consensus decision-making models. In the camp we don't have a formal leader or coordinator. Rather we have our committees with women who take responsibilities for different areas in the camp. When a decision has to be made fast, we alter the decision process a little. One of the major times when that happened was when we were choosing sites. It came down to a point where we had two weeks before a plant opening. That was to be a big deal, and we didn't have a site yet. Since we met only once a week, it fell upon the women who were at the last meeting to approach the mayor and say, "You know we need some land. Do you have any ideas? If you don't, we'll be there anyway."

In this case there were natural leaders in our group who took the initiative and said, "Look, it's got to be done. We've got to meet with the mayor. We're going to try to work something out." What we tried to do was to call as many people as we could when something came up really quickly and to work as hard as we could to contact people who we knew would want to be a part of that decision. But there were always decisions that were made with some members absent. And our premise was, if you are not there and if you do not attend, you are trusting those of us who are there. You trust us enough to have us be your voice. If it were a major, earthshaking decision then we often would hold it off to the next meeting so that people would have a week to contact people and alert them that the final decision would be made the following week.

A lot of times we have disagreements, but when we have a big split in the group, ultimately someone will say, "You know what we're working for is more important than this disagreement." Then we will overcome our differences.

I think as a bottom line we are very different. We are very different women in style, in background, in philosophy. But we also recognize that nuclear weapons and the violence that makes them possible and maintains them are threatening all of our lives on earth and that the powers that are keeping them in place are much stronger and much more well-monied than we are. So we have to go that extra mile in cooperation.

We've had disagreements over peoples' class backgrounds. Because we were set up as this consensus group, I think this created very high expectations in peoples' minds that if they came in, then their work would be appreciated, accepted, and not questioned. Yet what we found was that some of us are college educated and that we've had more experience in speaking and writing. Others who came into the group and didn't have the same kind of skills or who didn't have as much self-confidence thereby found themselves being shut off. They were kind of denied an active leadership role.

The working-class women and the poorer people said, "Look, this is going on," while those of us who were middle-class women were pretty much oblivious to it. It is the same in a lot of mixed groups. Blacks will be very aware of white culture and the differences with their own, whereas we as white people don't very often perceive or understand the difference.

Our major goal is to defeat nuclear weapons, especially those of a first-strike nature. When you spend money on these weapons, it's inflationary, and you're draining money from other areas which help people. In fact, the first victims of nuclear weapons are already dead or suffering greatly because all this money was and is taken from human services and put into weapons of human destruction. And it's creating greater unemployment, because military projects tend to employ very high tech people and to use more robotics and computers. We understand that these missiles *will* be used. They'll be used just as the ovens were used in Nazi Germany, to kill people.

In addition to opposing these weapons, we're also offering the world a different model for making decisions. About two thousand women passed through the camp over the summer months. Many of them came from other peace camps and from England, Denmark, and Japan. We had workshops almost every night. We had programs and meetings in which we discussed this new model.

There's a feeling in this country that the real power is in Washington and that the men and women there hold the reins of power. Our counter-model is modeled on a Gandhi campaign of nonviolence. We believe people can refuse to cooperate in this country and can exercise power without using violence at all. So I think we're accomplishing three things: we're showing women that women can accomplish something; we're opposing nuclear weapons; and we're offering a different, better way for making decisions.

In general, that's what turns me on about being a leader here. We're all making sacrifices, but we all have the joy of knowing that we're doing everything we can to stop this mad race to the sea. And that's a lot. There are a lot of people who do not believe that anything can be done at this point. Basically they're living half lives; their spirit is already gone. We're trying to alleviate that by being creative and colorful, offering analogies in history when people have overcome great obstacles, like in the civil rights movement and in the women's suffrage movement.

But I think the greatest reward to me is recognizing that people are changing very quickly and that also we all have this goodness inside us. We have the capability to see that we're going down the wrong path. I, for example, had this great experience when I was leafletting—that's what we call handing out leaflets. I had these motorcyclist gang members approach me with leather jackets and tattoos. I had this flickering fear, and then this one guy got off his cycle and said, "This is just great. I'm just so glad you're out here; can I help you?" And he stood there and passed out leaflets. A year ago if I'd seen him, I would have said, "This redneck is not going to have anything good to say to me" and would have written him off. Now I have this belief that people are basically good and that we all like to change. I think it's wonderful seeing people change and knowing that you can't second-guess people, that you have to give everyone the benefit of the doubt.

On the other side, I think that we're not as patient with one another as we could be. There's so much frustration that gets piled onto people working on this because of the apathy we see. Then we tend to take our frustrations out on one another. We're just human. And with so many people coming through the camp, there is a tension. They have to be oriented, and you do it over and over so that you develop a feeling that they're the peasants and we're the landlords. We had to take steps to eliminate that.

But a lot of little victories help to overcome the tensions and frustrations. For example, this woman picked up her husband from work and instead of driving home, drove down the little driveway to our camp. He said, "Where are you taking me?" And she said, "I've decided it's time we talked to these women at the peace camp about what Boeing is making."

This man was up for promotion and was scared to death that he was going to be seen in a peace camp; so he was slumped down in his seat as they drove down the road. She got out and said, "I told George it was time to come talk to you." So we had a wonderful conversation with the wife, and eventually George sat up in his seat and came to talk to us too. Once he saw that we weren't ten feet tall and that we didn't eat men, he got along well with us.

And there was this encounter with a farmer we were trying to lease land from. We gave him a thumbnail sketch of what we wanted to do on that land. Then he said, "What are you women up to, anyway? Are you mad at your husbands?" We said it went a little further than that—that we were mad at Boeing.

His reply was, "Now I don't understand why you're picking on Boeing. Boeing just fulfills government contracts and gives the government what it asks for."

We said, "Look, if we had $100 and we wanted to spend it on apples with razor blades, would you as a farmer sell them to us?"

"Well of course not. I wouldn't sell dangerous things like apples with razor blades."

"We see Boeing's production of cruise missiles as being in the same category as you as a farmer selling apples with razor blades."

Looking to the future, I think we'll have to centralize our leadership a little as our organization grows. Leaders will have more power then. I don't think we believe that leadership is corrupt. We are willing to experiment. The bottom line is effectiveness and productivity. But I don't know if we'd be willing to become *highly* centralized, because we believe strongly that excluding so many leads to a poorer decision.

A peace camp in upstate New York did have this experience. They had hundreds of people at one time; they were much larger than we are. They were highly transitory; people came for the big consensus decisions and then they were gone. And what happened was that they found it almost impossible to make decisions by consensus with that large a group. So they toyed around with more centralized techniques.

I think if you had that large a group, people would understand that decisions would be unwieldy and would delegate leadership or decision-making to those women who are most committed. Women will do this because they trust others more. Competitiveness is not quite so ingrained in women as it has been in men, and there's more trust. Therefore, if I hand it over to this woman, I trust that she will speak for me and not do something totally off the wall. You see, women are good followers as well as good leaders.

In spite of being both good leaders and workers, women are not advancing as rapidly as they should. I think what's happened is that structurally institutions are accepting women and encouraging women. But it's a problem of not enough women who can serve as mentors for women; that is, we need more role models.

There's also the situation that is subtle—women who step into leadership positions are often set up to fail because men will not follow them. Men are taught in this world that if you follow a woman you are some kind of sissy; you're less of a man. There's this built-in resistance to following a woman's lead on the job. So there's this subterfuge or sabotage that goes on sometimes; a woman is unsuited because she can't lead. In fact, the problem is that men have not been taught that it's okay to follow.

And there's another problem created by affirmative action. Successful women are perceived as rising to their positions because a woman was needed in that position. And women who fail are highly visible, whereas incompetent men are not seen as representing all of mankind.

Bar Manager

My girls think this place is their territory, and I let them run it.

Why run a bar? If I weren't here, I'd be in someone else's bar from 7:00 'til midnight. This way I just recycle my money. And I always wanted my own bar, so when this one was put on the block, my partners and I came up with the cash. One hundred grand, and we've put a lot into it—about twenty grand—to fix it up. Knocked out some walls. Added this nice cedar bar and tables over there. Expensive? Yeah, but we used scab carpenters—$6.00 an hour—and we laid the floor ourselves. Good idea, this tile floor. Just mop it once when we close up, and that's it.

As for our target market, we shoot for the unmarrieds. They spend money; it don't mean nothing to them. Marrieds, they count every penny and don't travel. Singles, now they come in, spend a few hours, drink with their friends. And they'll drive to get here. If a place is popular, they'll drive fifteen to twenty minutes to get here. Marrieds, they stick close to home, so get a place that's "in" with the singles and they'll pack the place every night, drive from all parts south of the city.

We keep this place pleasant, light, and airy. Open and loose, the way they like it. For example, see those potted plants hanging there? Good idea. Cheap, too. Spent less than $50 on all of them. Got some plants on sale at K-Mart and then rigged up some pots for them.

I'm an expert on bars, so I made this an easy place to drink. Customers can get a drink at the bar, circulate without stepping all over everybody's toes, play Pac Man, hit the juke. Like the juke? My idea with these large in-set speakers. Gives good sound without deafening you. And look at this counter here against the window. Nice place to lean on and look out the window—right? That's not half of it. Had the carpenters build this in front of the windows so that people don't go through them in fights. Nice little detail that saved us a window last week.

Fights? They come with the territory. We tell customers to take it outside or we'll call the cops and sign a complaint. Usually that works, but when it's off-duty cops, it can get hairy. We make sure to cut them off the next time they come in. We had some big Irish dudes—packers, loaders, steel men—come in a lot when we opened. You know, they like to drink a lot, arm wrestle, and fight. Geez, you and I like to sit here and talk; these guys like to fight. So they come in, drinking, fighting, and all that. How did we handle it? We didn't. All the other bars on the south side got together and banned them, so they thought we had too. Haven't seen them in a year.

When you run a place like this, you *got* to be here. You might not do a lot, but you've got to be here for whatever comes up. Like that broad who ordered a bourbon sour a few minutes ago. No way! I cut her off up front. She goes wacko with one drink, so we don't serve her. Some people can drink all night and be okay. Others you got to watch; one drink and they're crawling. Usually I leave that up to Kay or Norma. I stay out of the way. If someone is giving them too much grief, I step in and tell the fellow or gal to cool it or leave. That's my management philosophy. Let the employees run the place. They think it's their territory. That's fine with me.

You got to be cool with your employees, too. Take some ragging that you don't have to. Like last night I used Kay's keys to open up the stockroom. Then I took them home by mistake. Kay then has to ride with Mary; rather, she has to drive Mary's car, with Mary and her kid riding. Mary's kid keeps crying that it's too cold with the window down; it had to be down because the defroster doesn't work. So the window has to be up; the windshield fogs; Kay runs a stop sign, and a cop pulls her over. So I got to take some ragging for that. I just bought her a sandwich, and pretty soon we were all laughing.

Mainly I'm okay if I respect their territory. Like I use the pay phone up front and don't go behind the bar. Kay gets irritated if we go behind the bar. Like I said—her territory. My date last week went back behind the bar to make herself a cup of coffee. Kay hit the ceiling. Ragged on me for a week about that. I take it. It's her job; she's honest and good. Stands back there 6:00 'til 2:00 pouring drinks, on her feet all the time. It's dark and smokey, and at times it gets mighty heavy. Then Norma's in as a backup, and they've got to maneuver around each other. It's not a lot of fun, so I give them their space and let them handle their end. The job and customers tell them what to do, dictate the pace. So I stay off their cases.

Had one partner who couldn't keep his hands off the details. He was here from 5:00 'til 2:00 every night. Had to watch everything, money, beer, tables, customers, bouncers. Drinking too much, too. He was here for nine straight hours, making all the decisions, driving everybody nuts, plus himself. So he drank to calm down. We had to buy him out.

Sure, I use the stuff I learned in school, with some modifications. Take the EOQ [Economic Order Quantity] idea. In MBA school, we were taught that you order enough inventory so that carrying costs just equal the cost of lost sales. Well, I figure a more important factor into the model—cost of stolen inventory when you get robbed.

In this business, you also got to know a lot about PR. I always sit back here by the john, where I get to meet everyone. They come in, have a few drinks, and got to go to the john. I watch, see them coming, and call out their names. On a good night I see everybody two or three times.

And I buy free beer for our softball team when they win. Then for Friday or Saturday night I hire one or two of the beefier ones as bouncers. They're going to be in here anyway. They think it's cool—drinking beer and being paid for it. If there's big trouble, all their buddies jump in to help; so actually I got seven or eight bouncers on my hands for the price of one or two.

I set this place up to run itself. The girls run the show, pour the drinks, handle the customers, decide what drinks—beer especially—to order. They got an advantage; guys are nicer to them than they are to males. If somebody gets too heavy, I ask him to leave, and if he doesn't, I call the cops. If a guy comes in with a motorcycle jacket on, I tell him to take it off. We don't want that in here. Prostitutes, I just throw them out.

I handle the exceptions, and I help the girls with their personal problems, or if a keg is foaming, say, and they get behind in something. They help me when I'm down. Exceptions on customers I handle—the loud ones, drunks, fights, off-duty cops. Too many off-duty cops in here. I don't like it; they always want some handout. Some are okay, but too many want handouts.

I do the planning, too. Do we add another bar? A kitchen maybe. I think I'll add some food, then maybe we can catch the dinner crowd. We're running a good operation here. Guess I learned how to run a bar by spending a lot of time in them. And friends down here have helped me and given me advice.

Who to target? Unmarrieds. Where to locate? Away from homes and in a place with lots of parking around. Where to buy booze on the side? Friendly liquor stores. See, the IRS looks at our purchases and extrapolates what our sales are. So I buy a few extra cases on the side and don't list them as expenses. For example, from a liter we get about twenty drinks. That's about $40. Helps to buy on the side.

Video games? Don't have to ask about them. The mob puts them in and takes good care of them. Nicest guys in the world. They count the money right here on top of the counter and give us 50 percent. How much of that gets reported to the IRS? Who knows? And they take good care of the machines. One broke last night at 11:30. A guy was here in fifteen minutes to fix it. I'm not dumb enough to put in my own machines. They'd break up the place. It's their territory and not worth the risk. Besides, they're nice guys.

And payoffs. I had got all the information when I opened. Whose palm to grease. But that was old times. Can't pay off people anymore. Too bad; now we can't get anything done quickly.

Quality Circle Leader

Being a QC leader has permanently altered my supervisory style.

Quality circles are advised to attack smaller problems first, to get the feel of it. We didn't. We went with a large problem that had a large cost saving. It took us a long time to put everything together. There was a lot of data gathering required. And there were times when I think the circle, the members of the circle, were getting a little frustrated because we weren't moving. But the closer it got, when everything started fitting together, when the charts we were making were prepared, and when we were getting to the point that we were having dry runs on our presentations, then the enthusiasm really started building. Once we had our presentation, everyone just had a great feeling about it.

The problem was one of automating a job that previously had been done by hand. We get an engineering order to make some sort of engineering change, and on the back of the order you've got a place to indicate what you did to comply.

So what we did, okay, was to come up with a way to get that indication into the computer so you could punch a button and the computer would flash up the engineering order and what was done to respond to it.

We calculated out the savings, and from what we know about future business over the next three years, we calculated that we would be saving right around $650,000 a year. The cost for implementing this entire system is going to be about $450,000, so we're actually paying for the implementation of that system in the first year. The reason we went with this big, complex problem was that the further we got into it, the more cost savings we could see. We were really thrilled with what we could save the company.

There are ten men in my quality circle. What I did when I set it up was to take the names of everyone who volunteered and put them into piles, one for each department, so I would have a cross section from all departments. Then I just drew a name out of each pile, so that in my quality circle I have some of my own people but most come from other departments and are under other supervisors.

Once we're in the QC meeting, my job is to keep the meeting moving. I'm not supervising that group. I am a member just like they are, but I'm the chairman, who makes sure that things keep moving rather than getting bogged down. I'm both a supervisor within the department and the leader of the QC. I don't want to say I'm a QC supervisor because I don't want to impose my feeling on the circle. If they want recommendations from me, I want them to ask for them because of my experience. I can help them in making a decision, but I want the decision to be made by the circle, not by me.

The circle members and I work with the facilitator, who sits in on all our meetings. We meet once a week, and if we're having a problem somewhere—say we need help from another department somewhere, or we're not getting cooperation somewhere—it's his job to get with these people and straighten things out so that we can get some cooperation. He is a liaison for us and for the other QC's that he works with.

I'll tell you what I have done. I read about this really good idea in my quality circle training manual. I liked it, and I don't know of too many circles that use it. Using an alphabetical system, we have a new leader every week. Each person in my circle takes a turn at leading a session. So I think the members are finding out what it takes to lead somebody. For instance, you get ten or eleven people trying to say something at the same time and nobody is getting anywhere. They find out for themselves that somebody has to keep things organized, going, moving forward. So when a meeting starts, one person knows he is going to be the leader, so he just starts it. My role—I try to sit back and watch the circle move. If we get bogged down on an issue, I try to solve the issue so we can keep moving, so that we don't use the whole hour arguing a particular thing.

I serve as a mediator, pointing out that this is a problem here, and suggesting that we take some guys, investigate it, get some feedback on it, and move on to something else. Let's keep going. I don't want them to try and please me with their ideas; they're there to solve problems in the areas with their own techniques.

When we make our presentations to management, the whole circle does it. What I generally do is make the introduction; that is, I give a little speech as to what we're going to present to them. Then my circle members—we've already gone through our presentation several times to get all the bugs worked out before we actually give the real presentation—make the actual presentation. And I think this helps, too, because it exposes the members to upper management, who remember their names. They say, "Hey, this guy did a good job in there." And it follows the opposite way also. The members feel good being able to look a top manager they normally wouldn't see straight in the eye and say that we need this, this, and this. They get to see the persons behind some of the names they read and hear.

Savings—like our $1.5 million in three years—is one reason I am so enthusiastic about leading a quality circle. It also gives the average employee more visibility, more opportunity to do something about his conditions, and it is a "people-building" program. I think people building is the most important thing other than the cost savings. We are building people. It makes people better. It makes their job better, and it makes them feel better about themselves.

The circle, as it improves quality, really develops the personnel. The members of the circle learn problem-solving techniques: how to investigate problems, brainstorming, and other investigation approaches. They're becoming better decision makers and problem solvers on the job, not just in the circle. So it's beneficial to the company from that standpoint.

The QC is also good for me. It's good exposure, and along with the younger members, I've developed. If nothing else, it's a refresher to me on problem solving and solution finding. And I'm finding that it's broadening me, exposing me to technical areas that I previously knew little about.

My leadership position is a delicate one within the circle. I am in a dual role— a supervisor within the department but a leader in the QC. While we're in a room, just us—the QC—I try not to come on as a supervisor. I try to treat them as equals and don't overpower them. But a lot of subjects come up as we're leaving the room, walking down the hall, or coordinating during the week that require me to act as supervisor. Then they perceive or recognize that I have a great deal of power. The dual role doesn't confuse them, but it does create some stress for me.

I don't know how much the QC members appreciate the fact that I come down and give up my power in the QC. I think they might. But more importantly, out of that room they all know they can come up to me and talk to me about any problem, not just one related to our QC. Maybe it's a father image that I've achieved [laughs].

I am sure they appreciate the number of free hours I spend at night working on presentations. I'm not stating, "You guys do this, you do that." I'm in there doing. It's not participative management, it's participative QC, equalism.

I think my mode of managing my own group has changed since I've started being a leader in the QC. As a supervisor, I know my people have a firm, set schedule to meet, and we're almost constantly behind schedule. So here I have to be a little more firm in my direction. With a QC it's freer. Number one, it's voluntary and there's no schedule. There's no deadline to meet in the circle. You can drag opinions out from people. If you take the time frequently to draw out opinions, people will start to present the opinion along with the problem. That is, when they present the problem, they'll say, "I think we should do this or that to solve it." And they'll indicate how they personally feel about the problem and the solution.

Learning this has really changed me; its made me more participative. Because I get so participative with the circle (I see benefits from participation—my QC people are so free to let their ideas flow) I say, "Why can't it work over here in my group?" I've changed and developed a different vocabulary, a different way to express myself, and now I conduct myself interpersonally in a way that better taps the resources of my subordinates.

Now, when time is available, when people in my group ask me questions, I'll say, "What do you think?" or "Why don't you go here, there, or wherever, and find that out." I've always found that if you've got to dig it out yourself, you'll remember it. If someone just tells you, it's too easy. You'll just be back in a week asking the same question.

QC has not only affected my style; it's had an effect on my superiors. The company's management has preached participative management for a number of years and put us through seminars on it, but they never used it or gave us the opportunity to use it. They were just beating the drums. Now, with QC, it's starting to seep in to all levels of management. And it eases some of that shockwave. Instead of the vice president coming in, beating the fist, and saying, "You *will* have participative management"—you know, the old Theory X—they're helping us to ease into it. They still expect the same quick response [*laughs*], but the way it is presented and supported is different.

In a nutshell, and no one expected this, having quality circles around and being a leader of a quality circle has changed my supervisory style on the job and has even changed the supervisory style of my superiors.

Limestone Quarry Foreman

When you confide in people, they can start to think you can't do without them.

Within the span of two weeks, three quarries had turned me away. One manager volunteered the information that his quarry was so backward that I would not be interested in its operation. The other two had cited federal mine regulations forbidding persons without mine safety training to enter an operating quarry. So my expectations were at a low point as I called the fourth quarry. When I reached the owner/operator (after my tenth call), he asked tersely, "What do you want?" When I told him, he replied, "Sure, come on down." We discussed appropriate times for my visit. All the times I suggested appeared to be convenient for him, so I said I'd be there at 2:00 P.M. "Nope," he said, "that would be too late, because the quarrying crew gets off at 4:00, and I want you to be sure to spend plenty of time in the quarry. That's where the action is."

When I arrived at his office, I found he wasn't there. "Down at the quarry," the others said. So I absent-mindedly listened to the directions to the quarry, figuring that when I got somewhat close to it, I would be able to home in on the exact position by locating the derricks. That turned out to be a mistake. An hour later, I found the quarry and its owner. He was patiently reassembling a large air compressor.

I'm the only foreman here. Below me are working foremen with a person or two helping them. I'm the foreman and kind of the worker, too. It varies a lot from season to season.

During the winter I lay off all my workers for three months or so. Then the working foremen and I come into a new area, drill through to check the quality of limestone, depth, etc., and then drill blasting holes. We blow up all the overcover—dirt and shale—and bulldoze it off so that we're ready for spring. Come April, we have a wide floor of limestone exposed. When the workers come back on, we lay tracks on top of the stone and then mount this Perrier chain saw on the tracks. Its teeth are diamond-edged—$15,000 in diamonds per chain—and with it we cut a groove about eight feet deep. The chain cuts, and the machine, as it cuts, pulls its blade slowly through the limestone. After making that first cut, we set the track over about three feet, paralleling the first cut, and make a second long cut. We do this until we've cut all the stone in that direction. Then we set the tracks perpendicular to the first cuts and make cuts at right angles to the first series, about eight feet apart.

Now comes the fun; we've got the stone cut from the top in 8 by 3 feet blocks, and we've got to get it out; so we come in from the side. We drill holes along the bottom of each stone, then with the dozer we build up a pile of dirt about three feet beside the stone. We go back up on top again. Slip an air bag into the grooves we've cut; then we attach an air hose; the bag expands to eighteen inches and breaks the stone loose. We deflate the air bag; put two, side by side, into the groove; expand them (now to 36 inches) and the stone topples over.

Now that we've got the block broken away and lying on its side, we check what size the mill wants it to be. Seldom is it asking for an 8-by-8-by-3-feet block. We check their order, drill holes in the block with an air hammer, drive bits and feathers in by hand and split the block along its seams. The bit is driven in, then removed and driven in again with small, thin, wedge-shaped pieces of steel—"feathers"—sheathed down its sides. In comes the high lift—a huge tractorlike machine with forks on its front—which hoists up the stone and puts it on the semi, which hauls it to the mill. That's it; that's the way you quarry limestone.

Of course, I'm the only operation in the United States that quarries that way. I read about those chain saws in a trade magazine and then went off to France to see them in action. I bought me three—the current price is $160,000 each. The air bags? I saw them being used to pry out metal in automobile wrecks, so I asked a company representative to bring some out to the quarry. I was lucky; my chain saws made grooves just wide enough to get the bags in, and the air hoses were already there for my jackhammers.

My competitors use long wire saws to cut the limestone; therefore, their grooves are too narrow for the bags. So they have to use block and tackles to turn over their stones. It's interesting, but I bought the chain saws long before I heard about the air bags. You might say I just got lucky on that one. You could also say I made my luck! Right now I plan to quarry stone from the side. Leave the overburden and drag out the stone. I heard about a company in Alabama that's doing it that way; thought I'd give it a try.

I've always tried to be an innovator and to take advantage of doing things a new way. When I came out of high school, I went into professional baseball. I was a left-handed pitcher for the Pittsburgh Pirates and a good one, too. For two years I was at Waco in the class B, before I was drafted for the Korean War. Two years later, when I returned, a lot had changed in baseball, so I came back here. I'd never been in a quarry, other than to swim, but this other fellow and I went into business with his father-in-law.

I had no background at all, had to learn from my mistakes; I had to learn everything—about explosives, pumps, people, stone, derricks, finances, hogs, electricity, drills—anything and everything. We didn't have any money; so we borrowed money for one machine, paid for it, and then bought another piece. And we cut stone like everybody else; we cut channels in the stone, then set up big long wire saws. Then we would pile up dirt beside the stone by hand. On top, we'd use blocks, tackle, and quarry hogs to break the stones loose. We'd have to haul them to the derricks, cut notches for the hogs, and then hoist the blocks up with the derricks.

"Man," I said, "there's got to be a better way of doing this." I started innovating right there, and over twenty some years I've been improving. I like it. This business allows me to do what I want. If I get an idea, then I do it. I don't have to wait around for some boss, government, or somebody to think it over and say yes, no, or maybe. Here I run everything except the office; my wife handles that. But really I'm married to about fifty people. They depend on me, and I know that.

In this business, I have to know everything. I've done everything, and I teach the people below me what to do and then they do it. When I started, I had to work hard and learn everything, so I expect others to do the same.

But you can't think working hard will get you there. Back fifteen years ago, we worked mighty hard. It was backbreaking work, hammering, dragging blocks, tackles, and steel cables around. But I saw with all that hard work we weren't getting anywhere. We were just keeping up. I had to do more.

I wanted to take advantage of my opportunities and get a competitive edge. I spent a lot of money. I've got three high lifts, new ones, when I only need two. But you have to keep *plenty* of good updated equipment on hand. Lots of my competitors tried to get by with old equipment. They're bankrupted now because they fell behind.

That's not unusual. Actually, the stone business is so far behind you can't believe it. People are always doing things the same old way. I try to avoid that. Up 'til six years ago, I had thirty people in the quarry. Now I'm down to eight and getting 50 percent more stone out. We did $1.5 million in business last year, and my goal is to be up to $4.5 million in three years.

I'm innovative. For example, on these chain saws, I figured out what teeth were needed and got this fellow to pour them. Then we put on the diamonds, cut them to shape with lasers, and assembled our own chains. I want my people to turn out the best product in the best way.

And another idea I've got: at night I'm working on a new wire saw up at the mill. It'll be sixty feet long, and when I get it ready, it'll cut twelve and a half inches down in the stone—that's what most of our slabs are now—so in a year or so we'll be doing most of our sawing down here. So the milling operation comes down into the quarry, instead of the stone going to them.

My management style? In general, I manage by example and try to be fair and firm. My fellows know me. They've learned over the years that I'm a tough taskmaster. I let them get by with some things, but not many. There's a lot of stuff going on down there that could be done better. When I get these people to improve, I always try to involve them. For example, I'll say, "You know we've got to do this better," and they'll try. They know they can't kid me, because everything being done in this job I've done before.

I don't have or expect perfect harmony or happiness here. I don't think anyone who is in business and gets anything done does. And I don't try to be a perfectionist. When I started out, I was going to be one, but I learned when you're working with people you better back off a little or it'll put you in the graveyard.

My older people, trouble is, will stick to the basics and that's it. For example, this fellow working the saw knows what to do. He comes in, starts cutting stone as he has for years. He's learned a lot of old mistakes, and if there's a problem, he ignores it. He won't troubleshoot. He doesn't want to. He wants me to do it so it takes pressure off him. He, like too many others here, relies on me too much. And it extends into their management style. They'll say to the workers, "Do this or that because the boss said to." I try to impress on them that when they do this, they lose all their authority. They've got to learn to tell the fellows what to do, and if they don't do it, tell them to get their butts over the hill. Use your authority; don't say do it because someone else wants it done.

I've gone through this with my son-in-law. Told him he's on the other side of the fence now. He's no longer a worker. It's not all buddy-buddy. But he doesn't have to change; all he has to do is be fair. If a fellow isn't doing what he's supposed to, get on *him* right there. Don't use some whipping boy. I had some men who had whipping boys—people who will take it—so when something went wrong, they'd chew him out, thinking by some sort of osmosis it would get around to the others that he's a tough guy.

When you've got a problem, you go straight to the person to say, "Hey, you're screwing up, and you've got to quit screwing up or else." I've fired a lot of people, because one bad employee can put the place in an uproar. So when people cause a disruption, they're gone.

And you've got to watch when you manage. A lot of people start to think you can't do without them. On the one hand, you want to build confidence in your main people, so you confide in them and let them know they're important to you. On the other hand, they can start to think you can't do without them. There's a fine line there; some people can bridge it and some can't. For example, I had this office manager who I confided a lot in. Then he started acting like he owned part of the company. Thought I couldn't do without him.

Now I do without him, just like I do without those derricks.

Marijuana Dealer

In the drug culture there are no rules that say how I'm to lead.

Seems like I've always had trouble on my jobs because of the stupidity around me controlling the job. Like when I's in the marines, there was so many stupid rules and regulations that didn't apply to anything positive. It was too much of a control thing for me.

I didn't do good in the marines. I got out, had six children, and worked hard at a lot of jobs. Worked as an orderly in a hospital, worked for the city, worked for a car company, for a construction company, at a warehouse. Worked on a towboat for about six years. Started out as a deckhand and then made first deckhand. It's really hard work. I messed up there and went to this employment agency for some help. I took all these tests, and the lady's just flabbergasted with my scores. She's freaking out. "Wow, you got this and you got this. What do you want to be?"

"What can I be?"

"Well, you can be most anything other than a brain surgeon or a heart specialist."

So I said, "Well, can I go to a four-year college? I'd like to be a social worker. I'd like to work with young people who've been deprived and who've been misused and mistreated. I'm really compatible with that situation, coming from that environment." But she wasn't really qualified at her job. She didn't help me out. All she'd do was write on papers "not qualified." That was the depth of her intellect when it came to performing her job. It was a job 9 to 5 for her.

But to blow that off, I got me a job as a cook. That got me in the fast lane. One thing led to two—drugs, sex, rock 'n' roll, young gals—the good times.

The cooking job gave me a living, but not a good one. I was sustaining myself. Then I saw drugs as a way of earning some money, maybe getting a little house out in the country, maybe reestablishing my family. I saw drugs as a free-enterprise thing. I didn't see there's any way as a cook that I could get those things. There was no room for advancement. All the doors were closed within the whole system. So I got into drugs to make a better life for me and my family. I was getting too old and falling behind. I felt compelled to do better.

I started seeing people using drugs. You got two types of people. You got the family type, which is basically what I am. They stay at home and work. Then you got the rounders or partiers who smoke reefers, shoot dope, drink wine, and just lay around and have fun. So I seen this other group. They's using drugs. And it was like a different big economy, and I thought I was slick enough to be a kingpin in it. Even though I knew it was wrong as long as society was concerned, it didn't matter. I had the desire to have a house and to have a place for my family. That meant more to me than being wrong. I wanted a place that my family could feel was a home. And I wanted money for my family. I didn't want to knock anybody or hurt anybody. People just wanted drugs, and I wanted to supply them.

I just spent a lot of time around where people were getting high and observed who had the dope. Then I approached him and said, "Hey man, I'd like to get a hundred of them quaaludes." To begin with, I had to shoot in there and put a scam down to get a front. Like I had to get the drugs without money. Then after I sold them, I'd pay for them. So I ran this scam to get started. I guess I just became a dominant conversationalist—know all about this and all about that. I make myself appear equal to the suppliers. Let them know I could do the job. I's going to make them some money and get by myself.

Had to do this a lot. Knew me some people who was growers, who had the pills. The street buyers, they want a variety of drugs. You might have a pot smoker here, a downer freak over here, a speed freak here, a hallucinogenic freak here, heroin junkie here. I have to supply them with what they need. They don't want to shop around.

My suppliers aren't too easy to deal with. They're very cautious. They're not paranoid or tripping about undercover. But they don't want you to know how much drugs or money they got or how. It's such a free enterprise that that's where the real paranoia comes. People taking things from them; people pulling a gun and robbing them. I'll probably do that on down the line, but now I want to get in there and see what I can get. If I pull a gun and he's got only a pound of marijuana, then what kind of dumb move would that be? Then I lose myself a supplier.

I sell some of it myself and I have other people sell some. I'm not worried about them robbing me or beating me up. I think it's just the way I present myself. (I don't even have any problems with the real hard core people with monkeys on their back—those shooting on heroin.) I don't feel no pressure, because I'm so familiar with the drug scene now, so familiar with manipulating people—getting what I want.

What they say is that the first impression is a lasting one. So I put on my first impression to my people, and it's not usually a nice one. But I put it down thorough. It's a tough image. Good language, to the point, professional. Scare them. Then I tell them what to do and how to do it: "Here's what you're going to get, and here's what you'll pay me for it."

Sometimes it's a barter-type situation. A fellow wants to negotiate on a price or what he gets. Sometimes he just asks what price I'm getting on this, on that, on that. When they do that, they automatically make themselves vulnerable.

I got six working for me now. Some have the money. Like a fellow comes up on a Friday and buys a thousand quaaludes and a pound of marijuana. He pays and comes back when he runs out. With some it can be up front—like you take this pound of weed and bring me $1,000 later. Get another pound. That type of thing. If they've established themselves, we can do that. At first, though, he's got to have money, or something to let me know he can deliver.

When I first got into this, I had a lot of trouble with the up-front thing. I got phone calls, threats. I got beat up a lot because I didn't pay. Like there was a fight where I got set up in a bar. One guy called me out, and I go out. He's standing way over there, then other guys beat me up. See, I'd beat this guy—I'd got some drugs and hadn't paid him.

Now I know how to handle people who don't pay me, but I don't have to do much of that with my people. They know the score. I have a reputation. I'll get them. They can't get it off. I might not get them directly, but I always get them some way—a way they'll never be looking for—physical harm or some way.

They don't work a territory that I give them, and I don't tell them how to sell. My experience in the marines really affected my leadership style. I had all those dumb rules on my back, and I hated it. Like I'm your boss here, and we're involved in doing something; I'll say, "Hey man, let's do it this way. It's faster and more proficient." In the drug culture I can do that. But out there in the other world, I can't do it, because there are all of these rules and regulations.

Here, I'm the leader I want to be. Society says to manage with all these rules. When I see stupid things, I don't use any tact in getting it done. I'll say, "Hey man, if we do it this way then possibly . . ." I don't believe in all that easy going stuff. I just want the job done, and because of the nature of people in the drug culture, they can relate to it. Here it's a basic knowledge of who is, who isn't, what's right, and what's wrong. There's not all that formality. In the drug culture there are no rules that say how I'm to lead. I don't have to use rules that my boss gives me. I don't have to be tactful. We just relate and communicate as individuals. We just relate together as men in the best way to appropriately get something done, if it's selling drugs, loading trucks, building buildings or anything else. That's the way I operate, and my men respect me for it.

A leader on the job has got to be loose. Not all these rules. Rules is why people are breaking down on the job, nervous breakdowns. Nerves are shot, mental breakdowns, dying at fifty-five. Their jobs are driving them crazy. Trying to perform for the man so he'll give them enough to pay their punk taxes, utility bills, and what else. Leaders get their people's minds in their hip pocket. "Get out there and perform like I say."

I'm not that type a leader. I'm loose, and I try to make my people feel good about themselves. Lot of them are like me. Been held down by society. I tell them they did good. Little remarks like "We did good." I use the word *we*. Or if they did something particularly good, I say, "You *really* did good." Try to motivate them to have the same good feelings about themselves that I do about me. And if they feel good about themselves, then they're going to jump in there and help me get this little job—drug selling—done, to the best of their ability. If I compliment them on that, they're always going to perform on that high level.

I try to bring everything I can out of every individual I can. I want every individual to come up to his full potential. That helps put money in my pocket, puts money in his pocket, and makes him feel good about himself. Now, if he doesn't perform I just tell him, "Hey man, we got this job to do. Now, you can do it; I know you can. But if you don't want to, I got all these others over here to take your place."

I feel good about myself here. I'm moving up in this second economy. It seems I didn't have enough tact as far as what society won't let me do. But I don't need that tact in the drug scene.

Sure, I got good threads and all that now, but see, having a good feeling about yourself doesn't have anything to do with the clothes, car, or money. My success gives me a good superiority about myself. This wasn't the reason I went into drugs. I went in for the economy thing, the little bungalow, some money for my family, clothes, the dream, the pot of gold at the end of the rainbow. But it's the accomplishment that's made me feel good.

Here's another thing that makes me feel good. I'm accepted and recognized for what I am. All my other jobs have been like, "Go over there and sit in the corner, boy, until we tell you to start your machine, boy." I never was accepted as anything but a robot. Here I got people that depend on me to get their jobs done.

It's a downer, though, having this be illegal. It's got to be so secretive. Society says I'm an outlaw, but I don't force people to do anything they don't want to do. I don't kill people. I just have stuff here if they want to buy it. And for me to be shunned by society because I provide a service . . . only the people I get high with can talk to me about it. I don't like it, but there's no stress for me because of it. I accepted a long time ago that I do things that are not accepted by society. Although I don't enjoy doing them, I accepted a long time ago that I have to. Accept me for what I am. I don't hide anywhere.

I'm not hiding anymore, and I'm not being held down anymore. What I've always felt basically is that I could move up, in everything I've ever done. Lot of my frustrations in my earlier years was that it never came out the way it is coming out now. I want more. I can do more. I can. But there was always someone there to swat me [*slaps table*] like a fly. Maybe they were paranoid. Saw some potential I had, wanted to keep me down, saw me as another piece of meat or whatever.

That's over now. Those people are over in that "other" economy. Over here in mine, I'm doing good, and I'm moving up.

About the Author

J IM WALL, a professor of management at the University of Missouri, divides his time among teaching, writing, and advising leaders in diverse fields. He is the author of a book entitled *Negotiation* and numerous articles.

can come, to socialize with. Outside our society they have their friends, their good times, their fun, and they are not going to sacrifice this just to come and pray in the mosque or to be with us. So we begin and gradually, gradually, gradually socialize them. This is a sacred responsibility. We are the people who have got the right message, and if we let people slip away, we have not done the right thing.

When I find there is a conflict in the group, I act in a similar way. I am not very assertive. Consider the conflict over the role of women. I did not take the role of a chairman; rather, I just gave my opinion and discussed it as any one of the group. If the group comes to my side, that is fine, and if they reject that, it is also fine; I have to abandon what I have said and go with the consensus. I am not a mediator. I try to say my opinion, but go with the group.

But if the decision has practical consequences that are undesirable—maybe they would cause conflict in the group—then I would implement them in such a way that this problem does not occur. The issue might be agreed upon, but the way it is to be implemented is my decision. For example, if there is to be a change, I will implement it gradually. Or if I know one part of the group opposes a proposal, I would not implement it for them.

People always go along with what I say, because in our society—Islamic society—we have great respect for the person who is leading, because the qualifications on which he is chosen should give him that respect. So what you say is discussed almost automatically, because the *Koran* says:

> *O ye who believe!*
> *Obey God, and obey the Apostle,*
> *And those charged*
> *With authority among you.*